VOLUME 3

Victorious
Walking in Christ

The Living in Victory Series

BY MARILYN HICKEY

**Marilyn
Hickey
Ministries**

P.O. Box 17340 • Denver, Colorado 80217

Volume 3 - The Living in Victory Series

VICTORIOUS WALKING IN CHRIST

Copyright 1984
Marilyn Hickey Ministries
All rights reserved

Printed in the United States of America

(Formerly School of Ministries: Branching Out in Your Faith)

ISBN 1-56441-030-7

TABLE OF CONTENTS

PRAYER LIST

Prayer List of your cell members and needs that you agree to pray over.

(Be sure and date when God answers the need.)

_____

_____

_____

_____

_____

_____

_____

_____

_____

_____

_____

_____

_____

_____

_____

_____

SPIRITUAL FACT SHEET

1. When did you ask Jesus to be Lord of your life? Give the date and some of the details involved.

2. Do you speak in tongues? When did you begin to speak in tongues?

3. Give one reason you read the Bible.

4. What is your reason for prayer?

5. State briefly your relationship to God the Father, the Holy Spirit, and Jesus Christ.

6. Describe your view of the church.

7. What is the greatest area of need in your life?

1   What is Faith?

INTRODUCTION: "Without faith it is impossible to please God" (Hebrews 11:6, KJV). We must have faith to please God. We need to learn what it is and how to operate in it consistently. We want to grow in God's kind of faith--the kind of faith He lives in. That's the kind of faith that brings results, moves mountains, saves families, and supplies human needs. Most of all, that's the kind of faith that pleases God!

I.   CATEGORIES OF FAITH

   A. GENERAL FAITH

      1. Human faith

         People have human faith--faith that a business will succeed, faith in their mates or family, faith in certain banks, lawyers or doctors. They put their trust in these people or institutions. This is natural, human faith that works for people on a natural plane. People believe for human achievements, and they get them. People may have faith in an idea and become very wealthy.

      2. Religious faith

         Some people have faith in a creed, an organization, or a church. They follow the ordinances, rituals, or order of service explicitly because they have faith in what they are doing.

      3. Faith in experiences

         Many will believe only what they see, what they can prove to their own senses, or what they experience. If it happens to them, then they believe it. The faith of Thomas was based upon experience.

      4. Intellectual faith

         Believing with your mind, giving mental assent, while your heart isn't in it and your belief doesn't affect your life-style, is an intellectual faith. The rich young ruler believed the right things, and to a great extent lived them, but he was not willing to involve the heart, make Jesus Lord, and follow and obey Him.

      5. Temporary faith

         Faith that hears the Word, receives it joyfully, but later doubts, is temporary faith. It is the rocky ground of the "Sower and the Seed" parable.

> And the one on whom seed was sown on the rocky places, this is
> the man who hears the word, and immediately receives it with
> joy; yet he has no firm root in himself, but is only temporary,
> and when affliction or persecution arises because of the word,
> immediately he falls away.
> Matthew 13:20,21

B. REVELATION FAITH

1. Revelation faith is based on what God says, believing and acting on what He says
   without substantiation of the senses. Revelation affects the visible world but it
   does not originate with the visible. It is the result of the Word being quickened
   by the Holy Spirit.

2. This faith is saving faith, the good ground of the "Sower and the Seed."

   > For by grace you have been saved through faith; and that not
   > of yourselves, it is the gift of God.
   > Ephesians 2:8

3. This faith expects the miracle-working power of God to operate.

4. This faith is authoritative--it is in command of the situation. Jesus had
   authoritative faith. He commanded the winds to obey, diseases to flee, and the
   dead to rise.

5. At times this faith will come as a gift of faith--you will know that a miracle is
   about to happen.

6. This faith is creative. God shaped the worlds by faith. Jesus multiplied bread.

   > By faith we understand that the worlds were prepared by the
   > word of God, so that what is seen was not made out of things
   > which are visible.
   > Hebrews 11:3

   > And Jesus called His disciples to Him, and said, "I feel
   > compassion for the multitude, because they have remained with
   > Me now three days and have nothing to eat; and I do not wish
   > to send them away hungry, lest they faint on the way." And
   > the disciples said to Him, "Where would we get so many loaves
   > in a desolate place to satisfy such a great multitude?" And
   > Jesus said to them, "How many loaves do you have?" And they

said, "Seven, and a few small fish." And He directed the multitude to sit down on the ground; and He took the seven loaves and the fish; and giving thanks, He broke them and started giving them to the disciples, and the disciples in turn, to the multitudes. And they all ate, and were satisfied, and they picked up what was left over of the broken pieces, seven large baskets full.   And those who ate were four thousand men, besides women and children. And sending away the multitude, He got into the boat, and came to the region of Magadan.
Matthew 15:32-39

II.   THE FOUNDATION OF YOUR FAITH

A. GOD HIMSELF, AS THE AUTHOR, IS RELIABLE.

1. Our God is Supreme.

Our God is the Creator and the Ruler of the universe. He made the whole thing. He especially created each human being. He chose you to be His own.

You did not choose Me, but I chose you, and appointed you, that you should go and bear fruit, and that your fruit should remain, that whatever you ask of the Father in My name, He may give to you.
John 15:16

Our God loves us, has good plans for us, and wants us to grow up into maturity with wisdom. Our God is good. He does only good things and makes all things work together for our good.

And we know that God causes all things to work together for good to those who love God, to those who are called according to His purpose.
Romans 8:28

Our God is omniscient, He knows all things, and He is aware of everything that happens to you. Our God is omnipresent; no one can hide from Him. Our God is just; He does only righteous things. He can never be accused of evil or of being unfair. This is the God in whom we trust! He is the foundation of our faith, and He is the One that will never, never fail us. He is the one who gives us our faith!

> For nothing will be impossible with God.
> Luke 1:37

2. He keeps His Word.

    According to the dictionary, one meaning of faith is "belief without evidence." Christians do have faith, but it is not without evidence. Our faith is based on the promises of God--a God who has been found to be totally reliable! Our faith is not blind; it is based on a God who is righteous, trustworthy, and faithful.

    > Thy righteousness is an everlasting righteousness, And Thy law is truth. Trouble and anguish have come upon me; Yet Thy commandments are my delight. Thy testimonies are righteous forever; Give me understanding that I may live.
    > Psalm 119:142-144

    > When I am afraid, I will put my trust in Thee. In God, whose word I praise, In God I have put my trust; I shall not be afraid. What can mere man do to me?
    > Psalm 56:3,4

    > Let us hold fast the confession of our hope without wavering, for He who promised is faithful.
    > Hebrews 10:23

    It is the experience of knowing God this way that makes it possible for our faith to grow, at times without evidence for the senses. We can trust our God to mean what He says and to carry out what He declares. His Word will accomplish what it was sent to do. When God makes a promise, He will keep it!

    > So shall My word be which goes forth from My mouth; It shall not return to Me empty, Without accomplishing what I desire, And without succeeding in the matter for which I sent it.
    > Isaiah 55:11

3. He is a faith God.

    The world was created by faith (Heb. 11:3). God created the world out of things that were not seen. Because He operates by faith, His children know that they can also operate by faith, fulfilling the word which says, "the just shall live by faith" (Hab. 2:4 KJV).

4. He is faithful.

    a) God cannot deny Himself. He will remain faithful. His very character is faithfulness. God can require us to be full of faith because He is faithful.

        If we are faithless, He remains faithful; for He cannot deny Himself.
        II Timothy 2:13

    b) God is so faithful that He keeps His covenant to a thousand generations. If I walk in the light of God's Word, God will keep His Word and perform it to my generation.

        Know therefore that the Lord your God, He is God, the faithful God, who keeps His covenant and His lovingkindness to a thousandth generation with those who love Him and keep His commandment.
        Deuteronomy 7:9

    c) God's faithfulness is undeniable and unquestionable. We can count on Him. We have faith in what God says.

        Forever, O Lord, Thy word is settled in heaven. Thy faithfulness continues throughout all generations; Thou didst establish the earth, and it stands.
        Psalm 119:89, 90

        The Lord's loving-kindnesses indeed never cease, For His compassions never fail. They are new every morning; Great is Thy faithfulness.
        Lamentations 3:22,23

        God is faithful, through whom you were called into fellowship with His Son, Jesus Christ our Lord.
        I Corinthians 1:9

        Faithful is He who calls you, and He also will bring it to pass.
        I Thessalonians 5:24

    d) God's faithfulness is not tied to a person or ministry. It is entirely dependent on Himself. God's Word works because God is faithful. God is faithful, whether you are or not (II Tim. 2:13).

5. He guarantees His promises.

God's promises are sworn by God Himself--an oath to Himself for us!

> For when God made the promise to Abraham, since He could swear by no one greater, He swore by Himself, saying, "I will surely bless you, and I will surely multiply you." And thus, having patiently waited, he obtained the promise. For men swear by one greater than themselves, and with them an oath given as confirmation is an end of every dispute. In the same way God, desiring even more to show to the heirs of the promise the ...unchangeable things, in which it is impossible for God to lie, we may have strong encouragement, we who have fled for refuge in laying hold of the hope set before us.
> Hebrews 6:13-18

B. THE PROMISES OF GOD

1. His Word endures.

a) It is settled in heaven forever (Ps. 119:89).

b) It will never pass away.

> "Heaven and earth will pass away, but My words shall not pass away."
> Matthew 24:35

> The grass withers, the flower fades, But the word of our God stands forever.
> Isaiah 40:8

c) It can be part of you and your family forever.

> "And as for Me, this is My covenant with them," says the Lord: "My Spirit which is upon you, and My words which I have put in your mouth, shall not depart from your mouth, nor from the mouth of your offspring, nor from the mouth of your offspring's offspring," says the Lord, "from now and forever."
> Isaiah 59:21

2. His Word is valid.

    a) God's Word has been tried and tested.

        "As for God, His way is blameless; The word of the Lord is tested; He is a shield to all who take refuge in Him."
        II Samuel 22:31

        Every word of God is tested; He is a shield to those who take refuge in Him.
        Proverbs 30:5

    b) God's Word is pure and refined.

        The words of the Lord are pure words; As silver tried in a furnace on the earth, refined seven times.
        Psalm 12:6

        Thy word is very pure, Therefore Thy servant loves it.
        Psalm 119:140

    c) God's Word is right.

        The precepts of the Lord are right, rejoicing the heart; The commandment of the Lord is pure, enlightening the eyes.
        Psalm 19:8

        For the word of the Lord is upright; And all His work is done in faithfulness.
        Psalm 33:4

        Therefore I esteem right all Thy precepts concerning everything, I hate every false way.
        Psalm 119:128

    d) God's Word is truth.

        Sanctify them in the truth; Thy word is truth.
        John 17:17

    e) The promises are confirmed in Christ.

For I say that Christ has become a servant to the circumcision on behalf of the truth of God to confirm the promises given to the fathers.
Romans 15:8

3. His Word is powerful.

    a) With God nothing is impossible. "For with God nothing is ever impossible and no word from God shall be without power or impossible of fulfillment" (Luke 1:37, TAB).

    b) The Word heals.

        He sent His word and healed them, And delivered them from their destructions.
        Psalm 107:20

    c) The Word strengthens.

        My soul weeps because of grief; Strengthen me according to Thy word.
        Psalm 119:28

    d) The Word gives light and understanding.

        The unfolding of Thy words gives light; It gives understanding to the simple.
        Psalm 119:130

4. His Word is for you now.

    a) It is the Word that brings salvation.

        Many other signs therefore Jesus also performed in the presence of the disciples, which are not written in this book; but these have been written that you may believe that Jesus is the Christ, the Son of God; and that believing you may have life in His name.
        John 20:30,31

    b) God's Word is a way of life.

My son, observe the commandment of your father, And do not forsake the teaching of your mother; Bind them continually on your heart; Tie them around your neck. When you walk about, they will guide you; When you sleep, they will watch over you; And when you awake, they will talk to you. For the commandment is a lamp, and the teaching is light; And reproofs for discipline are the way of life.
Proverbs 6:20-23

c) You err if you don't know the Word.

But Jesus answered and said to them, "You are mistaken, not understanding the Scriptures, or the power of God.
Matthew 22:29

d) It brings forth fruit in your life.

"And the one on whom seed was sown on the good soil, this is the man who hears the word and understands it; who indeed bears fruit, and brings forth, some a hundredfold, some sixty, and some thirty."
Matthew 13:23

e) Christ's Word is to dwell in you.

Let the Word of Christ richly dwell within you, with all wisdom teaching and admonishing one another with psalms and hymns and spiritual songs, singing with thankfulness in your hearts to God.
Colossians 3:16

f) God says "yes" to His promises to you.

For as many as may be the promises of God, in Him they are yes; wherefore also by Him is our Amen to the glory of God through us.
II Corinthians 1:20

g) By God's promises you become a partaker of the divine nature.

For by these He has granted to us His precious and magnificent promises, in order that by them you might

become partakers of the divine nature, having escaped the corruption that is in the world by lust.
II Peter 1:4

h) It is for your teaching, equipping, and training.

...and that from childhood you have known the sacred writings which are able to give you the wisdom that leads to salvation through faith which is in Christ Jesus. All Scripture is inspired by God and profitable for teaching, for reproof, for correction, for training in righteousness; that the man of God may be adequate, equipped for every good work.
II Timothy 3:15-17

5. His Promises are conditional.

a) The Word must be mixed with faith.

For indeed we have had good news preached to us, just as they also; but the word they heard did not profit them, because it was not united by faith in those who heard.
Hebrews 4:2

b) Abraham received the promise through faith.

For the promise to Abraham or to his descendants that he would be heir of the world was not through the Law, but through the righteousness of faith. For if those who are of the Law are heirs, faith is made void and the promise is nullified; for the Law brings about wrath, but where there is no law, neither is there violation. For this reason it is by faith, that it might be in accordance with grace, in order that the promise may be certain to all the descendants, not only to those who are of the faith of Abraham, who is the father of us all.
Romans 4:13-16

c) Inheritance of the promises is through faith and patience.

And we desire that each one of you show the same diligence so as to realize the full assurance of hope until the end, that you may not be sluggish, but imitators of those who

through faith and patience inherit the promises.
Hebrews 6:11,12

d) Old Testament believers obtained by faith.

Who by faith conquered kingdoms, performed acts of
righteousness, obtained promises, shut the mouths of lions.
Hebrews 11:33

e) Even Jesus, the Son of God, could not activate the healing promises of God
where there was no faith.

And Jesus said to them, "A prophet is not without honor
except in his home town and among his own relatives and in
his own household." And He could do no miracle there
except that He laid His hands upon a few sick people and
healed them.
Mark 6:4-5

III. DEFINITION OF FAITH

A. REALIZING THAT THE INVISIBLE IS AS REAL AS THE VISIBLE

The things that are seen are temporal; the unseen is eternal.

...while we look not at the things which are seen, but at the things
which are not seen; for the things which are seen are temporal, but
the things which are not seen are eternal.
I Corinthians 4:18

When God shows us a truth from His Word and we do not see physical manifestation
with it, that does not mean it is unreal. That which is unseen is real and eternal.
The Word of God is often giving us truth that we cannot yet see with our eyes or
recognize with our senses; however, believing His Word puts our trust in something
more real than the tangible.

Christians are to walk by faith, not by sight. Faith is obeying the unseen--doing
what God says because He said it, not because we can always see immediate results.
Eternal results should determine our walk.

...for we walk by faith, not by sight--...
II Corinthians 5:7

But my righteous one shall live by faith; And if he shrinks back,
my soul has no pleasure in him.
Hebrews 10:38

B. THE EVIDENCE OF THINGS NOT SEEN

The Bible's definition of faith is found in Hebrews 11:1:

NAS "Now faith is the assurance of things hoped for, the conviction of things not seen."

PHILLIPS "Now faith means putting our full confidence in the things we hope for; it means being certain of the things we cannot see."

NEB "And what is faith? Faith gives substance to our hopes, and makes us certain of realities we do not see."

KJV "Now faith is the substance of things hoped for, the evidence of things not seen."

Vines Expository Dictionary: Faith (Pistis) is, primarily, firm persuasion, a conviction based upon hearing, is used in the N.T. always of faith in God or Christ, or things spiritual.

Thomas believed when he saw Jesus alive. Jesus said, "Blessed are they who did not see and yet believed."

> But Thomas, one of the twelve, called Didymus, was not with them when Jesus came. The other disciples therefore were saying to him, "We have seen the Lord!" But he said to them, "Unless I shall see in His hands the imprint of the nails, and put my finger into the place of the nails, and put my hand into His side, I will not believe." And after eight days again His disciples were inside, and Thomas with them. Jesus came, the doors having been shut, and stood in their midst, and said, "Peace be with you." Then He said to Thomas, "Reach here your finger, and see My hands; and reach here your hand, and put it into My side; and be not unbelieving, but believing." Thomas answered and said to Him, "My Lord and my God!" Jesus said to him, "Because you have seen Me, have you believed? Blessed are they who did not see, and yet believed."
> John 20:24-29

C. THE ASSURANCE OF THE THINGS HOPED FOR

   1. The necessity of hope

   Hope is not "I think so," or "I don't believe, but I hope so." It is not mere wishful thinking. According to Strong's, hope (elpis) means to "anticipate, usually with pleasure, expectation or confidence." Hope is the vision of your faith--the end result. Hope in itself will never come to pass. You need faith to feed the hope and faith to take action. But faith's action will bring to pass the things hoped for.

   Your hope may be your vision for the Body of Christ, a work that needs to be done, a need that must be met, a healing that needs to take place. Keep that hope before you, and add your faith to it. Act on it, and you will see it come to pass. To exercise faith in God, we must exercise faith in His Word. Act like God's Word is real. We can mentally assent to God's Word and never act on it. Faith is more than a mental assent. It is putting our actions in line with God's Word. Faith does not have to see, feel, smell, or taste. Faith believes when sense knowledge is not there. Faith states, "I have it now, even though I do not see it." As we consistently confess and act on God's Word, it materializes.

   We need hope. Faith gives substance to the things hoped for. We keep hope alive and keep that vision before us, then apply our faith to it. If there is no vision, no hope, we have nothing in which to apply our faith. We are to keep on hoping when all hope is gone. Abraham did, and he received his promise.

   > In hope against hope he believed, in order that he might become
   > a father of many nations, according to that which had been
   > spoken, "SO SHALL YOUR DESCENDANTS BE." And without
   > becoming weak in faith he contemplated his own body, now as
   > good as dead since he was about a hundred years old, and the
   > deadness of Sarah's womb.
   > Romans 4:18,19

   Hope will not be shattered if it is in God. God cannot change. If your hope is in circumstances, it will fall away when the circumstances change for the worse. With hope fallen, your faith will have nothing to put substance to, nothing to feed. The Psalmist says, "My hope is in Thee" (Psalm 39:7).

   God wants you to cherish and confess your hope. "So let us seize and hold fast and retain without wavering the hope we cherish and confess, and our acknowledgement of it, for He who promised is reliable (sure) and faithful to His Word" (Hebrews 10:23, TAB). Since our hope is in God, we are able to confess our hope, confess what we "hope" or expect God to do for us. As we do this, our faith has more and more to feed. Since both hope and faith are in God and His Word, it is essential that we know the Word and become saturated in it more and more.

Your hope can be developed. "But we do strongly and earnestly desire for each of you to show the same diligence and sincerity all the way through in realizing and enjoying the full assurance and development of your hope until the end" (Heb. 6:11, TAB). The more Word you receive into your spirit, the more your hope will be developed and the greater will be your active faith.

2. Incubation period of faith

Dr. Paul Yonggi Cho, Korean pastor of the world's largest church, has learned much about the operation of faith in his life. In his book, The Fourth Dimension, he describes faith as having an incubation period before the manifestation of it is seen with the senses. He points out four basic steps to the process of incubation:

a) First, one must envision a clear-cut picture of the objective of faith. Faith is the substance of clear-cut things that are hoped for. During his early ministry, Dr. Cho had been laboring under very poor circumstances without even his basic needs met. One day, while reading the Word, he began to realize that God wanted to fulfill His promises to him. He wanted to give to him those things that he needed. So Dr. Cho asked the Father for a chair, a desk, and a bicycle in order to more effectively preach the gospel. He believed God for them. He then began to wait expectantly for the visual fulfillment. He waited one, two, three, finally six months and nothing happened. Disappointed and somewhat dejected, he cried out to the Lord, asking Him what went wrong. Surely God would have to do something about answering His prayers if others were to believe in living a life of faith. The Father clearly showed him that he had not been specific. He had just said, "chair, table, and bicycle"--but there was no clear-cut vision. Immediately the young pastor clarified the request. He wanted a Philippine mahogany desk of a certain size, an iron-frame chair with rollers, and an American-made bicycle.

The next morning he was troubled. His heart felt empty. How was he to have faith until he received the answer? Romans 4:17 was quickened to his spirit: "God...calls those things which be not as if they were." He rushed out to tell everyone in the church tent of the three specifics he had received. To his frightened surprise, several men followed him home to see the things he had received. The Lord gave him wisdom to answer. He explained that just

14

as a baby is in the mother's womb nine months before it is born and seen by the world, so he had "conceived" a desk, a chair, and a bicycle. They were not visible yet, but he would receive them. They were growing inside of him. Though he had to contend with some ridicule, at the right time he received exactly what he had requested!

b) Have a burning desire for the thing requested. Proverbs 10:24 says, "The desire of the righteous will be granted." "Delight yourself in the Lord; and He will give you the desires of your heart" (Psalm 37:4). God rewards the earnest seeker, not the casual inquirer. Red hot desires get results!

c) Pray for the assurance of the answer. Faith is the "assurance of the things hoped for." It may take time to receive the assurance, but pray until you get it--then no one can take it from you. Your substance or assurance is like the title deed to "the thing hoped for."

d) Speak the Word. Just as Sarah and others called Abraham "father of many" long before he even had one son, so we speak the promises of God before we see them visibly come to pass. Speak the Word during the incubation period--speak it boldly! When Joshua and Caleb returned from spying out the land of Canaan they spoke out what they believed. They declared their faith: "We should by all means go up and take possession of it, for we shall surely overcome it" (Numbers 13:30). Faith in your heart is not sufficient. It must be released by your mouth.

> But what does it say? "The word is near you, in your mouth and in your heart"--that is, the word of faith which we are preaching,...
> Romans 10:8

IV. ACTION OF YOUR FAITH

Faith without works is useless. In other words, if we talk about our faith, but we don't act on what we believe, it means nothing, and nothing is accomplished.

In Joshua 2 we read the story of Rahab, a harlot who had heard the Word of the Lord. She had heard a rumor of what God was doing through the Israelites. She accepted God to be truly the God of heaven and earth and followed up with actions. When the spies came to her house, she hid and aided them in getting out of the city without being detected. As a new convert, she was not only concerned with her own salvation, but she also had an immediate burden for the members of her family. She pleaded that they be spared when the Israelites took the city.

The spies agreed to spare Rahab and her family. As a sign, they instructed her to hang a scarlet cord from her window. This cord was her hope. She hung it out of the window, knowing that the situation was not hopeless for her and her family. Along with hope was faith in her new-found God. The action she took, along with her faith, resulted in the salvation of her entire household. As an added blessing, she married an Israelite and became a "blessed one." Rahab had a son named Boaz and became an ancestor in the lineage of David and of the Lord Jesus Christ. Faith plus action will put you over!

If Rahab had merely believed that the Israelites worshiped the true God, but had never confessed it and taken corresponding actions, she would have been lost with the rest of the city (Joshua 2:14-24).

The paralytic man had been let down through the roof of the house by the faith of his companions; nevertheless, he was not healed until he acted on the words of Jesus, "Rise, take up your stretcher and go home" (Luke 5:18-26).

V. SUMMATION

A. The faith that pleases God is revelation faith. It is faith that believes and acts on God's Word regardless of visible circumstances. It is faith that is authoritative and creative. Only God can give this kind of faith.

B. The foundation of our faith is God Himself. He is not only the author of our faith, but He is also the example. He created the world by faith. God tells the righteous to live by faith; then He gives enough information in His Word to show us how. We can have faith because we have a faithful and reliable God. His Word is enduring, valid, true, and powerful for us today. Our faith is in God and His Word.

C. Faith is believing what God says even if visible manifestation is not seen. The unseen things are eternal. Christians are to walk by faith, not by sight. Faith is "perceiving as real fact what is not revealed to the senses." Faith is the confirmation of things hoped for. Use your hope to envision the answer you requested from God.

D. Faith has an incubation period. The four basic steps are: Ask specifically with a Scripture and have a clear-cut objective of faith. Second, have a burning desire for the thing requested. Third, envision the answer. Fourth, speak the Word. Now, be patient. God does keep His Word.

E. Faith has action. Believing without acting is not faith. We must believe what God says, speak it with our mouth, and then proceed to act like God is telling the truth. Act as though you have the answer to your prayer.

VI. ASSIGNMENTS

    A. Listen to the tape carefully.

    B. Complete the study guide questions.

    C. Recommended reading: <u>Changing the Seen and Shaping the Unseen</u>, by Charles Capps, and <u>Whatever Happened to Hope</u>? (Booklet), by Roy H. Hicks D.D.

STUDY GUIDE QUESTIONS

1. Briefly define four categories of faith.

    a. Human faith
    b. Religious faith
    c. Faith in experiences
    d. Revelation faith

2. Find a Biblical example of each category of faith.

3. Using Scripture, show how God is the foundation of your faith.

4. How do you know that God's Word is valid?

5. Describe three ways in which God's Word is powerful. Use Scripture.

6. List five things that God's Word does for you now. Share one thing that the Lord has done for you this week.

7. Give four Scriptures to explain what condition is necessary to receive the promises of God.

8. Choose a verse that speaks of the enduring power of God's Word and memorize it this week. Share it with the group.

9. Study Section III of your notes, and then give a definition of faith in your own words.

10. Explain why hope is necessary to faith.

11. From where should we get the material for our hopes?

12.   Name the four steps in the incubation period of faith.

13.   In Proverbs 10:24, it says "the desire of the righteous will be granted." Are these desires limited? If so, how?

14.   How can you get assurance for the answer to your request?

15.   Write out a clear-cut faith vision that the Lord has put on your heart.

2 How Faith Comes

I. FAITH COMES FROM GOD.

   A. AS AN ALLOTTED MEASURE

     Romans 12:3 says, "God has allotted to each a measure of faith." Every man has some faith as a direct gift from God. Man is responsible for how he uses this measure of faith. The verses following this one indicate that God has given this faith to be used in His service along with the foundational gift.

   B. THROUGH JESUS CHRIST YOUR SAVIOR.

     "Looking away, from all that will distract, to Jesus, Who is the Leader and the Source of our faith, giving the first incentive for our belief, and also its Finisher, bringing it to maturity and perfection" (Heb. 12:2, TAB).

     The more you know Jesus, the more your faith will grow. You know Him by what He says. As your Faith Source, He will take you through any situation. He will perfect and mature your faith. Jesus is the focal point of your faith.

   C. AS PART OF YOUR NEW NATURE

     Your new nature is a faith nature because it was born of God. We are the sons of God, and since God is a faith God, it is normal for His children to have His kind of faith.

       By faith we understand that the worlds were prepared by the word
       of God, so that what is seen was not made out of things which are
       visible.
       Hebrews 11:3

     Jesus told us to "have faith in God" (Mark 11:22), or, according to some translators, it could be, "Have the God-kind of faith." It is God's will for us to move in His kind of powerful, mountain-moving faith.

   D. AS A GIFT OF THE HOLY SPIRIT

     The Holy Spirit will at times drop a special gift of faith in your spirit for a specific task.

       ...to another faith by the same Spirit, and to another gifts of
       healing by the one Spirit,...
       I Corinthians 12:9

It will be faith to see a need met, a person saved, healed, or delivered. This faith is a known assurance that the event <u>will</u> come to pass.

II. FAITH COMES THROUGH YOUR SPIRIT.

According to Vine's Expository Dictionary, the heart is: "the chief organ of physical life ("for the life of the flesh is in the blood," Lev. 17:11); occupies the most important place in the human system. By an easy transition the word came to stand for man's entire mental and moral activity, both the rational and the emotional elements. In other words, the heart is used figuratively for the hidden springs of the personal life." The Scripture regards the heart as the sphere of Divine influence.

> ...in that they show the work of the Law written in their hearts, their
> conscience bearing witness, and their thoughts alternately accusing or
> else defending them.
> Romans 2:15

> ...and He made no distinction between us and them, cleansing their
> hearts by faith.
> Acts 15:9

Faith does not come through the senses; it comes through your heart or your spirit. In I Peter 3:4 the spirit is called "the hidden person of the heart." In Romans 7:22 it is called the "inner man." It is the part of you that believes, the part of you where faith takes place. "With the heart man believes..." (Rom. 10:10). This part of your being is re-created, renewed, and growing strong.

> Therefore we do not lose heart, but though our outer man is decaying,
> yet our inner man is being renewed day by day.
> II Corinthians 4:16

> That He would grant you, according to the riches of His glory, to be
> strengthened with power through His Spirit in the inner man;...
> Ephesians 3:16

There are times when your mind cannot grasp God's truth, but your heart or spirit is receiving it. That is the center of the Holy Spirit's indwelling, and He will cause your mind to comprehend what your spirit receives easily from God.

> For to us God revealed them through the Spirit; for the Spirit searches
> all things, even the depths of God. For who among men knows the
> thoughts of a man except the spirit of the man, which is in Him? Even
> so the thoughts of God no one knows except the Spirit of God. Now we

have received, not the spirit of the world, but the Spirit who is from God, that we might know the things freely given to us by God, which things we also speak, not in words taught by human wisdom, but in those taught by the Spirit, combining spiritual thoughts with spiritual words. But a natural man does not accept the things of the Spirit of God; for they are foolishness to him, and he cannot understand them, because they are spiritually appraised. But he who is spiritual appraises all things, yet he himself is appraised by no man. For who has known the mind of the Lord, that he should instruct Him? But we have the mind of Christ.
I Corinthians 2:10-16

But when He, the Spirit of truth, comes, He will guide you into all the truth; for He will not speak on His own initiative, but whatever He hears, He will speak; and He will disclose to you what is to come.
John 16:13

The Holy Spirit is your Faith Teacher. He teaches you through the Word. Let the Word feed your spirit in order for your faith to grow.

III.   FAITH COMES BY HEARING THE WORD OF GOD.

A. READ TO HEAR.

In your daily Bible reading you are hearing God's Word. Reading out loud gives you double hearing--with your outer ear and with your inner ear. Read as much of the Word as you can. Plan your schedule around God's Word. Every day, the receiving of God's Word into your spirit is the most important input of the day.

What you are reading is the general revealed Word of God, the "logos." But what brings faith is "rhema."

So faith comes from hearing, and hearing by the word of Christ.
Romans 10:17

"Logos" is the whole Word of God. "Rhema" is the singular Word--the spoken Word of God for a specific situation to you. When you fill your heart with the "logos," there is a reserve from which the Holy Spirit will bring to remembrance specific "rhema" for your situation. You will be able to speak the "rhema," and change your circumstances. Your faith will grow.

In Ephesians 6:17, the sword of the Spirit is the "rhema" of God. It is the individual Word used at the right time that will be as a sword to the enemy. Jesus said that man is to live by the "rhema" of God. Faith comes by hearing the "rhema" of God, but it starts with the "logos."

> And take the helmet of salvation, and the sword of the Spirit, which is the word of God.
> Ephesians 6:17

> But He answered and said, "It is written, 'Man shall not live on bread alone, but on every word that proceeds out of the mouth of God.'"
> Matthew 4:4

B. CONFESS TO HEAR.

God's Word is the Word of Faith.

> But what does it say? "The Word is near you, in your mouth and in your heart"--that is, the word of faith which we are preaching.
> Romans 10:8

You cannot separate God from His Word. Jesus was a part of all He said. Confess the following Scriptures:

> The Lord is my shepherd, I shall not want.
> Psalm 23:1

> "I am the good shepherd; and I know My own, and My own know Me."
> John 10:14

> "Do not fear, for I am with you; Do not anxiously look about you, for I am your God. I will strengthen you, surely I will help you, Surely I will uphold you with My righteous right hand."
> Isaiah 41:10

> What then shall we say to these things? If God is for us, who is against us?
> Romans 8:31

> I can do all things through Him who strengthens me.
> Philippians 4:13

The Lord is my light and my salvation; Whom shall I fear? The
Lord is the defense of my life; Whom shall I dread?
Psalm 27:1

And my God shall supply all your needs according to His riches in
glory in Christ Jesus.
Philippians 4:19

I will lift up my eyes to the mountains; From whence shall my help
come? My help comes from the Lord, Who made heaven and earth.
Psalm 121:1-2

How blessed is the man whose strength is in Thee; In whose heart
are the highways to Zion!
Psalm 84:5

Let God's Word get into every cell of your being and become part of you. Let God's
Word and you become one. God watches over His Word. He will watch over the Word
you confess.

You hear what you say! You will much more readily believe what you constantly hear
yourself saying. Say what God says!

C. LISTEN TO HEAR.

1. Take care how you listen.

Jesus said in Luke 8:18 that we should take care how we listen.

"Therefore take care how you listen; for whoever has, to him
shall more be given; and whoever does not have, even what he
thinks he has shall be taken away from him."
Luke 8:18

It is important to hear the Word, but it is more important that we really listen to
it--giving it importance in our attention. Our Lord had just finished explaining
the parable of the seed and the sower. The good soil had heard the Word in an
honest and good heart and held it fast. It was not passive hearing. It was
active listening and response! This was the successful and fruitful soil.

2. Isaac heard right.

In the blessing of Esau and Jacob, Isaac was deceived by his own smell, taste, and feelings. But, he was not deceived by his hearing--he heard the voice of Jacob. He should have given heed to what he heard!

> Then Isaac said to Jacob, "Please come close, that I may feel you, my son, whether you are really my son Esau or not." So Jacob came close to Isaac his father, and he felt him and said, "The voice is the voice of Jacob, but the hands are the hands of Esau." And he did not recognize him, because his hands were hairy like his brother Esau's hands; so he blessed him.
> Genesis 27:21-23

3. The Woman heard and acted.

The woman with the issue of blood heard about Jesus and gave heed to what she heard. That gave her faith to make her way through the crowd and dare to touch the hem of His garment, even though she had a condition that prohibited her from doing so. Her faith made her whole. It came from listening when she heard about Jesus.

> And a woman who had had a hemorrhage for twelve years, and had endured much at the hands of many physicians, and had spent all that she had and was not helped at all, but rather had grown worse, after hearing about Jesus, came up in the crowd behind Him and touched His cloak. For she thought, "If I just touch His garments, I shall get well." And immediately the flow of her blood was dried up; and she felt in her body that she was healed of her affliction.
> Mark 5:25-29

4. The lame man listened and responded.

"This man was listening to Paul as he spoke..." (Acts 14:9). The words the man heard were heeded to. He accepted them and faith came. Paul saw that faith and said, "Stand upright on your feet." His faith resulted in total healing.

> And at Lystra there was sitting a certain man, without strength in his feet, lame from his mother's womb, who had never walked. This man was listening to Paul as he spoke, who, when he had fixed his gaze upon him, and had seen that he had faith to be made well, said with a loud voice, "Stand upright on your

feet." And he leaped up and began to walk. And when the
multitudes saw what Paul had done, they raised their voice,
saying in the Lycaonian language, "The gods have become like
men and have come down to us."
Acts 14:8-11

D. MEDITATE TO HEAR.

The Bible says that faith comes by hearing the Word of God.

> So faith comes from hearing, and hearing by the word of Christ.
> Romans 10:17

Hearing the Word constantly is the best way for faith to come into our lives. God
has ordained a way which we can constantly hear the Word--by meditation. When we
meditate, we go over and over a thought in our mind. We think it, say it, then
think about it some more. Strong's says meditate means to: "mutter, ponder,
imagine, speak, study, talk, and utter." It is the same action as worry--only in
reverse! When we do all these things with the Word of God, our ears are bound to
hear it again and again. That is how faith comes. The best way to meditate is to
memorize a portion of God's Word; then several times a day "meditate" or ponder it.
Say it over and over again, asking God to reveal truth from it. Personalize it-- put
the Word into your present situation; then visualize the Word coming to pass.

Joshua needed faith to conquer the Promised Land. He had God's Word on it, yet
God gave him specific instructions to meditate on the Word.

> This book of the law shall not depart from your mouth, but you
> shall meditate on it day and night, so that you may be careful to do
> according to all that is written in it; for then you will make your
> way prosperous, and then you will have success.
> Joshua 1:8

The Word was not to depart from his mouth. He was to speak it again and again. He
did so and was able to lead Israel in faith. Also: "By faith, the walls of Jericho fell
down" (Heb. 11:30).

The righteous man of Psalm 1 meditates on the Word day and night.

> How blessed is the man who does not walk in the counsel of the
> wicked, Nor stand in the path of sinners, Nor sit in the seat of
> scoffers! But his delight is in the law of the Lord, And in His law
> he meditates day and night. And he will be like a tree firmly

planted by streams of water, Which yields its fruit in its season,
And its leaf does not wither; And in whatever he does, he
prospers.
Psalm 1:1-3

The Word causes him to be firmly planted, fruitful, and prosperous. It is the faith
that comes from God's Word that causes him to excel.

IV.   FAITH COMES BY SPEAKING IT.

A. MAKE YOUR FAITH YOUR OWN.

1.   Establish it.

It is essential that the faith we are speaking of becomes your very own. Do not
become dependent upon the faith of your pastor, teacher, or friend. God wants
your faith to belong to you and to work for you. He wants you to be established
in your faith.

> ...having been firmly rooted and now being built up in Him and
> established in your faith, just as you were instructed, and
> overflowing with gratitude.
> Colossians 2:7

One way to establish a thing is to declare it with your mouth. That is how you
were saved. You believed and you confessed. The word of faith is in your
mouth.

> But what does it say? "The word is near you, in your mouth
> and in your heart"--that is, the word of faith which we are
> preaching, that if you confess with your mouth Jesus as Lord,
> and believe in your heart that God raised Him from the dead,
> you shall be saved; for with the heart man believes, resulting
> in righteousness, and with the mouth he confesses, resulting in
> salvation.
> Romans 10:8-10

Believing involves the confession with your mouth. When you confess the
promises of God, you are claiming them as your own. You have been given a
measure of faith, the Logos of the Word, a will to choose, and a mouth to speak.
The more you choose to put the Word of God in your mouth the more faith will
become yours. It will become part of you, and no one can take it away.

2. Use it.

Once you have established your faith, claimed it as your own, begin using it. Use it to <u>receive</u> the promises of God. Remember, they are obtained by faith.

> ...who by faith conquered kingdoms, performed acts of righteousness, obtained promises, shut the mouths of lions.
> Hebrews 11:33

Receive the promises of healing:

> ...and He Himself bore our sins in His body on the cross, that we might die to sin and live to righteousness; for by His wounds you were healed.
> I Peter 2:24

> Surely our griefs He Himself bore, And our sorrows He carried; Yet we ourselves esteemed Him stricken, Smitten of God, and afflicted. But He was pierced through for our transgressions, He was crushed for our iniquities; The chastening for our well-being fell upon Him, And by His scourging we are healed.
> Isaiah 53:4-5

Receive the promise of your family's salvation:

> And they said, "Believe in the Lord Jesus, and you shall be saved, you and your household."
> Acts 16:31

Receive God's provision:

> And my God shall supply all your needs according to His riches in glory in Christ Jesus.
> Philippians 4:19

Receive wisdom in dealing with difficult situations:

> But if any of you lacks wisdom, let him ask of God, who gives to all men generously and without reproach, and it will be given to him.
> James 1:5

3. Hold fast to your confessions.

You know the promises of God. You have confessed them, you have received them, and you have received tangible evidence of the answers to your prayers. There are, however, other areas in which your faith is about to waver because you have confessed so long and nothing has happened. God wants you to "hold fast to your confession," and keep God's Words in "the midst of your heart."

Since then we have a great high priest who has passed through the heavens, Jesus the Son of God, let us hold fast our confession.
Hebrews 4:14

My son, give attention to my words; Incline your ear to my sayings. Do not let them depart from your sight; Keep them in the midst of your heart. For they are life to those who find them, And health to all their whole body.
Proverbs 4:20-22

B. SHARE YOUR FAITH.

"And I pray that the sharing of your faith may promote the knowledge of all the good that is ours in Christ" (Philemon 6, RSV).

It is difficult to share your faith without speaking it. Words are an indispensable means of communicating your faith. Your faith needs action, but is defined by your words. Share and speak your faith. It will grow and multiply--both in your life and in the lives of others. Share your doubts and they will do the same unless they are quenched with the water of the Word. Quit confessing your doubts, and begin confessing your faith. Real faith is built on God's Word. Don't let your words gain ascendancy over His Words! Promote the knowledge of all the good that is yours in Christ (Philemon 6).

V. FAITH COMES ACCOMPANIED BY LOVE.

Faith is not alone. It comes with love, and it works by love.

For in Christ Jesus neither circumcision nor uncircumcision means anything, but faith working through love.
Galatians 5:6

No believer should seek to be a person of great faith without seeking also to love much. The Word says that though you have the faith to remove mountains, if you have not love, you are nothing.

28

> And if I have the gift or prophecy, and know all mysteries and all
> knowledge; and if I have all faith, so as to remove mountains, but do
> not have love, I am nothing.
> I Corinthians 13:2

Kenneth Hagin, Jr. says, "If we are to live in line with God's Word, we must not only be the faith child of a faith God, but we must be a love child of a love God."

When Paul thanks God for the Thessalonians, he speaks of their "work of faith and labor of love."

> ...constantly bearing in mind your work of faith and labor of love and
> steadfastness of hope in our Lord Jesus Christ in the presence of our
> God and Father,...
> I Thessalonians 1:3

VI. SUMMATION

A. Faith comes from God as an allotted measure. Each person received enough faith to receive Christ and enough faith to operate in the foundational gifts that God gives him. Faith also comes through Christ, our Source, and is innate in the new nature because we are children of a faith God.

B. Faith comes through the heart or the spirit. Our mind must be renewed by the Word to receive God's truths. The reborn spirit readily accepts them. The Holy Spirit gives our spirits understanding and will also cause our minds to comprehend. Expect your spirit to receive much more than your mind can grasp!

C. Faith comes by hearing the Word of God. You can hear by reading, listening, confessing and meditating. Ask God to make the Logos of the written Word become the Rhema to you and give you specific words by which you are fed and with which you feed your enemies!

D. Faith becomes your own as you establish it with your mouth. Use your faith to receive God's promises, and hold fast to your confession of faith regardless of outward circumstances. Your faith also grows as you share it with others. Each truth of God that is shared is multiplied back to the giver.

E. Faith will come with love--it cannot work without it. Be a child of faith and of love. Your Heavenly Father is the Author of both.

VII. ASSIGNMENTS

    A. Listen to tape carefully.

    B. Complete the study guide questions.

    C. Recommended reading: <u>The Force of Faith</u>, by Kenneth Copeland.

STUDY GUIDE QUESTIONS

1. Study Romans 12:1-8. Why was the measure of faith given to you?

2. Christ is the Source of faith according to Hebrews 12:2. How can we cause this faith to grow?

3. One of the translations of Mark 11:22 says, "Have the God-kind of faith." How do we obtain this God-kind of faith (Mark 11:23, 24)?

4. Faith comes through our hearts, or spirits. How should we pray for our "inner man" according to the following verses:

    a. Ephesians 1:18
    b. Ephesians 3:16
    c. II Corinthians 4:16

5. Study I Corinthians 2:10-16.

    a. How does God reveal spiritual truth?
    b. For what specific reason did we receive the Spirit of God?
    c. Why does natural reasoning have difficulty accepting God's truth?
    d. What is the assurance that we will be able to comprehend even
       with our mind?

6. Explain in your own words "logos" and "rhema". Which brings faith according to Romans 10:17?

7. How does "confessing the Word" cause you to hear and, therefore, to believe?

8. Read several translations of Luke 8:18. What did Jesus mean when He said, "Take care how you listen?" From the context of the chapter, to what were they to listen?

9.   How can you make faith your own so you do not have to be dependent upon anothers' faith?

10.   Find at least four Scriptures to support this truth: "Speak your faith and not your doubts."

11.   Faith works through love. Using the Scripture given, tell how we can be love-children of a love-God?

      a. Galatians 5:6-14
      b. Ephesians 5:1,2
      c. Romans 14:12-23
      d. Ephesians 4:1-3
      e. Ephesians 4:15,29

12.   Choose one "love" verse to memorize this week. Share it with the class.

3   The Power of the Tongue

I. SPEAKING CAUSES ACTION.

A. GOD SPOKE AND THE UNIVERSE WAS CREATED.

1. Hebrews 11:3 tells us that the "worlds were prepared by the Word of God."

> By faith we understand that the worlds were prepared by the word of God, so that what is seen was not made out of things which are visible.
> Hebrews 11:3

When you read Genesis chapter 1, you notice that God spoke and matter was created. He said, "Let there be light" and there was light. He said, "Let there be an expanse in the midst of the waters, and let it separate the waters from the waters...and it was so." He said, "Let the earth sprout vegetation...and it was so." All of the universe was created by God's spoken Word; and even now all things are upheld by the Word of His power.

> And He is the radiance of His glory and the exact representation of His nature, and upholds all things by the word of His power. When He had made purification of sins, He sat down at the right hand of the Majesty on High.
> Hebrews 1:3

B. LUCIFER SPOKE AND WAS CAST OUT OF HEAVEN.

Isaiah 14:13 tells what happened to the mighty, high-level angel, Lucifer. He said, "I will ascend to heaven; I will raise my throne above the stars of God, and I will sit on the mount of assembly in the recesses of the north...I will make myself like the Most High."

Ever since that day, Satan has been existing with one purpose--to turn others in rebellion against the Most High. Every time he speaks, it is with lies and deception. Much, much destruction has taken place because of his words.

C. JESUS SPOKE AND PROVIDED YOUR FREEDOM.

Jesus said to the Father, "Thy will be done." The Father's will led Him to the cross. On the cross, some of His last words were, "It is finished." He had provided a way in which you could be free from the tyranny of sin. He gave His life that you might have yours. His death and resurrection stripped Satan of his power, giving you a new power--Christ as your very life source.

Having canceled out the certificate of debt consisting of decrees against us and which was hostile to us; and He has taken it out of the way, having nailed it to the cross. When He had disarmed the rulers and authorities, He made a public display of them, having triumphed over them through Him.
Colossians 2:14-15

"I have been crucified with Christ; and it is no longer I who live, but Christ lives in me; and the life which I now live in the flesh I live by faith in the Son of God, who loved me, and delivered Himself up for me."
Galatians 2:20

Now, Christ's words spoken by you overrule Satan each time he comes with his cunning lies! From Jesus' words come life and overcoming power!

II. YOUR TONGUE IS DYNAMIC.

A. IT GUIDES YOUR WHOLE LIFE.

Your tongue is the most powerful weapon and force of your life. James 3:5 states that you can control your whole body by that small member you have called the tongue--it is a tremendous power for good. As a rudder guides a ship and a bit in a horse's mouth causes him to go the right direction, so also your tongue can guide your thoughts, your emotions, and your body into paths of prosperity and success.

So also the tongue is a small part of the body, and yet it boasts of great things. Behold, how great a forest is set aflame by such a small fire!
James 3:5

B. IT CAN DESTROY.

Your tongue can be used to damage and destroy your physical body, your thought life, and your emotional reactions. Corrupt words can destroy those about us. Proverbs states that words are like the piercing of swords.

There is one who speaks rashly like the thrusts of a sword, But the tongue of the wise brings healing.
Proverbs 12:18

You set on fire the course of nature by what you speak because hell acts on your words. Eve had to speak wrong words before Satan could act. He can act only on

33

your words. Every negative word you speak sets hell into activity. This is why God spoke to Joshua and said, "Don't let _my_ words depart out of your mouth...."

"This book of the law shall not depart from your mouth, but you shall meditate on it day and night, so that you may be careful to do according to all that is written in it; for then you will make your way prosperous, and then you will have success."
Joshua 1:8

C. IT CAN DEFEAT THE WICKED ONE.

Revelation 12:11 states that God's children overcame the accuser of the brethren "because of the blood of the Lamb and because of the _word_ of their testimony." We overcome the wicked one by using our tongues against him.

What about words spoken against us and our loved ones? Will those negative confessions set hell into activity in our lives? As always, God's Word has an answer. It is found in Isaiah 54:17: "'No weapon that is formed against you shall prosper; and every tongue that accuses you in judgment you will condemn. This is the heritage of the servants of the Lord and their vindication is from Me,' declares the Lord." Condemn wrong words spoken against you and yours, in the Name of Jesus. Never condemn _a person_ who speaks, only _the words_ spoken against you; then those negative "word weapons" cannot harm you.

D. IT CAN YIELD PRECIOUS FRUIT.

Your tongue can yield precious fruit--words that are fitly spoken. Words can comfort the sad, heal the brokenhearted, cool anger, and bring order to confusion. Words can restore courage, calm the fearful, stir to right actions, and stop the work of the wicked one. But most of all, your words can announce God's Words! Words can heal the sick, release the imprisoned, and feed the poor. Your speaking the right thing will satisfy your life. God says those fitly spoken words are like "apples of gold in frames of silver."

With the fruit of a man's mouth his stomach will be satisfied; He will be satisfied with the product of his lips.
Proverbs 18:20

Like apples of gold in settings of silver is a word spoken in right circumstances. Like an earring of gold and an ornament of fine gold Is a wise reprover to a listening ear.
Proverbs 25:11-12

He sees "lips of knowledge" as "more precious than gold and precious jewels" (Proverbs 20:15). The treasure of your tongue can yield much power!

III. NEGATIVE USE OF THE TONGUE

A. GOSSIP

1. Harms friendships

He who covers a transgression seeks love, But he who repeats a matter separates intimate friends.
Proverbs 17:9

A man of violence entices his neighbor, And leads him in a way that is not good.
Proverbs 16:29

2. Warned against by God

"You shall not go about as a slanderer among your people, and you are not to act against the life of your neighbor; I am the Lord."
Leviticus 19:16

3. We are not to associate with gossips.

He who goes about as a slanderer reveals secrets, Therefore do not associate with a gossip.
Proverbs 20:19

4. Causes strife

For lack of wood the fire goes out, And where there is no whisperer, contention quiets down. Like charcoal to hot embers and wood to fire, So is a contentious man to kindle strife.
Proverbs 26:20-21

B. SPEAKING EVIL AND CURSING

1. Keep your tongue from evil and your lips from speaking deceit.

Keep your tongue from evil, And your lips from speaking
deceit.
Psalm 34:13

2. Put away from you a deceitful mouth, and put devious lips far from you.

Put away from you a deceitful mouth, And put devious lips far
from you.
Proverbs 4:24

3. Evil speaking can tear down a city.

By the blessing of the upright a city is exalted, But by the
mouth of the wicked it is torn down.
Proverbs 11:11

4. A worthless man digs up evil, while his words are a scorching fire.

A worthless man digs up evil, While his words are as a
scorching fire.
Proverbs 16:27

5. Let all evil speaking be put away.

Let all bitterness and wrath and anger and clamor and slander
be put away from you, along with all malice.
Ephesians 4:31

Therefore, putting aside all malice and all guile and hypocrisy
and envy and all slander,...
I Peter 2:1

For, "Let him who means to love life and see good days refrain
his tongue from evil and his lips from speaking guile."
I Peter 3:10

6. There should be no "filthiness, silly talk, or coarse jesting."

and there must be no filthiness and silly talk, or coarse jesting,
which are not fitting,...
Ephesians 5:4

C. PRIDE AND FLATTERY

1. The Lord is against the flattering lips.

> Help, Lord, for the godly man ceases to be, For the faithful disappear from among the sons of men. They speak falsehood to one another; With flattering lips and with a double heart they speak. May the Lord cut off all flattering lips, The tongue that speaks great things; Who have said, "With our tongue we will prevail; Our lips are our own; who is lord over us?" "Because of the devastation of the afflicted, because of the groaning of the needy, Now I will arise," says the Lord; "I will set him in the safety for which he longs."
> Psalm 12:1-5

2. A flattering mouth works ruin.

> A lying tongue hates those it crushes, And a flattering mouth works ruin.
> Proverbs 26:28

3. Let another praise you...not your own mouth.

> Do not boast about tomorrow, For you do not know what a day may bring forth. Let another praise you, and not your own mouth; A stranger, and not your own lips.
> Proverbs 27:1-2

D. TALKING TOO MUCH

1. When there are many words, transgression is unavoidable, but he who restrains his lips is wise.

> When there are many words, transgression is unavoidable, But he who restrains his lips is wise.
> Proverbs 10:19

> A fool always loses his temper, But a wise man holds it back.
> Proverbs 29:11

Do you see a man who is hasty in his words? There is more
hope for a fool than for him.
Proverbs 29:20

2. The one who guards his mouth preserves his life; the one who opens wide his lips
    comes to ruin.

    The one who guards his mouth preserves his life; The one who
    opens wide his lips comes to ruin.
    Proverbs 13:3

3. The fool multiplies words.

    Words from the mouth of a wise man are gracious, while the lips
    of a fool consume him; the beginning of his talking is folly, and
    the end of it is wicked madness. Yet the fool multiplies words.
    No man knows what will happen, and who can tell him what will
    come after him?
    Ecclesiastes 10:12-14

E. LYING AND DECEIT

1. The lying tongue is only for a moment.

    Truthful lips will be established forever, But a lying tongue is
    only for a moment.
    Proverbs 12:19

2. An evildoer listens to wicked lips. An evildoer pays attention to a destructive
    tongue.

    An evildoer listens to wicked lips, A liar pays attention to a
    destructive tongue.
    Proverbs 17:4

3. Though men may try to cover the deceit of their heart with their lips, it will not
    be successful.

    The words of a whisperer are like dainty morsels, And they go
    down into the innermost parts of the body. Like an earthen
    vessel overlaid with silver dross Are burning lips and a wicked
    heart. He who hates disguises it with his lips, But he lays up
    deceit in his heart. When he speaks graciously, do not believe

him, For there are seven abominations in his heart. Though his hatred covers itself with guile, His wickedness will be revealed before the assembly.
Proverbs 26:22-26

4. A lying tongue hates those it crushes (Proverbs 26:28).

IV. POSITIVE USE OF THE TONGUE

A. PRAISING THE LORD

1. We are created to praise and worship God. God <u>seeks</u> those who will worship Him in spirit and in truth.

> "But an hour is coming, and now is, when the true worshipers shall worship the Father in spirit and truth; for such people the Father seeks to be His worshipers.
> John 4:23

The Psalms are full of exhortations to praise the Lord for His mighty works, to magnify His Name. Let everything that hath breath praise the Lord (Psalm 150:6). What a way to use your tongue!

2. There is power in praise. Many people are baptized in the Holy Spirit while praising the Lord. Also, many physical healings take place while God's people are praising Him. And there is no question that the assurance of answered prayer often comes during praise. Praise was powerful according to Scripture:

a) The Baptism of the Holy Spirit fell on a group of disciples who were "continually in the temple praising God."

> And they returned to Jerusalem with great joy, and were continually in the temple, praising God.
> Luke 24:52-53

> And when the day of Pentecost had come, they were all together in one place. And suddenly there came from heaven a noise like a violent, rushing wind, and it filled the whole house where they were sitting. And there appeared to them tongues as of fire distributing themselves, and they rested on each one of them. And they were all filled with

the Holy Spirit and began to speak with other tongues, as the Spirit was giving them utterance.
Acts 2:1-4

b) Numbers were added to the early church when there was an atmosphere of praise among the believers.

And day by day continuing with one mind in the temple, and breaking bread from house to house, they were taking their meals together with gladness and sincerity of heart, praising God, and having favor with all the people. And the Lord was adding to their number day by day those who were being saved.
Acts 2:46-47

c) Praise opened prison doors and brought salvation to the jailer.

But about midnight Paul and Silas were praying and singing hymns of praise to God, and the prisoners were listening to them; and suddenly there came a great earthquake, so that the foundations of the prison house were shaken; and immediately all the doors were opened, and everyone's chains were unfastened. And when the jailer had been roused out of sleep and had seen the prison doors opened, he drew his sword and was about to kill himself, supposing that the prisoners had escaped. But Paul cried out with a loud voice, saying, "Do yourself no harm, for we are all here!" And he called for lights and rushed in and, trembling with fear, he fell down before Paul and Silas, and after he brought them out, he said, "Sirs, what must I do to be saved?" And they said, "Believe in the Lord Jesus, and you shall be saved, you and your household."
Acts 16:25-31

3. We are to enter into God's presence with praise.

Enter His gates with thanksgiving, And His courts with praise. Give thanks to Him; bless His name. For the Lord is good; His lovingkindness is everlasting, And His faithfulness to all generations.
Psalm 100:4-5

B. EDIFYING ONE ANOTHER

1. We are to speak the truth to one another, in love, letting nothing corrupt come out of our mouths, only that which brings edification, which is needed for the moment.

> Therefore, laying aside falsehood, speak truth, each one of you, with his neighbor, for we are members of one another.
> Ephesians 4:25

> Let no unwholesome word proceed from your mouth, but only such a word as is good for edification according to the need of the moment, that it may give grace to those who hear.
> Ephesians 4:29

2. Pleasant words heal.

> Pleasant words are a honeycomb, Sweet to the soul and healing to the bones.
> Proverbs 16:24

3. Timely words bring joy.

> A man has joy in an apt answer, And how delightful is a timely word!
> Proverbs 15:23

C. SPEAKING WISELY

1. The tongue of the wise makes knowledge acceptable.

> The tongue of the wise makes knowledge acceptable, But the mouth of fools spouts folly.
> Proverbs 15:2

> The lips of the wise spread knowledge, But the hearts of fools are not so.
> Proverbs 15:7

2. The mouth of the righteous utters wisdom and speaks justice.

The mouth of the righteous utters wisdom, And his tongue
speaks justice.
Psalm 37:30

The mouth of the righteous flows with wisdom, But the
perverted tongue will be cut out.
Proverbs 10:31

She opens her mouth in wisdom, And the teaching of kindness is
on her tongue.
Proverbs 31:26

3. The wise person conceals instead of reveals private information.

He who goes about as a talebearer reveals secrets, But he who
is trustworthy conceals a mattèr.
Proverbs 11:13

A man's discretion makes him slow to anger, And it is his glory
to overlook a transgression.
Proverbs 19:11

4. He turns away wrath with a soft answer.

A gentle answer turns away wrath, But a harsh word stirs up
anger.
Proverbs 15:1

5. His speech is always with grace. He knows how to answer each person.

Let your speech always be with grace, seasoned, as it were,
with salt, so that you may know how you should respond to each
person.
Colossians 4:6

...but sanctify Christ as Lord in your hearts, always being
ready to make a defense to everyone who asks you to give an
account for the hope that is in you, yet with gentleness and
reverence;...
I Peter 3:15

6. He is not quick to speak. He bridles his tongue.

This you know, my beloved brethren. But let everyone be
quick to hear, slow to speak and slow to anger;...
James 1:19

If anyone thinks himself to be religious, and yet does not bridle
his tongue but deceives his own heart, this man's religion is
worthless.
James 1:26

For we all stumble in many ways. If anyone does not stumble in
what he says, he is a perfect man, able to bridle the whole body
as well.
James 3:2

He who guards his mouth and his tongue, Guards his soul from
troubles.
Proverbs 21:23

D. PRESENTING REQUESTS

1. We are to do away with anxiety and worry by letting God know of our needs and
then receiving His peace.

> Be anxious for nothing, but in everything by prayer and
> supplication with thanksgiving let your requests be made known
> to God. And the peace of God, which surpasses all
> comprehension, shall guard your hearts and your minds in
> Christ Jesus.
> Philippians 4:6-7

2. We are to pray and intercede especially for those in authority.

> First of all, then, I urge that entreaties and prayers, petitions
> and thanksgivings, be made on behalf of all men, for kings and
> all who are in authority, in order that we may lead a tranquil
> and quiet life in all godliness and dignity.
> I Timothy 2:1-2

3. We are to pray for one another for both spiritual and physical health.

> Is anyone among you sick? Let him call for the elders of the
> church, and let them pray over him, anointing him with oil in
> the name of the Lord; and the prayer offered in faith will

restore the one who is sick, and the Lord will raise him up, and if he has committed sins, they will be forgiven him. Therefore, confess your sins to one another, and pray for one another, so that you may be healed. The effective prayer of a righteous man can accomplish much. Elijah was a man with a nature like ours, and he prayed earnestly that it might not rain; and it did not rain on the earth for three years and six months. And he prayed again, and the sky poured rain, and the earth produced its fruit. My brethren, if any among you strays from the truth, and one turns him back, let him know that he who turns a sinner from the error of his way will save his soul from death, and will cover a multitude of sins.
James 5:14-20

E. TALKING ABOUT THE LORD

1. I will muse (talk) about Thy deeds.

    I will meditate on all Thy work, And muse on Thy deeds.
    Psalm 77:12

    On the glorious splendor of Thy majesty, And on Thy wonderful works, I will meditate.
    Psalm 145:5

2. Speak of the Lord's power and glory and mighty acts.

    All Thy works shall give thanks to Thee, O Lord, And Thy godly ones shall bless Thee. They shall speak of the glory of Thy kingdom, And talk of Thy power; To make known to the sons of men Thy mighty acts, And the glory of the majesty of Thy kingdom.
    Psalm 145:10-12

3. The righteous man's mouth is filled with the Word of the Lord.

    With my lips I have told of all the ordinances of Thy mouth.
    Psalm 119:13

    I will also speak of Thy testimonies before kings, And shall not be ashamed.
    Psalm 119:46

Thy statutes are my songs In the house of my pilgrimage.
Psalm 119:54

Let my tongue sing of Thy word, For all Thy commandments are
righteousness.
Psalm 119:172

V. THE NECESSITY OF TONGUE CONTROL

A. YOUR WORDS REFLECT YOUR CHARACTER.

"A tree is known by its fruits...for the mouth speaks out of that which fills the
heart."

> "Either make the tree good, and its fruit good; or make the tree
> bad, and its fruit bad; for the tree is known by its fruit. You
> brood of vipers, how can you, being evil, speak what is good? For
> the mouth speaks out of that which fills the heart. The good man
> out of his good treasure brings forth what is good; and the evil
> man out of his evil treasure brings forth what is evil. And I say to
> you, that every careless word that men shall speak, they shall
> render account for it in the day of judgment. For by your words
> you shall be justified, and by your words you shall be condemned."
> Matthew 12:33-37

What you say is powerful because you show to the world what is inside your heart.
If your heart is filled with the Word of God, your mouth will speak the Word. If the
all-powerful God is in charge of your life and His Word fills your being, your life will
reflect that power, and your prayer life will be dynamic. If the holy, good God
dwells within your heart, then your words will be holy and good. If the Creator of
the universe is your constant companion, you will speak creative and constructive
words. If the only wise God is abiding in the inner man, your words will be
saturated with wisdom. This God is also loving, just, and faithful. How can your
words be otherwise?

We pray, "Lord, you have control of my life, now live my life for me. May all my
words and actions forever be pleasing to you." This is a correct prayer; however,
our will is constantly at work. We are daily making choices to live with His Life and
not ours. It is our task to yield almost exclusively with our tongue! We make a
decision in our heart and then announce it with the words we express. Assurance of
tongue control is the speaking of God's Word. When our conversation is in line with
God's Word, we know it is also revealing the character of God, which is our new
nature. That is why you need to fill your heart with the Word of God! Then speak

it with your mouth. You will find that your actions will reflect what you know to be in your heart--the Holy Spirit of God Himself. That is powerful living! Believe the Word, then speak what you believe!

> But having the same spirit of faith, according to what is written, "I believed, therefore I spoke," we also believe, therefore also we speak.
> II Corinthians 4:13

B. YOU WILL ACCOUNT FOR YOUR WORDS.

Jesus said that we will render account for every careless word we speak. We will be justified or condemned by the words we speak (Matthew 12:36,37).

That is very strong language and may tend to sting until we realize that God meant for the tongue to be an avenue of strength and creativity. He said that a good tree brings forth good fruit. You have the righteousness of Christ. His goodness is your fountain, your vine. The fruit you bear comes straight from the Vine Himself. There is no lack of quality, no lack of resource. Our will needs to be put into actions to have our words reveal the quality of His life. Jesus did not give us an impossible task. Without Him it is impossible. With Him, however, our words can be a fountain of blessing every time we open our mouth. Your words can work for you or against you. The Word in your mouth will make your words a positive, powerful force!

C. YOU NEED HELP TO TAME YOUR TONGUE.

In James 1:26 the Bible says, "If anyone thinks himself to be religious, and yet does not bridle his tongue but deceives his own heart, this man's religion is worthless." And James 3:2 says, "For we all stumble in many ways. If anyone does not stumble in what he says, he is a perfect man, able to bridle the whole body as well." It is very clear that taming the tongue is necessary to success in God's eye. Yet, in James 3:8 he says, "But no one can tame the tongue; it is a restless evil and full of deadly poison." That means you <u>cannot</u> completely control your tongue and harness the energy and power within it for good. <u>You</u> cannot--but the Holy Spirit can! He wants the fountain of your tongue to bring forth fresh water and produce good fruit at all times.

You can do all things through Christ who strengthens you (Philippians 4:13). You <u>can</u> allow the Holy Spirit to control your tongue. In Romans 6 we are exhorted to present the members of our body to God as instruments of His righteousness. We are the instruments, and He provides the power and knowledge. Our yielding to Him regulates the control!

46

For the death that He died, He died to sin, once for all; but the life
that He lives, He lives to God. Even so consider yourselves to be
dead to sin, but alive to God in Christ Jesus. Therefore do not let
sin reign in your mortal body that you should obey its lusts, and
do not go on presenting the members of your body to sin as
instruments of unrighteousness; but present yourselves to God as
those alive from the dead, and your members as instruments of
righteousness to God. For sin shall not be master over you, for
you are not under law, but under grace. What then? Shall we sin
because we are not under law but under grace? May it never be!
Do you not know that when you present yourselves to someone as
slaves for obedience, you are slaves of the one whom you obey,
either of sin resulting in death, or of obedience resulting in
righteousness? But thanks be to God that though you were slaves
of sin, you became obedient from the heart to that form of teaching
to which you were committed, and having been freed from sin, you
became slaves of righteousness. I am speaking in human terms
because of the weakness of your flesh. For just as you presented
your members as slaves to impurity and to lawlessness, resulting in
further lawlessness, so now present your members as slaves to
righteousness, resulting in sanctification. For when you were
slaves of sin, you were free in regard to righteousness. Therefore
what benefit were you then deriving from the things of which you
are now ashamed? For the outcome of those things is death.
Romans 6:10-21

Yielding to the Lord necessarily involves submission to His Word. This in turn, as
we have already seen several times, means being _full_ of the Word of God.

Pray these prayers for tongue control: "Set a guard, O Lord, over my mouth; keep
watch over the door of my lips" (Psalm 141:3). "Let the words of my mouth and the
meditation of my heart be acceptable in Thy sight O Lord, my rock and my
Redeemer" (Psalm 19:14).

VI.   USE YOUR TONGUE TO SEND THE WORD OF GOD.

A. GOD'S WORD ACCOMPLISHES AND PERFORMS.

1.   In Jeremiah 1:12 the Lord says that He will hasten His Word to perform it. If we
are sending God's Word, it has a built-in guarantee with it. God's Word carries
God's promise to perform!

> Then the Lord said to me, "You have seen well, for I am watching over My word to perform it."
> Jeremiah 1:12

2. God promises that His Word would prosper in the thing to which He sent it. God's Word will accomplish its purpose!

> So shall My word be which goes forth from My mouth; It shall not return to Me empty, Without accomplishing what I desire, And without succeeding in the matter for which I sent it.
> Isaiah 55:11

B. GOD'S WORD-POWER ANNIHILATES DISTANCE.

1. The centurion

> And when He had entered Capernaum, a centurion came to Him, entreating Him, and saying, "Lord, my servant is lying paralyzed at home, suffering great pain." And He said to him, "I will come and heal him." But the centurion answered and said, "Lord, I am not worthy for You to come under my roof, but just say the word, and my servant will be healed. For I, too, am a man under authority, with soldiers under me; and I say to this one, 'Go!' and he goes, and to another, 'Come!' and he comes, and to my slave, 'Do this!' and he does it." Now when Jesus heard this, He marveled, and said to those who were following, "Truly I say to you, I have not found such great faith with anyone in Israel."
> Matthew 8:5-10

A centurion came to Jesus. Jesus said, "I will come and heal your servant." But the centurion answered, "I am not worthy. Just speak the word and he will be healed." Jesus spoke the Word, and the healing traveled to the servant. The distance was no obstacle. His Word knows no distance! You, too, can speak the Word for distant friends and relatives.

2. The healing of the Nobleman

> He came therefore again to Cana of Galilee where He had made the water wine. And there was a certain royal official, whose son was sick at Capernaum. When he heard that Jesus had come out of Judea into Galilee, he went to Him, and was requesting Him to come down and heal his son; for he was at the point of

death. Jesus therefore said to him, "Unless you people see signs and wonders, you simply will not believe." The royal official said to Him, "Sir, come down before my child dies." Jesus said to him, "Go your way; your son lives." The man believed the word that Jesus spoke to him, and he started off. And as he was now going down, his slaves met him, saying that his son was living. So he inquired of them the hour when he began to get better. They said therefore to him, "Yesterday at the seventh hour the fever left him."
John 4:46-52

The man believed the Word of Jesus, and his son was healed even though he was quite a distance away. When the Word of God is spoken in faith at one point, miracles can be happening at another place!

C. GOD'S WORD WILL BE A POSITIVE FORCE.

1. To restore right attitudes

There are times when we share negative feelings and problems, but we must not stop at that. Where there are negative feelings, remember who you are in Christ and who your source is, and speak the positive feeling. For example, perhaps you "feel" hatred for a brother who has misused you. You may express that feeling to God, confess your hatred as sin, and then speak the answer: "I have the love of God shed abroad in my heart for my brother. I forgive him. I will be kind and "not take into account the wrong suffered."

...and hope does not disappoint, because the love of God has been poured out within our hearts through the Holy Spirit who was given to us.
Romans 5:5

Love does not act unbecomingly; it does not seek its own, is not provoked, does not take into account a wrong suffered.
I Corinthians 13:5

As you confess that a few times, you will begin to feel love for that person; however, you do it in faith before any feeling comes.

2. To heal--anything!

Psalm 107:20 says, "He sent His Word and healed them, And delivered them from their destruction." And Proverbs 4:20-22 goes on to say, "My son, give attention to my words; Incline your ear to my sayings. Do not let them depart from your sight; Keep them in the midst of your heart. For they are life to those who find them, And health to all their whole body." Use your mouth to activate the Word of God. Send it into broken homes, to sick friends, tired workers, dried up finances, ungodly relatives, and see the Word heal the situation.

Speak the Word to your own body when sickness attacks. When you speak to your body, use verses on healing and renew your mind to think health and not sickness. If your healing does not manifest immediately, do not allow Satan to condemn you over the use of medication. As Charles Capps says, "Take your pills in the Name of Jesus, and you will find your pills work twice as good." Soon you will find that you don't need them. God _does_ want you well, not suffering for years, claiming you are trusting God.

> Beloved, I pray that in all respects you may prosper and be in
> good health, just as your soul prospers.
> III John 2

D. JESUS ALWAYS SPOKE GOD'S WORD.

Jesus spoke what He heard the Father say. That is how He overcame the world. Jesus spoke words of truth and life. Ephesians 5:1 tells us to be imitators of God. Like Jesus, we should talk like our Father.

> Jesus therefore answered and was saying to them, "Truly, truly, I
> say to you, the Son can do nothing of Himself, unless it is
> something He sees the Father doing; for whatever the Father does,
> these things the Son also does in like manner."
> John 5:19

> "I can do nothing on My own initiative. As I hear, I judge; and My
> judgment is just, because I do not seek My own will, but the will of
> Him who sent Me."
> John 5:30

> "I have many things to speak and to judge concerning you, but He
> who sent Me is true; and the things which I heard from Him, these
> I speak to the world." They did not realize that He had been
> speaking to them about the Father. Jesus therefore said, "When

you lift up the Son of Man, then you will know that I am He, and I
do nothing on My own initiative, but I speak these things as the
Father taught me."
John 8:26-28

"These things I have spoken to you, that in Me you may have
peace. In the world you have tribulation, but take courage; I have
overcome the world."
John 16:33

"It is the Spirit who gives life; the flesh profits nothing; the words
that I have spoken to you are spirit and are life."
John 6:63

Therefore be imitators of God, as beloved children;...
Ephesians 5:1

E. YOUR DEEDS MUST CORRESPOND WITH YOUR WORDS.

Hear the Word, say the Word, and practice the Word. If your tongue is harnessed
up to God's Word power, your deeds will have to adjust to be in oneness with your
mouth!

"And why do you call Me, 'Lord, Lord,' and do not do what I say?
Everyone who comes to Me, and hears My words, and acts upon
them, I will show you whom he is like: he is like a man building a
house, who dug deep and laid a foundation upon the rock; and
when a flood rose, the torrent burst against that house and could
not shake it, because it had been well built."
Luke 6:46-48

Therefore putting aside all filthiness and all that remains of
wickedness, in humility receive the word implanted, which is able to
save your souls. But prove yourselves doers of the word, and not
merely hearers who delude themselves. For if anyone is a hearer of
the word and not a doer, he is like a man who looks at his natural
face in a mirror; for once he has looked at himself and gone away,
he has immediately forgotten what kind of person he was. But one
who looks intently at the perfect law, the law of liberty, and abides
by it, not having become a forgetful hearer but an effectual doer,
this man shall be blessed in what he does. If anyone thinks himself
to be religious, and yet does not bridle his tongue but deceives his
own heart, this man's religion is worthless. This is pure and

undefiled religion in the sight of our God and Father, to visit
orphans and widows in their distress, and to keep oneself unstained
by the world.
James 1:21-27

VII. SUMMATION

A. When God spoke, the worlds were made. When Satan spoke, he caused his whole
    existence to change; He destroyed his position. Jesus spoke to give us a choice: we
    are free to speak God's words of creation and life, or Satan's words of doubt,
    defeat, and destruction.

B. Your tongue is the key to how your life is expressed. You can destroy yourself and
    others with negative and biting remarks, or you can defeat the enemy and produce
    precious and lasting fruit to enjoy. Speak fitting and wise sayings!

C. The Bible is full of examples of how not to use the power of your tongue. For every
    negative word, however, there is a life-giving word from God. Praise the Lord
    instead of cursing and speaking evil. Edify one another rather than gossip. Ask
    the Lord to give you wise words in place of those filled with pride and flattery.
    Speak more to the Lord than to people about your needs. Make the Lord the center
    of your conversation!

D. You must control your tongue. It is the rudder for the rest of your life! Your
    character is revealed by your word; your heart is exposed by what you say. Christ
    said that you will be held accountable for all your words. Since the taming of your
    tongue is such a monumental task, the only way it can be accomplished is to present
    it to God as an instrument of righteousness; then keep it busy speaking that which
    is in line with God's Word!

E. Keeping the Word in your mouth means that your speech will be effective, since
    God's Word accomplishes and performs that which it was sent to do. Send His Word
    to your friends and relatives in need--His Word overcomes any distance. Send His
    Word to heal--His Word is greater than any circumstances. Follow Jesus' example,
    and speak your Father's words--then do them!

VIII. ASSIGNMENTS

A. Listen to the tape carefully.

B. Complete the study guide questions.

C. Suggested reading: <u>The Tongue--A Creative Force</u>, by Charles Capps.

STUDY GUIDE QUESTIONS

1. Find three examples of Biblical people speaking their faith, followed by definite action.

2. Besides Lucifer, can you find two examples of negative talk resulting in catastrophe?

3. Why is it possible for you to overrule Satan with your mouth?

4. What can you do with a destructive tongue?

5. Using Scripture, write two ways you can defeat the enemy with your tongue.

6. Describe three ways for your tongue to "yield precious fruit."

7. Make a list of five negative uses of the tongue. Beside each of them, write out a Scriptural prayer that can overcome it.

8. Give three promises of God concerning His own Word.

9. Illustrate how God's Word can be used as a positive force. Give three examples, either Biblical or personal.

10. If we are to be imitators of our Father, we will talk like Him. Show three ways to talk like our Father. For example, "God loves the world; therefore, 'I love those around me.'"

11. Study Matthew 12:33-37. What three important truths did you learn about your words in this scripture?

12. Read James 1:26 and 3:1-12 in several versions. Explain briefly what James meant by "bridling the tongue."

13. Rewrite the following verses in your own words:

a. Proverbs 21:23   b. Proverbs 18:13   c. Proverbs 17:9

4 Turn Your Faith Loose

I. CHOOSE THE RIGHT WORDS.

    A. YOUR WORDS AFFECT YOUR OWN PERSONALITY AND HEALTH.

        1. Words are powerful. They can turn you into an arena of life or death.

> Death and life are in the power of the tongue, And those who
> love it will eat its fruit.
> Proverbs 18:21

        2. Words do affect the bones. "Sticks and stones may break my bones, but words will never hurt me." This is an old, old adage we all chanted and mocked to one another on playgrounds and in school rooms; however, the Bible totally refutes our childish words. In fact, God's Word swings to the other end of the pendulum and tells us that our bones are very much involved with our words.

> Pleasant words are a honeycomb, Sweet to the soul and healing
> to the bones.
> Proverbs 16:24

> Bright eyes gladden the heart; Good news puts fat on the
> bones.
> Proverbs 15:30

        3. They are dynamic. They can pierce you like a sword, bringing health or sickness.

> There is one who speaks rashly like the thrusts of a sword, But
> the tongue of the wise brings healing.
> Proverbs 12:18

        4. Words can cause you to be satisfied and productive in your vocation.

> A man will be satisfied with good by the fruit of his words, And
> the deeds of a man's hands will return to him.
> Proverbs 12:14

    B. YOUR WORDS INFLUENCE OTHERS.

        1. Words can cause people to love you.

Righteous lips are the delight of kings, And he who speaks right is loved.
Proverbs 16:13

He kisses the lips Who gives a right answer.
Proverbs 24:26

2. You can exert powerful influence through your words. They can affect national leadership.

By forbearance a ruler may be persuaded, And a soft tongue breaks the bone.
Proverbs 25:15

3. Right words can put joy in your spirit and lift depression.

A man has joy in an apt answer, And how delightful is a timely word!
Proverbs 15:23

4. Your words can turn on or off the temper tantrums of others.

A gentle answer turns away wrath, But a harsh word stirs up anger.
Proverbs 15:1

C. YOUR WORDS CAN MOVE GOD.

1. Your words move God to give you wisdom beyond yourself.

For if you cry for discernment, Lift your voice for understanding; If you seek her as silver, And search for her as for hidden treasures; Then you will discern the fear of the Lord, And discover the knowledge of God.
Proverbs 2:3-5

2. You have what you say.

"Truly I say to you, whoever says to this mountain, 'Be taken up and cast into the sea,' and does not doubt in his heart, but

believes that what he says is going to happen, it shall be granted him."
Mark 11:23

3. You are justified and condemned by your words.

"For by your words you shall be justified, and by your words you shall be condemned."
Matthew 12:37

D. YOUR WORDS ARE THE DOMINANT FORCE IN YOUR LIFE.

There is not one doubt in God's Word that your words can make you or break you in every area of your life. It is not sticks and stones we have to fear--it is the words which we speak. We should not speak words of our opinion, the success opinions of others, or "positive" words. It is not MIND OVER MATTER, but God's eternal, creative Word over every circumstance of life. The earth you walk on, the air you breathe, the water you drink, the sun that warms you, God spoke into being with His Word. Do you ever doubt any of these four will be here tomorrow? God keeps the earth with His Word; you are also kept with His Word.

How can you take the Word and make it effective in all areas of your life? You have the best facility God ever created to make the Word work--your mouth. The tiny book of Philemon, verse six, states that you make your faith effectual by acknowledging everything in you in Christ Jesus. How do you acknowledge it? With your mouth!

II. ACTIVATE YOUR FAITH.

A. LIKE JOSHUA, SPEAK THE WORD DAY AND NIGHT.

A man named Joshua put his mouth into practice and literally became successful in every area of his life. God told him to meditate in the Word day and night and to speak it day and night. God told Joshua to do what the Word says and he would prosper and be successful in every area of his life. And he was successful--in his spiritual life, his military life, his family life, his finances--even in commanding nature!

What did Joshua meditate on? He only had the first five books of the Bible from which to meditate and speak. Can you imagine meditating and speaking the book of Leviticus or Numbers day and night? He did! Do you realize he was over 80 when God commanded him to do this? Most of us feel we are "down the drain" at 40. Our memory is gone, and we have lost our retention. Joshua proves otherwise. You will never meet a busier man. He had over a million people to lead spiritually. As a military leader, he had the responsibility to clothe, feed, and provide water for the people. The provision of the wilderness stopped when they crossed the Jordan. Joshua took the time to meditate and speak God's Word first. How do I know? Because every need of the Israelites was met in the Promised Land. They ate food they never planted, they drank from wells they never dug, they lived in houses they never built. The Promised Land was taken in $6\frac{1}{2}$ years.

There was no military leader like Joshua. The walls of Jericho fell simply because he directed the people to shout. And shout they did! (What do you shout over, your troubles or God's Word?) One time God sent hail into one of Joshua's battles. The hail stones were huge, which in itself was most unusual. The greatest miracle was that the hail hit the enemy and missed Joshua and his men. Imagine yourself with the hand of a Caananite on your throat and suddenly he is on the ground senseless, knocked there by a huge piece of hail. How did it miss you and hit him? One late afternoon, Joshua said, "Sun, stand still, Moon stay in the valley of Ajalon." Others may have said it, but did it work? The word from Joshua's mouth stopped the sun and the moon. Was Joshua successful? Was he ever! When the Promised Land was taken, he became a very wealthy man. He asked for Timnath-Serath, a large mountainous tract of land whose name means "double-portion--city of the sun." He was successful in battle, successful in business, but was he successful at home? After all, isn't that where it really counts? Do you remember it was Joshua at the close of his book who said, "As for me and my house, we will serve the Lord." Our answer is "Yes, a thousand times, yes!" If it worked for Joshua, it can work for you. God made it possible for you, too. He gave you his Word. He created your mouth. Now you must open it, speaking His Word, His provision, in every situation of life. Try it! You'll like it!

"The Word of God is nigh Thee even in Thy mouth" (Deuteronomy 30:14). Activate your faith with your mouth by saying what God says!

B. LIKE DAVID, OVERCOME YOUR GIANT WITH YOUR MOUTH.

   1. Discover your position.

      Your giant may be a physical problem, a marital situation, lack of finances, a problem with your children, or strife with your employer or employee--any problem which overwhelms you. I Samuel 17:1 tells the location of the giant, which in your case would be your position in the problem you are facing. Once you have discovered your position, realize you are not a grasshopper in the sight of your problems and are assured that God is on your side. Practice your covenant relationship with God, whose promises are for you!

Then Caleb quieted the people before Moses, and said, "We should by all means go up and take possession of it, for we shall surely overcome it." But the men who had gone up with him said, "We are not able to go up against the people, for they are too strong for us." So they gave out to the sons of Israel a bad report of the land which they had spied out, saying, "The land through which we have gone, in spying it out, is a land that devours its inhabitants; and all the people whom we saw in it are men of great size. There also we saw the Nephilim (the sons of Anak are part of the Nephilim); and we became like grasshoppers in our own sight, and so we were in their sight." Numbers 13:30-33

2. Build a hedge.

The Philistines were the enemies of Israel, and they lived in Canaan, which was promised to Israel. They stayed around because they were not driven out. They gathered their armies to battle at a place called Socoh, which means "hedge, enclosure, or shut-in place." Socoh was located in Judah, which means "praise." When you begin to praise the Lord there is a hedge built around you and God, shutting you in with Him. Nehemiah 8:10 tells us, "The joy of the Lord is your strength." James 1:2 says, "Consider it all joy, my brethren, when you encounter various trials." So you are going through a trial? You are not to rejoice because of the trial, but you are to rejoice because of the victory over the trial!

There was also a place called Azekah, which means "a breach." God makes a breach between you and Satan, where the devil cannot cross over and overwhelm you. Another interesting word here is Ephesdammim, which means "the border of blood." Now, if you have a heavy problem, you are going to praise the Lord because the Lord told you to. You have also shut yourself in a place of praise, and you have a breach between you and your enemy--the problem. There is also a border around you which is the Blood of Jesus Christ which the devil cannot cross! Revelation 12:11 resolutely maintains that you have overcome Satan "by the Blood of the Lamb, and by the word of your testimony of faith."

3. Let your problem take you some place in God where you've never been.

Saul and the men of Israel were gathered together and set against the Philistines who stood on a mountain on one side while Israel stood on the other side, with a valley between them.

Goliath said, "We'll be your servants if somebody whips us." Your problem can become your servant, taking you to ever higher heights in God! It is important to realize this fact. Let God's Word be your weapon, and let that problem take you some place in God where you have never been before!

Goliath wouldn't disappear (verse 8). For 40 days he kept haranguing over and over, shouting epithets to the Israelites, challenging them to send someone to fight with him. In verse 10 the Philistine said, "I defy the armies of Israel this day; give me a man that we might fight together." When Saul and all Israel heard those words, they were dismayed and greatly afraid. Isn't that what the devil wants--for you to be afraid the problem will overwhelm you instead of you overwhelming the problem?

The devil shows us every detail of what "might happen" before we fight against him. The devil also tries to tell us that following God is not prosperous and that the devil's way is most prosperous. The Philistines talked of how mighty they were. (David, however, was not impressed with the enemy; he was impressed with the Lord of Hosts!)

4. Establish your position--with your mouth!

Now enters a young lad who is sent by his father to take food to his brothers in the army. I Samuel 17:26 describes young David upon seeing Goliath for the first time, asking, "Who is this man everyone is afraid of--this uncircumcised Philistine who defies the armies of the living God?" David knew who the Israelites were and who their God was, and he was not afraid to proclaim it for all to hear! David saw the battle where it was--not the Philistines against the Israelites, but the devil against God's army.

5. Rehearse your victories.

In verse 33 Saul said to David, "You are not able to go against this tough, experienced Philistine to fight with him, for you are but a youth." But one of the most important things in knocking out giants is to rehearse your victories. David said, "The Lord who delivered me out of the paw of the bear, He will deliver me out of the hand of this Philistine." David had made a confession of faith; therefore Saul said to him, "Go, and the Lord be with thee" (verse 37).

You need to confess your faith when problems come to you. Say, "I remember when He saved me. I remember when He filled me with the Holy Spirit. I remember when He healed me, and God won't fail me now!"

Calmly, David selected five smooth stones from the brook and put them in his shepherd's bag, and with his sling in his other hand, he drew near to the Philistine--ready to go! When Goliath looked about and saw David, he disdained him saying, "Come to me and I will give your flesh unto the fowls of the air and the beasts of the field" (verse 44). David answered, "You come to me with a sword, a spear and a shield, but I come to you in the Name of the Lord of Hosts, the God of the armies of Israel, whom thou hast defied" (verse 45). In other words, "You are not defying me; you are defying God, and you had better watch out!"

6. Have more than one stone ready.

David went to the brook to get five stones. It was not because he thought he might miss. He probably wanted to be prepared in case any of the giant's relatives came in to fight. Goliath had four sons. You, too, need more than one Scripture to handle each situation. Satan knows how to add problems. We know how to throw the "stones" of the Word at them--and win the victory!

David used the method God gave him--one he already had proven. King Saul sought to give him a more sophisticated way to fight--his way. It didn't work-- David went depending on the Word of God, not someone else's armor!

7. Cut the problem off.

Remember the helmet of brass Goliath wore on his head? Well, when David took a stone from his bag and threw it with his sling, it hit the Philistine in the forehead, and the stone sunk into his forehead. He fell on his face to the earth. How many rocks did it take? Just one! The greatest miracle occured when the stone actually penetrated the helmet of brass which covered the giant's forehead! Usually, when we throw a rock at a piece of metal, it bounces off. But, David's confession of faith made that rock pierce through the brass, through the flesh, through the bone, and knock the giant down in one fell swoop! Then David ran and stood upon the Philistine, and upon taking the giant's sword from the sheath, he slew him and cut off his giant head! It is very important that you remember it is not enough to knock-out a problem, you also need to cut off the problem at its source so it will not come back and attack you again.

The Philistines ran to the valley of Ekron. Ekron means "eradication." Throw the stone of the Word, and eradicate the enemy!

8. Give God the Glory.

David did not try to preserve his victory. He brought the head of Goliath to Jerusalem, city of peace. He took his victory back to where God was worshiped. God received the glory and the praise. Victory goes right back to the Source!

III. LEARN TO CONFESS GOD'S WORD.

A. IN WHATEVER YOU SAY

In his book, The Fourth Dimension, Dr. Paul Yonggi Cho gives the findings of a neuro-surgeon on the relationship of the tongue to the actions of the rest of the body: He said that the speech nerve center had such power over all of the body that simply speaking can give one control over his body, to manipulate it in the way he wishes. He said, "If someone keeps on saying, 'I'm going to become weak,' then right away all the nerves receive that message, and they say, 'Oh, let's prepare to become weak, for we've received instructions from our central communication that we should become weak.' They then in natural sequence adjust their physical attitudes to weakness.

"If someone says, 'Well, I have no ability. I can't do this job,' then right away all the nerves begin to declare the same thing. 'Yes' they respond, 'we received instruction from the central nervous system saying that we have no abilities, to give up striving to develop any capacity for capability. We must prepare ourselves to be part of an incapable person.'"

Jesus says in Mark 11:23 that "whoever says to this mountain, 'Be taken up and cast into the sea,' and does not doubt in his heart, but believes that what he says is going to happen, it shall be granted him." What you say and believe shall happen! How important then to say true and right things--to say the things that God said! Instead of, "I'm going to become weak," say, "I am strong because God is my refuge and strength" (Psalm 46:1). Instead of "I have no ability," say, "I can do all things through Christ who strengthens me" (Philippians 4:13).

B. IN TEMPTATION

1. When Jesus Christ was tempted by Satan, he answered with the Word, "It is written." Satan said, "If you are the Son of God, command that these stones become bread." But Jesus answered, "It is written, 'Man shall not live on bread alone, but on every word that proceeds out of the mouth of God.'"

Satan tried again, this time even quoting Scripture himself: "If you are the Son of God throw Yourself down; for it is written, 'He will give his angels charge concerning you'; and 'On their hands they will bear you up, lest you strike your foot against a stone.'" Jesus simply answered from the Word: "On the other hand, it is written, 'You shall not put the Lord your God to the test.'"

Would you believe that the devil tempted our Lord a third time? "All these things will I give you, if you fall down and worship me." This time Jesus said, "Begone, Satan! For it is written, 'You shall worship the Lord your God, and serve Him only.'" (Matt. 4:3-10)

What should you do in time of temptation? Quote the Word! Jesus gave us the example, and none can be stronger than His!

2. God will make a way of escape with every temptation. That way of escape is His Word. Use the Word on the enemy and he must flee. Use the Word on any temptation and you will escape. God will honor His Word and show you a way out of the situation, a way to overcome.

> No temptation has overtaken you but such as is common to man; and God is faithful, who will not allow you to be tempted beyond what you are able, but with the temptation will provide the way of escape also, that you may be able to endure it.
> I Corinthians 10:13

C. IN FAITH CONFESSIONS

Christ is the High Priest of your confession.

> Therefore, holy brethren, partakers of a heavenly calling, consider Jesus, the Apostle and High Priest of our confession.
> Hebrews 3:1

When you confess, make sure it is God's Word. The more we say God's Word, the more our faith rises to the level of our confession.

Hold fast to your confession.

> Since then we have a great high priest who has passed through the heavens, Jesus the Son of God, let us hold fast our confession.
> Hebrews 4:14

You are to stay with God's Word, watch what you say, what you confess with your mouth. Hold on to what the Word says, but let God work out the strategy of how He will perform it. He said that He would watch over His Word to perform it. We proclaim His Word, believe it, obey it, and hold on to it. The working out of results is God's department!

Putting dates on what you are confessing can cause your faith to waver. Let God settle your own heart as to whether or not you put a date on your confession.

D. NOT IN ANGER

    1. In anger we can confess bad things for others. When we call someone a fool, we say they are living as though there is no God.

> "You have heard that the ancients were told, 'You shall not commit murder' and 'Whoever commits murder shall be liable to the court.' But I say to you that everyone who is angry with his brother shall be guilty before the court; and whoever shall say to his brother, 'Raca,' shall be guilty before the supreme court; and whoever shall say, 'You fool,' shall be guilty enough to go into the fiery hell."
> Matthew 5:21,22

> The fool has said in his heart, "There is no God." They are corrupt, they have committed abominable deeds;
> Psalm 14:1

    2. There are three types of anger:

        Thumos--quick anger
        Orge--long-lived and brooding anger
        Rocca--contempt of others

        Any one of these can be destructive to another person's character and be harmful to the angry person himself.

    3. We should not damage another's character--confess good for them instead. This will be done by faith on what you know to be true, not on how you feel at the moment. Claim for them the positive quality of the negative one they are manifesting. For example, instead of being angry over someone's stubborn disposition, ask God to make them persevering in their faith.

    4. Claim for yourself self-control, peace, love--all that you know you have in Christ. Ask God for wisdom instead of venting angry words over a frustrating situation. Ask God to show you why you are angry. Perhaps He would reveal a weakness in your own character that He is anxious to mend and strengthen.

5. Acknowledge and confess your anger as sin. Confess the following verses: "Christ is made to me wisdom. His wisdom will work righteousness in this situation, not my anger" (I Corinthians 1:30). "I will be quick to hear, slow to speak, and slow to anger, for my anger does not achieve the righteousness of God" (James 1:19,20).

"Since I have knowledge, I will restrain my words. I have a cool spirit because in Christ I have understanding and can do all things."

He who restrains his words has knowledge, And he who has a cool spirit is a man of understanding. Even a fool, when he keeps silent, is considered wise; When he closes his lips, he is counted prudent.
Proverbs 17:27,28

I can do all things through Him who strengthens me.
Philippians 4:13

6. Be filled with the Holy Spirit. Allow Him to control you; then anger cannot be in control.

And do not get drunk with wine, for that is dissipation, but be filled with the Spirit, speaking to one another in psalms and hymns and spiritual songs, singing and making melody with your heart to the Lord;...
Ephesians 5:18,19

IV. PRAY YOUR FAITH.

A. THE LORD'S PRAYER

1. This prayer is for the follower of Jesus. Christ taught it as an example of prayer, an illustration of praying in the will of God. The words, "Thy will be done" is not a "cop out" phrase, but it means expecting the very best in a supernatural way in a situation. When you pray according to the will of God, and know it, your faith is turned loose.

"Pray, then, in this way: 'Our Father who art in heaven, Hallowed be Thy name. Thy kingdom come. Thy will be done, On earth as it is in heaven. Give us this day our daily bread. And forgive us our debts, as we also have forgiven our debtors. And do not lead us into temptation, but deliver us

from evil. For Thine is the kingdom, and the power, and the
glory, forever. Amen.'"
Matthew 6:9-13

And this is the confidence which we have before Him, that, if
we ask anything according to His will, He hears us. And if we
know that He hears us in whatever we ask, we know that we
have the requests which we have asked from Him.
I John 5:14,15

2.   This prayer is also a "confession of faith," knowing as you pray that God will
     take care of these needs. Of the six petitions, three have to do with God and
     His glory, and three have to do with our own needs.

3.   When we pray to "our Father," we are not using a Name exclusive to a few. He
     is the Father of the entire Body of Christ. There is power and divinity in that
     Name. It also shows the close relationship we have with God--we are family!

4.   The kingdom of God is past, present and future, and He is able to do the same
     mighty things in the present and future as He has done in the past. Confess
     that God will meet these needs in your life.

5.   "Daily bread" shows that God is able to meet our present needs.

6.   "Forgive us our debts as we forgive our debtors" shows that He is able to meet
     our past needs.

7.   "Lead us not into temptation, but deliver us from evil" provides for future
     needs. (Temptation is a testing and trying time which is done by the devil.
     Testings show us how strong we are in the Lord.)

B. PAUL'S PRAYERS

Paul's prayers for others were faith confessions for them. Make these prayers part
of your own prayer life as you confess them to the Lord:

"I pray that the God of our Lord Jesus Christ, the Father of glory, would give to me
(or anyone you are praying for) a spirit of wisdom and of revelation in the
knowledge of Him. I pray that the eyes of my heart would be enlightened so that I
might know what is the hope of His calling, what are the riches of the glory of His
inheritance in the saints, and what is the surpassing greatness of His power toward
us who believe" (Ephesians 1:17-19).

"I ask that I may be filled with the knowledge of His will in all spiritual wisdom and understanding, so that I might walk in a manner worthy of the Lord, to please Him in all respects, bearing fruit in every good work, and increasing in the knowledge of God; strengthened with all power, according to His glorious might, for the attaining of all steadfastness and patience" (Colossians 1:9-11).

V.   ABIDE IN THE VINE.

A.   JESUS IS THE VINE AND THE TRUTH.

Jesus is the Vine (John 15:1). He gives life to the branches; He is the total source for their existence; He is the measure of truth for everything they say. Your ability to turn your faith loose is one hundred percent dependent upon your ability to allow His life to flow through you. Your faith confessions--or any work that is of eternal value--will have its beginning in the Vine. If your confessions begin with you and are not originating in the WORD (Jesus is the Word: John 1:1) they will not be life-giving.

B.   BEARING FRUIT IS THE EXPECTED RESULT.

1.   God gives new beginnings.

"I am the true vine, and My Father is the vinedresser. Every branch in Me that does not bear fruit, He takes away; and every branch that bears fruit, He prunes it, that it may bear more fruit. You are already clean because of the word which I have spoken to you. Abide in Me, and I in you. As the branch cannot bear fruit of itself, unless it abides in the vine, so neither can you, unless you abide in Me. I am the vine, you are the branches; he who abides in Me, and I in him, he bears much fruit; for apart from Me you can do nothing. If anyone does not abide in Me, he is thrown away as a branch, and dries up; and they gather them, and cast them into the fire, and they are burned. If you abide in Me, and My words abide in you, ask whatever you wish, and it shall be done for you. By this is My Father glorified, that you bear much fruit, and so prove to be My disciples. Just as the Father has loved Me, I have also loved you; abide in My love. If you keep My commandments, you will abide in My love; just as I have kept My Father's commandments, and abide in His love. These things I have spoken to you, that My joy may be in you, and that your joy may be made full. This is My commandment, that you love one another, just as I have loved you. Greater love has no one

than this, that one lay down his life for his friends. You are My friends, if you do what I command you. No longer do I call you slaves, for the slave does not know what his master is doing; but I have called you friends, for all things that I have heard from My Father I have made known to you. You did not choose me, but I chose you, and appointed you, that you should go and bear fruit, and that your fruit should remain, that whatever you ask of the Father in My name, He may give to you."
John 15:1-16

Fruit is referred to eight times. Eight always has to do with new beginnings. A new beginning (salvation) must occur before a fruit can be produced. The Life of the Vine is essential!

2. God purges the branches.

    God prunes and cleanses the branches, guides them in the best way through the Word so that the branch can bring forth fruit and produce. The Word comes to us through Jesus Christ, and it cleanses us as we apply it and use it (John 15:2). We obey that Word by our actions and by our words. That Word comes again out of our mouths and brings forth fruit because Christ, the Living Word, dwells within.

3. Jesus produces the fruit.

    Jesus is the producer of the fruit in us, not we ourselves, because we can do nothing without Him (John 15:5). The life of the Vine produces the fruit, not the branches. Trust in the Christ of your confession--not merely in your confession!

4. God continually answers prayers.

    One of the manifestations of fruit-bearing is answered prayer: "Ask whatever you wish, and it shall be done for you" (John 15:7). And again Jesus said, "Whatever you ask of the Father in My Name, He will give it to you" (John 15:16).

C. ABIDING IN THE VINE IS THE CONDITION.

"Abiding in Him" means having a sustained communion with Him in His Word (John 15:7). If His Words abide in us, we will be continually confessing them, for "out of the abundance of the heart the mouth speaketh." His Word will teach us how to ask, and we will be asking what we wish and receiving. If we continue to confess His Word, He will give us what we confess, even if He has to create it.

VI. SUMMATION

A. It is essential to choose the right words; they can affect your own health and personality--can both pierce and heal. Your words can make or break you, influence others to love or hate you, and move God to answer or not answer your prayers.

B. The most successful way to activate your faith is to speak the Word of God day and night. Meditate on the Word, and literally fill your life with it. When your tongue is bridled by the Word, you will "Be perfect, able to bridle the whole body as well" (James 3:2).

C. Know who you are in Christ when "giants" come your way. Be impressed with the power of God to put you over, not with the threats of the enemy. Use your mouth to state your position of victory, and then watch that "giant" problem become your servant to take you to a higher place in your service to God.

D. Confess God's Word in whatever you say. Say what God says about the situation, rather than how you feel about it. In temptation, use God's Word to send the enemy fleeing. In anger, confess God's ability to keep your tongue--to restrain your words. Don't allow anger to force you to confess evil for others. Remember, your faith is not in your "faith confession," but in the God of your confession.

E. The Lord's prayer and the Apostle Paul's prayers are examples of how to pray the will of God and the Word of God.

F. Your faith confessions will have their origin in Jesus the Word, your Life. You cannot make your mouth bear good fruit unless you are abiding in the Vine. As you maintain sustained communion with the Lord in His Word, you will speak as He does. His Word is fruitful and does not return void!

VII. ASSIGNMENTS

A. Listen to the tape carefully.

B. Complete the study guide questions.

C. Recommended reading: The Power of Positive Confession of God's Word, by Don Gossett and E. W. Kenyon.
What You Say is What You Get! by Don Gossett.

REFERENCES:

1. Cho, Dr. Paul Yonggi, The Fourth Dimension, Logos International, Plainfield, 1965, p. 68.

STUDY GUIDE QUESTIONS

1.   Write four reasons why you should choose your words wisely.

2.   Write out three faith confessions on the subject of using your mouth positively to influence others.

3.   Give at least three verses that tell how your words can move God.

4.   Using the concordance and Bible, do a word study on "meditation." Give the definition, the reasons for doing it, when to do it, the results of it, and the subject of meditation.

5.   List the eight steps of David's victory over Goliath, then apply each to your own Christian life.

6.   Look up Scriptures to use in time of temptation. Now write them out as faith confessions. Do at least four.

7.   Write out four faith confessions to use in overcoming anger.

8.   Make a list of ten things that you can pray for in faith. Include a Scripture for each.

9.   Study the following **Scriptures** and describe the abiding Christian: John 15:4-7; 6:53-58; I John 2:4-6; 3:24; 4:15,16.

10. What are three results of abiding according to John 15?

5 Fear: Hindrance to Faith

I. DEFINITION OF FEAR

A. ROOT WORD MEANINGS

1. Phobos: to be intimidated by the enemy, to be in dread, terror, or flight
2. Deilia: cowardice and timidity, fearfulness

> For God has not given us a spirit of timidity, but of power and
> love and discipline.
> II Timothy 1:7

3. Eulabeia: caution and reverence, godly fear, holy, reverent fear
4. Entromos: trembling with fear
5. Aphobos: without fear

> To grant us that we, being delivered from the hand of our
> enemies, Might serve Him without fear, ...
> Luke 1:74

> Now if Timothy comes, see that he is with you without cause to
> be afraid; for he is doing the Lord's work, as I also am.
> I Corinthians 16:10

6. Pachad: (Old Testament word) to be on guard, a life companion--Hebrews 2:15
    says we were all our lifetime in bondage to fear--fear of death. Jesus delivers us
    from this lifetime companion.

> ...and might deliver those who through fear of death were
> subject to slavery all their lives.
> Hebrews 2:15

B. FEAR IN RELATION TO FAITH

Don Gossett compares fear and faith this way: "Fear is believing something bad.
Fear is actually faith in something you don't want to happen. Just as we use the
word "faith" to express believing something good, we use the word "fear" to express
believing in something bad. That is why fear cancels out faith, and faith cancels out
fear."

Doubt is a form of fear. Remember when Peter was walking on the water? He began
to be afraid. Later Jesus said, "Why did you doubt?"

And He said, "Come!" And Peter got out of the boat, and walked on the water and came toward Jesus. But seeing the wind, he became afraid, and beginning to sink, he cried out, saying, "Lord, save me!" And immediately Jesus stretched out His hand and took hold of him, and said to him, "O you of little faith, why did you doubt?"
Matthew 14:29-31

In his book, Relief from Unbelief, Francis P. Martin describes fear and faith in similar ways: "Faith is built on information from God, and fear is built on information from Satan, or demons, your neighbors, doctor, newspapers, weather reports, a phone call at midnight from the police concerning an accident involving your car...depression, gas shortage, epidemic report...fear comes by receiving information.

"Both faith and fear will motivate you; will cause you to move. Faith from God's Word will enable you to move, causing you to step out in faith and act on God's Word...fear will cause you to move, but in the opposite direction of faith. You will run from the problem...to be in flight from the enemy means that the devil is chasing you: and, in fact, we are supposed to chase him.

"Fear will cause you to run: to the doctor, to the finance company, to the insurance company. Faith will cause you to run to God, then run towards the problem and run over it.

"Both faith and fear will produce in your life. Faith will produce the desired outcome of what God's Word said, and fear will produce the thing that the devil said."

"For what I fear comes upon me, And what I dread befalls me."
Job 3:25

"God continually warns us not to fear, because we will produce in our life the thing which we fear. So then refuse to fear; do NOT fear, abstain from nurturing fear from the wrong information."

II. DANGERS OF FEAR

A. IT DRIVES OUT FAITH.

A childhood fear of heights can drive out your faith in airplanes. Dwelling on the fears of what Satan, the world, friends, or disease could do to you will drive out your faith in what God can and wants to do. Fear of the Enemy prevents you from speaking words of faith and conquering promised territory. The ten Israelite spies had the Word of God concerning the land of Canaan. They also had sense information as to the size of the enemies and their walled cities--that information drove out their faith in God's Word.

> But the men who had gone up with him said, "We are not able to go up against the people, for they are too strong for us." So they gave out to the sons of Israel a bad report of the land which they had spied out, saying, "The land through which we have gone, in spying it out, is a land that devours its inhabitants; and all the people whom we saw in it are men of great size. There also we saw Nephilim (the sons of Anak are part of Nephilim); and we became like grasshoppers in our own sight, and so we were in their sight."
> Numbers 13:31-33

B. IT BECOMES YOUR MASTER.

Like the Old Testement word "pachad", fear would like to become your life's companion. That is Satan's desire. With fear as your ruler you will not be acting on faith, you will be in enemy territory, afraid to claim your inheritance, afraid to use your weapons, afraid to declare Whom you serve. God inside you is greater than he that is in the world. God will overcome that fear; allow Him to do so.

> You are from God, little children, and have overcome them; because greater is He who is in you than he who is in the world.
> I John 4:4

Fear keeps some people in bondage to sickness. They are afraid to ask for healing, for fear they won't receive. Some are afraid of new responsibilities if they suddenly become healthy. Fear is a crippling, cruel taskmaster!

C. IT WILL CAUSE YOU TO WORRY.

A fearful person is anxious and constantly wondering what terrible event will occur next. When you fear, you cannot trust God. God wants you to cast all your cares on Him and to give Him all your anxieties.

> ...casting all your anxiety upon Him, because He cares for you.
> I Peter 5:7

Be anxious for nothing, but in everything by prayer and

supplication with thanksgiving let your requests be made known to
God.
Philippians 4:6

Worry is a product of fear and a hindrance to your faith. Eradicate worry by
casting your burdens on the Lord and leaving them there--receiving in return His
provisions. Trust and know that God is faithful to His Word! Count God's promises,
not your fears.

D. IT LEADS TO DEATH.

"But for the cowardly and unbelieving and abominable and
murderers and immoral persons and sorcerers and idolaters and all
liars, their part will be in the lake that burns with fire and
brimstone, which is the second death."
Revelation 21:8

In this verse the fearful head the list of those going to eternal death. Those who
were afraid to trust Jesus for life will have to be without Him for eternity. Living a
life of fear brings death to many areas of a person's life!

E. IT DESTROYS YOUR SELF-IMAGE.

Fear causes you to see yourself as a grasshopper--that is an evil report. When you
see yourself as a grasshopper, something to step on, then others see you that way
too, even your enemy.

"There also we saw the Nephilim (the sons of Anak are part of the
Nephilim); and we became like grasshoppers in our own sight, and
so we were in their sight."
Numbers 13:33

Locust and grasshoppers were to be eaten--roasted and salted--and the spies said,
"We will be meat for the giants." They had a bad self-image. They saw themselves
as grasshoppers, being eaten by the enemy.

From God's point of view it is the enemy who is the grasshopper.

For they would come up with their livestock and their tents, they
would come in like locusts for number, both they and their camels
were innumerable; and they came into the land to devastate it.
Judges 6:5

Satan is the grasshopper, not the faith-filled Christian! Now, grasshoppers lay eggs, and Satan acts like a grasshopper when he plants a little egg of fear inside of us. Fears like, "You'll always be clumsy" or "You can't do that; you're too weak." Then the egg hatches and begins to chew--and it chews on you. We know that God got rid of grasshoppers several times by sending a strong wind and blowing them away. He will do the same for you. By the wind of the Holy Spirit, He will blow those fears away if you will expose your fears to Him.

And then, Joel 2:25 tells us that God will restore the years that the locusts have eaten. With God you will come out ahead! The things that keep us from God's plan for us are the grasshoppers of sin and fear, not the obstacles we look at. Eat your grasshoppers! Eat up your fears by looking at God's Word!

> "Then I will make up to you for the years That the swarming locust has eaten, The creeping locust, the stripping locust, and the gnawing locust, My great army which I sent among you."
> Joel 2:25

III. HOW JESUS DEALS WITH FEAR

A. FEAR OF SIN

1. THE MAN SICK WITH PALSY

> And behold, they were bringing to Him a paralytic, lying on a bed; and Jesus seeing their faith said to the paralytic, "Take courage, My son, your sins are forgiven." And behold, some of the scribes said to themselves, "This fellow blasphemes." And Jesus knowing their thoughts said, "Why are you thinking evil in your hearts? For which is easier, to say, 'Your sins are forgiven,' or to say, 'Rise and walk'? But in order that you may know that the Son of Man has authority on earth to forgive sins"--then He said to the paralytic--"Rise, take up your bed, and go home." And he rose, and went home. But when the multitudes saw this, they were filled with awe, and glorified God, who had given such authority to men.
> Matthew 9:2-8

Some friends brought a man sick with palsy (a trembling disease--trembling like fear) to Jesus. Those friends believed, and Jesus saw their faith. He said to the sick man, "Take courage My son, your sins are forgiven you. The thing that had made this man sick, fearful, and trembling was his sin; he was afraid of the consequences of his sin. Jesus stepped into the situation-- between man and his fear of God--and said, "Your sins be forgiven you." When he was set free from sin, he was set free from fear; then he was set free from sickness.

2. YOUR FEAR OF CONSEQUENCES--If sin is causing you to fear, see Jesus standing between you and God. He is your Mediator. He is interceding for you and is willing to forgive.

> For there is one God, and one mediator also between God and men, the man Christ Jesus.
> I Timothy 2:5

> ...but if we walk in the light as He Himself is in the light, we have fellowship with one another, and the blood of Jesus His Son cleanses us from all sin.
> I John 1:7

Do you have friends who are sick with fear concerning their sins? Use your faith to bring them to Jesus!

B. FEAR OF PHYSICAL ILLNESS

1. THE WOMAN WITH THE ISSUE OF BLOOD

> And behold, a woman who had been suffering from a hemorrhage for twelve years, came up behind Him and touched the fringe of His cloak; for she was saying to herself, "If I only touch His garment, I shall get well." But Jesus turning and seeing her said, "Daughter, take courage; your faith has made you well." And at once the woman was made well.
> Matthew 9:20-22

> And He went off with him; and a great multitude was following Him and pressing in on Him. And a woman who had had a hemorrhage for twelve years, and had endured much at the hands of many physicians, and had spent all that she had and was not helped at all, but rather had grown worse, after hearing about Jesus, came up in the crowd behind Him, and touched His cloak. For she thought, "If I just touch His garments, I shall get well." And immediately the flow of her blood was dried up; and she felt in her body that she was healed of her affliction. And immediately Jesus, perceiving in Himself that the power proceeding from Him had gone forth, turned around in the crowd and said, "Who touched My

garments?" And His disciples said to Him "You see the multitude pressing in on You, and You say, 'Who touched me?'" And He looked around to see the woman who had done this. But the woman fearing and trembling, aware of what had happened to her, came and fell down before Him, and told Him the whole truth. And He said to her, "Daughter, your faith has made you well; go in peace, and be healed of your affliction."
Mark 5:24-34

Faith has to be involved for Jesus to move. This woman said, "If I touch His garment I will be whole." But she was sneaky about it, because a woman with an issue of blood was not allowed in the general public. She was ostracized from home, society, and the temple as "unclean." She had faith for healing, but feared to be open about it because of the nature of her disease.

Much money had been spent on physicians looking for a cure. Now she lived in fear of poverty and saw no future but death.

She had, however, heard Jesus, and it brought faith to her heart. She spoke her faith and released the power of the Word, Jesus Christ. He said to her, "Daughter, take courage; your faith has made you well." She became well, or whole--whole physically, spiritually, emotionally and socially. Jesus majors in taking nobodies and making them into somebodies! The devil specializes in taking somebodies and making them nobodies. When she faced Jesus, all her fears had to leave!

2. YOUR FEAR OF PHYSICAL ILLNESS--How can you deal with your fear of physical illness? You need not fear; Jesus has already dealt with physical sickness. He bore your diseases on the cross. Since He already bore them, you don't have to. See your physical sicknesses, as well as your sins, on Jesus.

> He was despised and forsaken of men, A man of sorrows, and acquainted with grief; And like one from whom men hide their face, He was despised, and we did not esteem Him. Surely our griefs He Himself bore, And our sorrows He carried; Yet we ourselves esteemed Him stricken, Smitten of God, and afflicted. But He was pierced through for our transgressions, He was crushed for our iniquities; The chastening for our well-being fell upon Him, And by His scourging we are healed.
> Isaiah 53:3-5

> And when evening had come, they brought to Him many who were demon-possessed; and He cast out the spirits with a word,

and healed all who were ill in order that what was spoken
through Isaiah the prophet might be fulfilled, saying, "He
Himself took our infirmities, and carried away or diseases."
Matthew 8:16-17

...and He Himself bore our sins in His body on the cross, that
we might die to sin and live to righteousness; for by His
wounds you were healed.
I Peter 2:24

There are several things you can do about physical illness:

a) Ask God for healing.

"If you abide in Me, and My words abide in you, ask
whatever you wish, and it shall be done for you."
John 15:7

"And whatever you ask in My name, that will I do, that the
Father may be glorified in the Son. If you ask Me anything
in My name, I will do it."
John 14:13-14

b) Speak to your mountain of illness.

And Jesus answered saying to them, "Have faith in God.
Truly I say to you, whoever says to this mountain, 'Be
taken up and cast into the sea,' and does not doubt in his
heart, but believes that what he says is going to happen, it
shall be granted him. Therefore I say to you, all things for
which you pray and ask, believe that you have received
them, and they shall be granted you."
Mark 11:22-24

c) Have the elders anoint you with oil and pray the prayer of faith.

Is anyone among you sick? Let him call for the elders of the
church, and let them pray over him, anointing him with oil
in the name of the Lord; and the prayer offered in faith will
restore the one who is sick, and the Lord will raise him up,
and if he has committed sins, they will be forgiven him.
James 5:14-15

d) Confess the Word of life over your body.

> He sent His word and healed them, And delivered them from their destructions.
> Psalm 107:20

> For I give you sound teaching; Do not abandon my instruction. When I was a son to my father, Tender and the only son in the sight of my mother, Then he taught me and said to me, "Let your heart hold fast my words; Keep my commandments and live; Acquire wisdom! Acquire understanding! Do not forget, nor turn away from the words of my mouth. Do not forsake her, and she will guard you; Love her, and she will watch over you. The beginning of wisdom is: Acquire wisdom; And with all your acquiring, get understanding. Prize her, and she will exalt you; She will honor you if you embrace her. She will place on your head a garland of grace; She will present you with a crown of beauty." Hear, my son, and accept my sayings, And the years of your life will be many. I have directed you in the way of wisdom; I have led you in upright paths. When you walk, your steps will not be impeded; And if you run, you will not stumble. Take hold of instruction; do not let go. Guard her, for she is your life. Do not enter the path of the wicked, And do not proceed in the way of evil men. Avoid it, do not pass by it; Turn away from it and pass on. For they cannot sleep unless they do evil; And they are robbed of sleep unless they make someone stumble. For they eat the bread of wickedness, And drink the wine of violence. But the path of the righteous is like the light of dawn, That shines brighter and brighter until the full day. The way of the wicked is like darkness; They do not know over what they stumble. My son, give attention to my words; Incline your ear to my sayings. Do not let them depart form your sight; Keep them in the midst of your heart. For they are life to those who find them, And health to all their whole body.
> Proverbs 4:2-22

C. FEAR OF CIRCUMSTANCES (WEATHER)

1. THE DISCIPLES IN A STORM

> And immediately He made the disciples get into the boat, and go ahead of Him to the other side, while He sent the multitudes away. And after He had sent the multitudes away, He went up to the mountain by Himself to pray; and when it was evening, He was there alone. But the boat was already many stadia away from the land, battered by the waves; for the wind was contrary. And in the fourth watch of the night He came to them, walking on the sea. And when the disciples saw Him walking on the sea, they were frightened, saying, "It is a ghost!" And they cried our for fear. But immediately Jesus spoke to them, saying, "Take courage, it is I; do not be afraid." And Peter answered Him and said, "Lord, if it is You, command me to come to You on the water." And He said, "Come!" And Peter got out of the boat, and walked on the water and came toward Jesus. But seeing the wind, he became afraid, and beginning to sink, he cried out, saying, "Lord, save me!" And immediately Jesus stretched out His hand and took hold of him, and said to him, "O you of little faith, why did you doubt?"
> Matthew 14:22-31

Jesus saw His disciples rowing in the dark, battling a storm. He had sent them out there; they were in the will of God, yet, they were in fearful circumstances. Jesus did not leave them in the circumstances alone; He followed to help. They were frightened when they saw Him; they did not recognize Him. Jesus knew their fear and immediately calmed them with His words, "Take courage, it is I, do not be afraid."

Then Peter had an idea. He said, "Lord if it is you, command me to come to You on the water." He knew he had to have the WORD to walk on the water. Jesus said, "Come," and Peter enjoyed a few glorious moments of doing the impossible by standing on the Word of Jesus! Then he looked at the circumstances and became afraid. As he began to sink, Jesus again came to the rescue of his fear and pulled him up.

2. YOU AND HELPLESSNESS--When darkness and storms come upon you, it may be that you are in the perfect will of God--doing His work. Don't give in to fear and despair. Jesus sees into your darkness and is well aware of your helplessness. He is right there to get into the circumstance with you. Invite

Him in--He will calm your fears and overcome that darkness and storm with light and peace. You are not really in darkness when Jesus is present! Upon His Word you will do the impossible as you walk with Him. With His strength you cannot be helpless!

> "Peace I leave with you; My peace I give to you; not as the world gives, do I give to you. Let not your heart be troubled, nor let it be fearful."
> John 14:27

> "These things I have spoken to you, that in Me you may have peace. In the world you have tribulation, but take courage; I have overcome the world."
> John 16:33

D. FEAR OF MAN

1. PAUL AND THE ANGRY MOB

> And as great dissension was developing, the commander was afraid Paul would be torn to pieces by them and ordered the troops to go down and take him away from them by force, and bring him into the barracks. But on the night immediately following, the Lord stood at his side and said, "Take courage; for as you have solemnly witnessed to My cause at Jerusalem, so you must witness at Rome also."
> Acts 23:10-11

This mob is dangerous--they may even kill Paul. Paul could have been afraid, not only of losing his life, but also of not being able to fulfill the Word of God and go to Rome with the Gospel. Again, Jesus comes during a time of fear: "Take courage; for as you have solemnly witnessed to My cause at Jerusalem, so you must witness at Rome also." The Lord made a special visit to Paul, his servant, to encourage him and eradicate any fear he may have of the men around him and of the future.

2. YOU AND YOUR PEERS--Are you ever afraid of what those in your family, neighborhood, place of employment, or even church, say or do against you? Your fears may, in the natural, be well-founded, as they were with Paul. Jesus, however, wants to say to you, "Fear not, be of good courage, I will complete what I have begun with you." His purpose in your life will not be thwarted by men around you; the Lord is for you. Do not fear. What can man do to you?

For I am confident of this very thing, that He who began a good
work in you will perfect it until the day of Christ Jesus.
Philippians 1:6

The Lord is for me; I will not fear; What can man do to me?
Psalm 118:6

You can say with confidence:

When I am afraid, I will put my trust in Thee. In God, whose
word I praise, In God I have put my trust; I shall not be
afraid. What can mere man do to me?
Psalm 56:3-4

The fear of man brings a snare, But he who trusts in the Lord
will be exalted.
Proverbs 29:25

E. FEAR OF THE WORLD AROUND YOU

1. JESUS' DISCIPLES--The disciples were beginning to understand that Jesus would
not always be physically with them. It was also becoming clear that it might not
always be popular to be His followers. Persecution from society in general was
not appealing--in fact, it was frightening. Jesus sensed that fear in His
disciples. He even predicted that they would leave Him alone during His time of
trial. Yet, with that statement, He declared His purpose: "These things I have
spoken to you, that in Me you may have peace. In the world you have
tribulation, but take courage; I have overcome the world" (John 16:33). He was
saying in essence, "I stand between you and every attack that the world will
ever launch against you."

2. YOU AND SOCIETY--Jesus' message is the same for you. No matter how bad it is
in the world, nor how corrupt the world system gets, He says, "Take courage, I
have overcome the world."

You needn't let the world squeeze you into its mold through fear or any other
intimidating forces. You have overcoming power within you. You need the
Word, but you also need a vision of seeing Jesus in your situation, seeing Him
overcome the fear that can paralyze you.

IV.   PETER OVERCOMES FEAR.

A. THE DOWNWARD PATH OF FEAR

1. FEAR OF THE CROSS--

> And Peter took Him aside and began to rebuke Him, saying, "God forbid it, Lord! This shall never happen to You." But He turned and said to Peter, "Get behind Me, Satan! You are a stumbling block to Me; for you are not setting your mind on God's interests, but man's." Then Jesus said to His disciples, "If anyone wishes to come after Me, let him deny himself, and take up his cross, and follow Me."
> Matthew 16:22-24

After making the greatest statement that man has ever made, Peter also made the worst: "I do not know this man that you are talking about!"

> And Simon Peter answered and said, "Thou art the Christ, the Son of the living God."
> Matthew 16:16

> But he began to curse and swear, "I do not know this man you are talking about!"
> Mark 14:71

He cursed and swore because he was afraid. Most of our wrong statements are made out of fear. Right from the beginning, he tried to put away the cross: "God forbid, Lord, this shall never happen to you." It was fear. He wanted a crown and a kingdom, but not the cross. We are sometimes afraid of the cross in our own lives, afraid to die to our own desires. Be willing to be crucified with Christ, to die to self.

2. BOASTING IN HIMSELF

> But Peter answered and said to Him, "Even though all may fall away because of You, I will never fall away."
> Matthew 26:33

Peter said, "Even though all may fall away because of You, I will never fall away." He had confidence in the flesh, not in the Word in him. He put confidence in the wrong thing. The Bible says to have no confidence in the flesh.

> ...for we are the true circumcision, who worship in the Spirit
> of God and glory in Christ Jesus and put no confidence in the
> flesh,...
> Philippians 3:3

3. TRIES TO PROTECT JESUS FROM THE CROSS

    > But a certain one of those who stood by drew his sword, and
    > struck the slave of the high priest, and cut off his ear.
    > Mark 14:47

Peter cuts off the ear of the slave of the high priest in an effort to keep Jesus
from going to the cross.

4. FOLLOWS JESUS AFAR OFF

    > And Peter had followed Him at a distance, right into the
    > courtyard of the high priest; and he was sitting with the
    > officers, and warming himself at the fire.
    > Mark 14:54

Fear puts a distance between you and the Lord. Peter followed Him "afar off."

5. DENIES AND CURSES OUT OF FEAR

    > And as Peter was below in the courtyard, one of the servant-
    > girls of the high priest came, and seeing Peter warming himself,
    > she looked at him, and said, "You too, were with Jesus the
    > Nazarene." But he denied it, saying, "I neither know nor
    > understand what you are talking about." And he went out onto
    > the porch. And the maid saw him, and began once more to say
    > to the bystanders, "This is one of them!" But again he was
    > denying it. And after a little while the bystanders were again
    > saying to Peter, "Surely you are one of them, for you are a
    > Galilean too." But he began to curse and swear, "I do not know
    > this man you are talking about!"
    > Mark 14:66-71

Fear gets bigger and bigger. Peter didn't yet know that the cross was a place of
victory--not defeat.

B. HIS STEPS OUT OF FEAR AND DEFEAT

1. JESUS PRAYED FOR HIM.

> "Simon, Simon, behold, Satan has demanded permission to sift
> you like wheat; but I have prayed for you, that your faith may
> not fail; and you, when once you have turned again, strengthen
> your brothers."
> Luke 22:31-32

Simon means "hearing one." Jesus wanted him to be a hearing one. Jesus prayed
for him that his faith would not fail--and it didn't. What failed was his courage.
The first thing that you should remember when you are afraid is that Jesus is
praying for you.

> Hence, also, He is able to save forever those who draw near to
> God through Him, since He always lives to make intercession for
> them.
> Hebrews 7:25

2. JESUS "LOOKS THROUGH" HIM.

> And the Lord turned and looked at Peter. And Peter
> remembered the word of the Lord, how He had told him, "Before
> a cock crows today, you will deny Me three times."
> Luke 22:61

Jesus comes by and sees Peter. Jesus looked through Peter. His look could
have said, "Peter, don't do that to yourself." Peter saw Jesus looking through
him, wanting to help, not condemn.

3. JESUS GAVE PETER A PERSONAL MESSAGE.

> "But go, tell His disciples and Peter, 'He is going before you
> into Galilee; there you will see Him, just as He said to you.'"
> Mark 16:7

> ...and that He appeared to Cephas, then to the twelve.
> I Corinthians 15:5

Jesus wanted Peter to have a personal message: "I know all about that which happened, but it was right for Me to go to the cross." Jesus has a personal message for you every time you are afraid, and it includes, "Be of good courage, I will never leave you nor forsake you" (Hebrews 13:5).

4. JESUS DEALS WITH HIS FEAR (John 21). After the resurrection, Peter says, "I'm going back to the fishing business." There is still something about the cross that frightens him. As a leader, he takes several of the key disciples with him. They went fishing all night and caught nothing.

In the morning, Jesus asked them, "Children, you do not have any fish, do you?" When He told them where to cast the net, they listened without knowing that it was Jesus because men on the shore could often see schools of fish from the shore. John, however, recognized that it was the Lord and said so. Peter didn't waste a minute--he dove into the sea and swam to shore.

Jesus had built a fire. It was by a fire that Peter had denied Jesus. (We don't have to camp by the enemy fire. We can have the Spirit's fire in our soul.) Jesus fed their hungry bodies and set them by a warm fire--He met their physical needs first.

Now He began to deal with Peter. Again He called him Simon, "the listening one." "Do you love me more than these (fish), more than this trade? Do you love me with a love that gives (agape)?" "Yes," said Peter, "I love you with phileo" (like a friend). "Feed the lambs," said Jesus (give them the best of nourishment).

The second time: "Simon, do you love (agape) me?" Peter answered, "Yes, Lord, you know that I love (phileo) you." "Then," said Jesus, "Feed, train, discipline my sheep."

The third time: "Simon, do you love (phileo) me?" Peter was grieved, "You know all things. You know that I love (phileo) you." "Tend my sheep," Jesus said (give them the best nourishment that you can).

Peter had denied Jesus three times. Three times he said, "You know I love you, Jesus." Next, Jesus dealt with the place where Peter's fears began--the cross. Jesus revealed that Peter would one day die on the cross to glorify the Lord. Jesus so delivered Peter from fear that he was willing to die for Him. Silently, Jesus had said, "In that day, you won't be afraid, Peter." He wasn't. History records that Peter was crucified for his faith, but he insisted on being hung upside down because he was unworthy to die in the same manner as his Lord. Peter truly triumphed over fear!

5. JESUS RENEWED HIS COMMISSION.

> But Peter, taking his stand with the eleven, raised his voice
> and declared to them: "Men of Judea, and all you who live in
> Jerusalem, let this be known to you, and give heed to my
> words.
> Acts 2:14

He got him back into the ministry. Peter went from fishing to feeding sheep. After the day of Pentecost, this Peter, restored from fear, preached, and three thousand were saved!

If you are afraid of the cross, you have not been there. The cross is the place of victory, the place where your old self died. Now you are free to live your new life unhindered by the fears of the old life and filled with power from the New.

V. BE A DANIEL--NEVER BE DOMINATED BY FEAR.

A. HE PURPOSED IN HIS HEART.

Despite the fact that he had been physically conquered, Daniel let the Word of God within him make <u>him</u> the conqueror! Daniel was taken during the first captivity, along with other royal children from the tribe of Judah. They were extremely good-looking, well built, had a high IQ, and they knew how to conduct themselves.

Immediately, Daniel's name was changed in an attempt to change his image of himself. Daniel means "my judge is God"; his new name was Belteshazzar, which means "one whom Bel judges or lives big in." But this did not change Daniel's image of himself! The world tries to change our image of ourselves, but we must continue to see ourselves as God sees us.

The first thing that Daniel did to keep his image, to overcome fear, was to purpose in his heart, "I am <u>not</u> going to be like Bel. I will <u>not</u> defile myself! My judge is God, not the king, <u>not</u> Bel." When he purposed in his heart, God gave him a good image in the sight of the eunuch. Daniel had favor. At the end of ten days, he and his friends looked better than everyone else. Christians ought to look better than anyone else because they eat the Word--not chew on other Christians!

The results of purposing in his heart were: favor with men and wisdom and knowledge from God! Now that is a winning combination to overcome any fear--even that of being kidnapped and taken to a strange country!

Daniel had a prayer meeting about the king's dream (Daniel 2). Later on we see that this was a pattern with Daniel. He prayed regularly--three times a day. This is good pattern for Christians, first thing in the morning, at noon, and last thing at night. Make your prayer time a two-way conversation by letting God speak through His Word each time. Good communication is continuous! Regular prayer is essential in overcoming fear!

C. HE RECEIVED PERCEPTION.

When you purpose in your heart and pray, God will give you perception. Daniel was given the ability to describe the dream as well as interpret it. Instead of reacting with fearful panic when the decree came for all wise men to be killed, Daniel had "replied with discretion and discernment." God came through for him!

D. HE BECAME POWERFUL.

Daniel became a man of power. How much power did Daniel have? "Daniel's life in Babylon...extended from the first year of Nebuchadnezzar, through the reign of the succeeding five kings, past the Fall of Babylon, into the Persian Empire, through the reign of Darius the Mede, even unto the third year of Cyrus the Persian...in all from 606 B.C. to 534 B.C., 72 years from the first year of the Jews' captivity until 2 years after their Return from the Captivity--God's witness in the palace of the empire that ruled the world."

What made Daniel powerful? He was dominated by what God said, not by the fear of man's word--even if they were the most powerful rulers in the world!

VI. SUMMATION

A. Both fear and faith come from receiving information. The information has two distinct sources. Both will motivate you. Faith will cause you to move toward God and His Word; fear will cause you to run from the problem (the enemy). Both will produce in your life. Faith will produce life; fear will produce death-like fruit.

B. Fear is dangerous. Fear drives out faith, which is your lifeline as a believer. Fear causes you to worry and not trust your Heavenly Father. It will lead to ways of death, never life. Fear seeks to present your enemy's image of you--not God's image of you.

C. When Jesus was on earth, He dealt with fearful men, not condemningly, but with compassion and understanding. He set people free from the fear of sin's consequences by forgiving them, from the fear of physical illness by healing them, from the fear of circumstances by His calming presence, and from the fear of man and the world by His overcoming promises.

D. Peter denied his Lord because of fear--fear of the cross. He learned, as Jesus dealt with him patiently, that the cross was a place of release and freedom--not terror. So freed was he, that he became a bold preacher of the Gospel who later gave his life for his Lord--on a cross!

E. ·Daniel never allowed fear to dominate him, though as a young child he was kidnapped from his home and taken to a strange country. The Word of God already in his heart grew bigger and bigger as he allowed it to dominate him. Because he purposed in his heart to stay true to God's Word and pray to Him, he overcame any fears that came his way. God rewarded him with divine perception and influential power.

VII. ASSIGNMENTS

A. Listen to the tape carefully.

B. Complete the study guide questions.

C. Recommended Reading: Deliverance from the Bondage of Fear, by Bob Buess.

REFERENCES:

1. Gossett, Don, What You Say Is What You Get, Whitaker House, Springdale, 1976, p. 163.

2. Martin, Francis P., Relief From Unbelief, Harrison House, Tulsa, 1980, pp. 8-9.

3. Halley, Henry H., Halley's Bible Handbook, Zondervan, Grand Rapids, 1965, p. 340.

STUDY GUIDE QUESTIONS

1. Compare fear and faith in three ways: Source of information, Motivation to action, Product or result.

2. Phobos, or fear, means "being in dread of the enemy." Find three places where the Word tells us we should be putting the enemy to flight!

3. Give four dangers or results of fear. What is a Scriptural antidote for each?

4. Find three "trust" verses to eradicate worry.

5. Using Scripture, give a brief outline of God's image of you.

6. Study the following Scriptures, and make a list of specific things you are not to fear: Isa. 37:6-7; Jer. 1:6-9; Ps. 91:5,10; Deut. 20:1,3; II Chron. 20:15; Ps. 23:4; Prov. 3:24-26.

7. In the following verses are found some ways or principles with which to overcome fear. Study the **Scriptures** and briefly describe each principle: John 8:32,36; 15:7; Ps. 112:7,8; Matt. 8:17-20,25,26; Isa. 35:3,4; Ex. 14:13,14; II Chron. 20:15,22; Acts 16:25; Neh. 8:10; Prov. 17:22; Rom. 6:16; Isa. 54:14; Ps. 34:4; I John 4:12-18; Eph. 3:19.

8. Why should we not be fearful? State the reason given in each of these verses: Deut. 31:6; Heb. 13:6; Deut. 3:22; Ps. 23:4; Eph. 2:5,6; 3:17; Gen. 15:1; Ps. 46:1-3; Isa. 41:10, 13-15; Ps. 27:1-3; Col. 2:15; II Tim. 1:7; Rom. 8:15; II Kings 6:15,16.

6 Faith Overcomes Tests, Trials, and Temptations

I. DEFINITIONS

The English words test, trial, and temptation are used interchangeably in the various translations of the Bible. Here are some of the root word meanings:

A. TEMPTATION (From the verb PEIRAZO)

1. To try, attempt, assay

2. To test, try, prove

a) Tempting believers:

-Christ was tempted.

> For since He Himself was tempted in that which He has suffered, He is able to come to the aid of those who are tempted.
> Hebrews 2:18

> For we do not have a high priest who cannot sympathize with our weaknesses, but one who has been tempted in all things as we are, yet without sin.
> Hebrews 4:15

-Old Testament saints were tempted.

> They were stoned, they were sawn in two, they were tempted, they were put to death with the sword; they went about in sheepskins, in goatskins, being destitute, afflicted, ill-treated...
> Hebrews 11:37

b) To tempt in a bad way:

-Attempts to ensnare Christ in His speech.

> And the Pharisees and Sadducees came up, and testing Him asked Him to show them a sign from heaven.
> Matthew 16:1

And some Pharisees came to Him, testing Him, and saying, "Is it lawful for a man to divorce his wife for any cause at all?"
Matthew 19:3

But Jesus perceived their malice, and said, "Why are you testing Me, you hypocrites?
Matthew 22:18

-Temptations to sin

Brethren, even if a man is caught in any trespass, you who are spiritual, restore such a one in a spirit of gentleness; each one looking to yourself, lest you too be tempted.
Galatians 6:1

Let no one say when he is tempted, "I am being tempted by God"; for God cannot be tempted by evil, and He Himself does not tempt anyone. But each one is tempted when he is carried away and enticed by his own lust.
James 1:13,14

Then Jesus was led up by the Spirit into the wilderness to be tempted by the devil.
Matthew 4:1

c) Trying or challenging God:

-Testing God by placing a yoke on disciples

"Now therefore why do you put God to the test by placing upon the neck of the disciples a yoke which neither our fathers nor we have been able to bear?"
Acts 15:10

-Some tried the Lord and were destroyed by serpents.

Nor let us try the Lord, as some of them did, and were destroyed by the serpents.
I Corinthians 10:9

-Putting the Holy Spirit to the test

> Then Peter said to her, "Why is it that you have agreed together to put the Spirit of the Lord to the test? Behold, the feet of those who have buried your husband are at the door, and they shall carry you out as well."
> Acts 5:9

B. TEST

In the Old Testament one of the root words translated as test in the NAS and as prove in the KJV is NICAH which means "to test, to attempt, to prove, to tempt, to try, to assay."

Examples: -The Israelites were tested at the waters of Marah.

> And when they came to Marah, they could not drink the waters of Marah, for they were bitter; therefore it was named Marah.
> Exodus 15:23

-They were tested again in the Wilderness of Sin.

> Then the Lord said to Moses, "Behold, I will rain bread from heaven for you; and the people shall go out and gather a day's portion every day, that I may test them, whether or not they will walk in My instruction.
> Exodus 16:4

-Abraham was tested concerning his son, Isaac.

> Now it came about after these things, that God tested Abraham, and said to him, "Abraham!" and he said, "Here I am."
> Genesis 22:1

God's testing never brings an inducement to sin--it brings forth the provision of His Word.

C. TRIAL

A trial is a test, testing our faith in God's Word. When you take God's Word into a trial, it makes you victorious. We are to go from faith to faith.

II.   RESPONDING TO TRIALS

A. RECOGNIZE YOUR TASK.

1.   Determine to pass the test.

In each trial or difficulty, there is the temptation to disregard God's Word, to face it in your own wisdom and strength, or to give way under it. God wants to show you what His Word in you can do and show you how strong you are in Christ. Satan's purpose is to sift you, make you ineffective, and cause you to give up. God is your teacher. In each trial there is an opportunity to prove to yourself, the world, and the devil that you have learned the principles that God has taught you and that God's Word really does work. Receive victory in every trial. If it appears that you are defeated, tell Satan that the game is not over-- you are playing until you win!

2.   Quench the fiery darts.

Some trials are clearly attacking, fiery darts of the enemy to kill our ministry and to get us off course. The water of God's Word will quickly quench them! Use your faith as a shield against these attacks.

> ...in addition to all, taking up the shield of faith with which
> you will be able to extinguish all the flaming missiles of the evil
> one.
> Ephesians 6:16

3.   Resist Satan's lures.

Others trials are the tempting work of the enemy seeking to lure you into his territory so that he can misuse you. These trials are never from God.

> Blessed is a man who perseveres under trial; for once he has
> been approved, he will receive the crown of life, which the Lord
> has promised to those who love Him. Let no one say when he is
> tempted, "I am being tempted by God"; for God cannot be
> tempted by evil, and He himself does not tempt anyone.
> James 1:12,13

Sometimes they strike a responding cord from our flesh and we sin. The answer, again, is the Word. If the Word controls our minds, there will be no responding cord from our flesh. The temptation will be resisted, and Satan will flee! There is always a way out of these temptations. It is never more than we can handle.

> Submit therefore to God. Resist the devil and he will flee from you.
> James 4:7

> No temptation has overtaken you but such as in common to man; and God is faithful, who will not allow you to be tempted beyond what you are able, but with the temptation will provide the way of escape also, that you may be able to endure it.
> I Corinthians 10:13

B. AVOID NEGATIVE RESPONSES--THEY CAUSE MORE TRIALS.

When the children of Israel crossed the Red Sea, God was praised, the people were jubilant and filled with faith and trust in God. They probably had no fear of an enemy army at that point. Their very next trial, however, was different--a lack of water. Their response should have been, "If God can part the Red Sea, surely He can provide water for us." Instead they murmured and complained, wondering what was going to happen. God performed another miracle and turned the bitter waters of Marah into sweet water and then provided in abundance: twelve springs of water and seventy date palms. The Israelites murmured, but Moses prayed. Murmuring will never bring victory, but prayer will.

> So the people grumbled at Moses, saying, "What shall we drink?" Then he cried out to the Lord, and the Lord showed him a tree; and he threw it into the waters, and the waters became sweet. There He made for them a statute and regulation, and there He tested them. And He said, "If you will give earnest heed to the voice of the Lord your God, and do what is right in His sight, and give ear to His commandments, and keep all His statues, I will put none of the diseases on you which I have put on the Egyptians; for I, the Lord, am your healer." Then they came to Elim where there were twelve springs of water and seventy date palms, and they camped there beside the waters.
> Exodus 15:24-27

The next chapter brings another test--there is no food. The positive response, "I know God will supply our need because He just did with the water," would have ended this trial; however, they grumbled and complained, wished they were back in Egypt, and accused Moses of bringing them out to the desert to kill them. All through the wilderness experience, there were trials and tests. They could have had real victory in every situation by simply speaking God's Word back to Him, trusting Him to supply.

If they had passed the test, they could have been in the Promised Land in less than a year (the journey takes less than two weeks on foot), living in the land of milk and honey. It was their negative responses that caused trials to come again and again. Because of grumbling, rather than trusting and obeying God, a whole generation failed the tests and never made it to the Promised Land!

> So the Lord said, "I have pardoned them according to your word; but indeed, as I live, all the earth will be filled with the glory of the Lord. Surely all the men, who have seen My glory and **My** signs, which I performed in Egypt and in the wilderness, yet have put Me to the test these ten times and have not listened to My voice, shall by no means see the land which I swore to their fathers, nor shall any of those who spurned Me see it."
> Numbers 14:20-23

You can become a servant to your problems or your problems can become a servant to bring you greater victories. The children of Israel tested God instead of passing their tests. God wanted them to pass, to be victorious, to win and conquer. They, instead, hardened their hearts and tested (provoked) God.

> Do not harden your hearts, as at Meribah, As in the day of Massah in the wilderness; "When your fathers tested Me, they tried Me, though they had seen My work. For forty years I loathed that generation, and said they are a people who err in their heart, And they do not know My ways. Therefore I swore in My anger, Truly they shall not enter into my rest."
> Psalm 95:8-11

Many times it is not the circumstances that are causing the problem, but our own heart attitude. That is what God wants to change! There are at least three ways to face the tests: (1) Complain, and have to take it over again; (2) Complain, fail and miss God's promises and provisions for you; (3) Praise God, stand on God's Word, pass the test, and enter the Promised Land. Joshua and Caleb did the latter! They enjoyed the land of milk and honey. You can too.

C. USE THE TRIAL TO GROW.

Sometimes we are not growing in faith because we are failing in the tests that are coming our way. We cannot progress until we master some of the fundamentals of faith! For example, financial tests are passed by tithing and giving. If we hold on to our money for fear of not having our needs met, we have failed the test and stopped prosperity and growth in this area.

A difficult situation is the entry way to God's provision! Walk through in faith! That does not mean that you must have difficulty to claim and receive God's provision. It does mean that at any point of difficulty in which you find yourself, "Look up!" God has His hand extended towards you, filled with all that you need to meet the crisis. It is by <u>practice</u> that you have your senses trained to discern good and evil. Then you grow, becoming mature and ready for solid food. The strong meat of God's Word can be yours when you discern the difference between what is flesh, Satan, or God.

> But solid food is for the mature, who because of practice have their
> senses trained to discern good and evil.
> Hebrews 5:14

III.   OVERCOMING FIERY TRIALS

A. HAVE YOUR MOUTH CLEANSED BY GOD'S FIRE.

1.   The situation may be bleak, but God is still on the throne.

> In the year of King Uzziah's death, I saw the Lord sitting on a
> throne, lofty and exalted, with the train of His robe filling the
> temple.
> Isaiah 6:1

In the year of King Uzziah's death, the throne of Judah was vacant. The people, in general, were hardened and unfaithful to God. It would have been easy at this time to speak negatively--the nation lived negatively. Amidst the dark picture of Judah's situation, Isaiah received a vision of what it is like in heaven: GOD IS STILL ON THE THRONE--LOFTY AND EXALTED!

2.   In the light of God's glory, Isaiah's lips were unclean.

> Seraphim stood above Him, each having six wings; with two he
> covered his face, and with two he covered his feet, and with
> two he flew. And one called out to another and said, "Holy,
> Holy, Holy, is the Lord of hosts, The whole earth is full of His
> glory." And the foundations of the thresholds trembled at the
> voice of him who called out, while the temple was filling with
> smoke. Then I said, "Woe is me, for I am ruined! Because I

am a man of unclean lips, And I live among a people of unclean
lips; For my eyes have seen the King, the Lord of hosts."
Isaiah 6:2-5

Gazing at the splendor of the King of the Universe, hearing the seraphims call
out His glory, feeling the trembling of the temple at the voice of God, and then
seeing the smoke of His presence caused Isaiah to unashamedly admit the
uncleaness of his lips (Isaiah 6:2-5). He saw that God was on top of everything
and he knew that he had been saying the wrong things. Your conversation
changes when you are looking up! Hallelujah!

3. The seraphim purges his mouth.

> Then one of the seraphim flew to me, with a burning coal in his
> hand which he had taken from the altar with tongs. And he
> touched my mouth with it and said, "Behold, this has touched
> your lips; and your iniquity is taken away, and your sin is
> forgiven."
> Isaiah 6:6-7

Immediately a serpahim flew to Isaiah and touched his mouth with a live coal from
the altar. His lips were cleansed and his sin forgiven. According to James 3:2
our mouth causes us to stumble. Our mouths must be cleansed by God.

> For we all stumble in many ways. If anyone does not stumble in
> what he says, he is a perfect man, able to bridle the whole body
> as well.
> James 3:2

4. He was willing to be God's messenger.

> Then I heard the voice of the Lord, saying, "Whom shall I send,
> and who will go for Us?" Then I said, "Here am I. Send me!"
> And He said, "Go, and tell this people: 'Keep on listening, but
> do not perceive; Keep on looking, but do not understand.'"
> Isaiah 6:8,9

Once he had been cleansed, Isaiah was ready to be sent to the rest of the people.
His lips had been touched by the fire of God and he would speak faith. When you
are in a difficult situation, ask God to first cleanse your way of talking, and then
you can be used by Him to deal with the problem.

B. LIVE IN THE FIRE OF GOD.

1. The righteous can live with continual burning.

> Sinners in Zion are terrified; Trembling has seized the godless. "Who among us can live with the consuming fire? Who among us can live with continual burning?" He who walks righteously, and speaks with sincerity, He who rejects unjust gain, And shakes his hands so that they hold no bribe; He who stops his ears from hearing about bloodshed, And shuts his eyes from looking upon evil;...
> Isaiah 33:14-15

Have you ever been afraid of the judgment of God? He is like a consuming fire. Who can live in this fire? Many may sojourn for a while as a guest, but who can live and take up permanent residency there? Verse 14 asks the question, "Who can come and live (sojourn) in the fire?" The answer is "the righteous, those who speak with sincerity." The Bible goes on to say in verse 16 that they will dwell (take up permanent residency) on the heights, with the Rock, with the Lord who is the consuming fire. He who lives righteously and speaks uprightly will be at home with God all the time. You will not be afraid of God if you are speaking the Word all the time. When we speak the same thing that God speaks, we can dwell in peace and rest; we are not madly trying to take care of the tests and trials. We let the Word in us do the work.

God is a fire, and we are living in His presence. He will consume in us that which is dross, and bring out the good. When we live in the fire, the Word will destroy the responding chord to temptation. We will be purified. What will be left is what God is doing in us. Fire can consume you or you can consume God's Word and put out the fire.

2. The Holy Spirit came in tongues of fire.

> And there appeared to them tongues as of fire distributing themselves, and they rested on each one of them. And they were all filled with the Holy Spirit and began to speak with other tongues, as the Spirit was giving them utterance.
> Acts 2:3-4

The believers were filled with the Holy Spirit. He was visible as tongues of fire. From this time forward, we begin to see the fire of the Word in their lives. Peter preached God's Word with conviction and fire, and many were saved. Those early Christians, filled with the fire of God, got results!

3. The Word causes hearts to burn.

> And beginning with Moses and with all the prophets, He
> explained to them the things concerning Himself in all the
> Scriptures. And they approached the village where they were
> going, and He acted as though He would go farther. And they
> urged Him, saying, "Stay with us, for it is getting toward
> evening, and the day is now nearly over." And He went in to
> stay with them. And it came about that when He had reclined at
> the table with them, He took the bread and blessed it, and
> breaking it, He began giving it to them. And their eyes were
> opened and they recognized Him; and He vanished from their
> sight. And they said to one another, "Were not our hearts
> burning within us while He was explaining the Scriptures to
> us?"
> Luke 24:27-32

The two disciples on the road to Emmaus heard Jesus explain the Scriptures to
them, and it caused their hearts to burn within them. Did not Jeremiah say,
"God's Word is like a fire" (Jeremiah 23:29)?

4. Enemy fire only burns binding ropes (Daniel 3).

The fiery furnace was to consume and terrorize the three Hebrew children into
bowing to the golden image. It didn't work. They said, "Our God is able to
deliver us, but if He doesn't, we still won't bow down." They spoke the right
things and lived in the fire because one like the Son of God was there. (When
you hit trials, keep your conversation right and you will be comfortable in the
fire.) When they came out, they didn't even have the smell of fire on them. All
that the fire had done was burn the ropes that bound them!

5. God's fire will consume wrong.

> Fire also came forth from the Lord and consumed the two
> hundred and fifty men who were offering the incense.
> Numbers 16:35

Fire came from the Lord and consumed 250 men. Because of the evil in their own
hearts, the righteous fire of God consumed them. God's desire is for us to allow
His fire to cleanse us, then we will be able to live in His presence, in His fire.

6. God led His people in the fire.

> And the Lord was going before them in a pillar of cloud by day
> to lead them on the way, and in a pillar of fire by night to give
> them light, that they might travel by day and by night. He did
> not take away the pillar of cloud by day, nor the pillar of fire
> by night, from before the people.
> Exodus 13:21-22

God led His people in the fire. They were comfortable when they were obedient and could dwell there, but very uncomfortable when they did not speak what God wanted. Neither are we comfortable with God when we are speaking that which is contrary to the way He speaks!

C. CONSIDER IT ALL JOY.

1. When you encounter various trials

> Consider it all joy, my brethren, when you encounter various
> trials,...
> James 1:2

Your first response to a trial should be joy because there is victory ahead. You can rejoice in total joy because your faith will bring you through--it overcomes! There is strength in rejoicing!

> For whatever is born of God overcomes the world; and this is
> the victory that has overcome the world--our faith.
> I John 5:4

2. The testing of your faith produces endurance.

> ...knowing that the testing of your faith produces endurance.
> James 1:3

This knowledge is obtained through observation. Remember all the times that God brought you through! Testing is proving. Every step of faith in your trial will prove you to have a higher faith.

3. Endurance will lead to perfection.

> And let endurance have its perfect result, that you may be
> perfect and complete, lacking in nothing.
> James 1:4

Becoming perfect means maturing, being entire without blemish, lacking in nothing. You won't be left behind by any other Christian!

4. You can ask for wisdom (James 1:5).

"But if any of you lack wisdom and most of us do, during a trial let him ask of God who gives to all men generously and without reproach, and it will be given to him." This wisdom is "sophia," wisdom to see the whole picture.

5. You are blessed when you perservere (James 1:12).

> Blessed is a man who perseveres under trial; for once he has
> been approved, he will receive the crown of life, which the Lord
> has promised to those who love Him.
> James 1:12

You can consider it all joy when you encounter trials because:

a) You will be blessed: receive prosperity, favor, wholeness, happiness, and benefits.

b) You will be approved.

c) You will receive a crown: a wreath of victory. A crown always means victory. We always triumph in Christ.

The best way to perservere is to praise the Lord and pray in the Spirit.

6. God won't ever tempt you.

> Let no one say when he is tempted, "I am being tempted by
> God"; for God cannot be tempted by evil, and He Himself does
> not tempt anyone. But each one is tempted when he is carried
> away and enticed by his own lust.
> James 1:13-14

Temptation is spawned by Satan and conceived by our own lusts when we respond! It is the lust of your flesh, the back-up plans, the self efforts, and the methods to help God out. These cause us to sin.

7. You have an opportunity to be a doer of the Word.

> But prove yourselves doers of the word, and not merely hearers
> who delude themselves.
> James 1:22

You may have all the answers to the difficulties that might arise, but when the trials come your way, you prove the Word and become a doer!

IV. TYPES OF TEMPTATIONS

A. QUESTIONING GOD'S WORD

From the Garden of Eden, Satan has been occupied with tempting the believer to question God's Word. He said to Eve, "Yea, Hath God said, you shall not eat of...." Satan was causing Eve to question what God had really said. Eve had understood very clearly, but now she was <u>listening</u> to the enemy, and she began to doubt that God really meant what He said, or that the consequence was really death.

> Now the serpent was more crafty than any beast of the field which
> the Lord God had made. And he said to the woman, "Indeed, has
> God said, 'You shall not eat from any tree of the garden'?" And
> the woman said to the serpent, "From the fruit of the trees of the
> garden we may eat; but from the fruit of the tree which is in the
> middle of the garden, God has said, 'You shall not eat from it or
> touch it, lest you die.'" And the serpent said to the woman, "You
> surely shall not die! For God knows that in the day you eat from it
> your eyes will be opened, and you will be like God, knowing good
> and evil."
> Genesis 3:1-5

The enemy will use the same tactic on us. Every time we face a choice there is the opportunity for Satan to say, "Did God really say you should not do that? Did He really say that He would provide <u>all</u> your needs?" If God's Word is in our hearts and mouth, our immediate response will be: "Yes, He said, 'My God shall supply <u>all</u> my need according to <u>His</u> riches in glory'" There will be no hesitation, just pure faith in His Word. A faith-filled believer should never allow himself the option of doubting God's Word!

B. CLAIMING A PROMISE WITHOUT MEETING THE CONDITION

With each promise comes a condition. We can live in the Promised Land if we meet the conditions. Resist the temptation to see the glowing promise and overlook the attached condition.

"And all these blessings shall come upon you and overtake you, if you will obey the Lord your God."

"The Lord will establish you as a holy people to Himself, as He swore to you, if you will keep the commandments of the Lord you God, and walk in His ways."

"And the Lord shall make you the head and not the tail, and you only shall be above, and you shall not be underneath, if you will listen to the commandments of the Lord your God, which I charge you today, to observe them carefully."
Deuteronomy 28:2,9,13

C. GIVING UP WHEN THERE IS A TIME LAPSE

When we have met the condition, we receive the promise by faith. Often, before the manifestation of that promise, there is a time lapse, and a test occurs. Now we face a decision: Will I keep on believing God's promise, or will I give up? God allows this test to prove to you that you can obtain the promise, that in Him is all the provision. Yet, it takes an act of faith, stepping out on His Word regardless of what one feels and what the circumstances say. In this test time we hold on to our confession, we hope against hope, and continue with faith believing that God will see us through. KEEP THE WORD IN YOUR MOUTH and you WILL see the fulfillment of God's promise. Don't walk by what your sense knowledge tells you. Walk by God's Word.

In hope against hope he believed, in order that he might become a father of many nations, according to that which had been spoken, "SO SHALL YOUR DESCENDANTS BE."
Romans 4:18

D. DISREGARDING GOD'S WORD

There are times when this time lapse produces a temptation from the enemy to disregard God's Word and do it your own way. You may think, "I guess it wasn't God's will after all." If God makes a promise to the believer in His Word, it is His will. That should never be an issue for debate to the faith-filled believer!

For as many as may be the promises of God, in Him they are yes; wherefore also by Him is our Amen to the glory of God through us.
II Corinthians 1:20

How do you deal with this temptation? Regard God's Word highly; put it in your heart and in your mouth. Insist on doing it His way. In Christ you do have the necessary power!

"Not every one who says to Me, 'Lord, Lord,' will enter the kingdom of heaven; but he who does the will of My Father, who is in heaven" (Matt. 7:21).

"Therefore every one who hears these words of Mine, and acts upon them, may be compared to a wise man...." Jesus warned us strongly about disregarding the Words of God (Matt. 7:24-27).

E. RECEIVING COUNTERFEIT PROVISION

When God promised to supply all our needs according to His riches, He meant it. But He will never supply any provision in violation of the principles of His Word. At times, during the lapse between our promise and the provision, Satan will come with a counterfeit provision. It will look so good, but not be quite in line with the Word. At this time we need to be aware of his schemes. Much Christian failure is due to accepting Satan's counterfeit instead of waiting for the real thing.

Abraham had this experience. God had promised him an heir, a son. After a long waiting time, the suggestion came that perhaps he would have a son through Hagar, the Egyptian maid, and not Sarah. He went ahead, and they had a son, but he was NOT the fulfillment of the promise. He was a counterfeit! Ishmael was born. He was also blessed in many ways, but he did not carry the Seed of promise, and he and his descendants were problems for Isaac and his sons later on (Gen. 16).

V. FAITH'S PROVISION FOR TEMPTATION

A. YOU ARE FREED.

1. From condemnation (Rom. 8:1)

   "There is therefore now no condemnation." We need never live under guilt or self pity, or fall prey to Satan's "You-will-never-be-good-enough" syndromes! The past and its failures are gone--you are free!

2. From the law of sin and death (Rom. 8:2)

   Sin has no more power over you, and neither does any evil temptation. You live under a higher law--that of the law of Spirit and life!

> There is therefore now no condemnation for those who are in
> Christ Jesus. For the law of the Spirit of life in Christ Jesus
> has set you free from the law of sin and of death.
> Romans 8:1-2

B. YOU HAVE ABILITY.

1. To be obedient

> For what the Law could not do, weak as it was through the
> flesh, God did: sending His own Son in the likeness of sinful
> flesh and as an offering for sin, He condemned sin in the flesh,
> in order that the requirement of the Law might be fulfilled in
> us, who do not walk according to the flesh, but according to
> the Spirit. For those who are according to the flesh set their
> minds on the things of the flesh, but those who are according to
> the Spirit, the things of the Spirit. For the mind set on the
> flesh is death, but the mind set on the Spirit is life and peace.
> Romans 8:3-6

Being born-again, you now set your mind on things above, according to the
Spirit, and the result is fulfilling God's purpose in your life. You are also living
a life of peace. You can overcome every temptation because of the Spirit in you!

2. To please God

> ...and those who are in the flesh cannot please God. However,
> you are not in the flesh but in the Spirit, if indeed the Spirit of
> God dwells in you. But if anyone does not have the Spirit of
> Christ, he does not belong to Him.
> Romans 8:8-9

Those who walk after the flesh cannot please God, but those who walk after the
Spirit can please God...and they can overcome temptation.

> No temptation has overtaken you but such as is common to man;
> and God is faithful, who will not allow you to be tempted beyond
> what you are able, but with the temptation will provide the way
> of escape also, that you may be able to endure it.
> I Corinthians 10:13

3. To be Spirit-controlled (Rom. 8:9,14)

"But you are not living the life of the flesh, you are living the life of the Spirit, if the (Holy) Spirit of God really dwells within you--directs and controls you. But if any one does not possess the (Holy) Spirit of Christ, he is none of His--he does not belong to Christ is not truly a child of God" (Rom. 8:9, TAB). It is the mark of the believer to be led and controlled by the Holy Spirit! The Spirit's control in us will always overcome temptation.

> For all who are being led by the Spirit of God, these are the
> sons of God.
> Romans 8:14

Learning to consciously live controlled by the Spirit is a daily growing process. We learn to give up our own will, and will to do God's will. This is not instantaneous, but the more we practice, the easier it becomes.

4. For an energy-filled life

> But if the Spirit of Him who raised Jesus from the dead dwells
> in you, He who raised Christ Jesus from the dead will also give
> life to your mortal bodies through His Spirit who indwells you.
> Romans 8:11

> "I have been crucified with Christ; and it is no longer I who
> live, but Christ lives in me; and the life which I now live in the
> flesh I live by faith in the Son of God, who loved me, and
> delivered Himself up for me."
> Galatians 2:20

The same Spirit who raised Jesus from the dead quickens our mortal bodies. He gives our bodies life. Someday we will have immortality--now we have a taste of immortality because our bodies are the dwelling place of the Life-giving Spirit. Our bodies are healthier and more energetic because of the Life Source within us. Satan cannot deceive you with "You are too weak to do that." You have Divine energy!

5. To put to death the evil deeds of the body (Rom. 8:13, TAB)

"For if you live according to the dictates of the flesh you will surely die. But if through the power of the (Holy) Spirit you are habitually putting to death--make extinct, deaden--the evil deeds prompted by the body, you shall (really and genuinely) live forever." Praise God you can do it, you have the power!

C. YOU HAVE A POSITION.

1. As God's child

> For you have not received a spirit of slavery leading to fear
> again, but you have received a spirit of adoption as sons by
> which we cry out, "Abba! Father!" The Spirit Himself bears
> witness with our spirit that we are the children of God,
> Romans 8:15-16

The Holy Spirit Himself tells you that you are the child of God. That constant reassurance does much to strengthen us in temptation--a reminder of who we are and what our nature is really like!

2. As joint-heir with Christ

> ...and if children, heirs also, heirs of God and fellow heirs
> with Christ, if indeed we suffer with Him in order that we may
> also be glorified with Him.
> Romans 8:17

Picture yourself as joint-heir with Christ. Envision the glory of the future if your present situation is less than glorious. No matter what the temptation or trail, you can go through it like a child of God and know that what is in store for you in the future is more than you can imagine.

No lying promise of Satan's for pleasure of the moment can even slightly compare with the value and worth of what we are to inherit. Your victories in the present are an education and preparation for your inheritance.

D. YOU HAVE A HOPE.

Although we can have a daily victory over sin, we are still living in the presence of sin in the world around us. It hurts our spirits to see how Satan and sin try to destroy people. We can be part of the process that sets men free from his power in this life. Tell them of the Savior! Yet a part of us is longing to be forever free from even the sight of sin. That is our heritage! Soon we will be changed, given a glorified body, and enjoy the complete redemption of creation. This hope gives you another overcoming incentive when temptation comes your way!

> For the anxious longing of the creation waits eagerly for the revealing of the sons of God. For the creation was subjected to futility, not of its own will, but because of Him who subjected it, in hope that the creation itself also will be set free from its slavery to corruption into the freedom of the glory of the children of God. For we know that the whole creation groans and suffers the pains of childbirth together until now. And not only this, but also we ourselves, having the first fruits of the Spirit, even we ourselves groan within ourselves, waiting eagerly for our adoption as sons, the redemption of our body.
> Romans 8:19-23

E. YOU HAVE HELP.

1. Intercession of the Holy Spirit

> And in the same way the Spirit also helps our weakness; for we do not know how to pray as we should, but the Spirit Himself intercedes for us with groanings too deep for words; and He who searches the hearts knows what the mind of the Spirit is, because He intercedes for the saints according to the will of God.
> Romans 8:26-27

God knows our weaknesses, knows we don't even know how to pray sometimes, and He makes provision for even that. The Holy Spirit helps us in our praying. He intercedes for us. He prays for us according to God's will. Pray in the Spirit often and allow the Holy Spirit to pray through you. Prayer is the most effective weapon against temptation. Jesus said in the garden of Gethsemene to His disciples, "Why are you sleeping? Rise, and pray that you may not enter into temptation" (Luke 22:46).

2. Knowledge that God causes all things to work together for good

> And we know that God causes all things to work together for good to those who are called according to His purpose.
> Romans 8:28

Once you have prayed and committed something to God, allowed the Holy Spirit to intercede for you; then you can rest assured that all will work together for good. If you have resisted temptation, and circumstances still look bad, hang in there, because God will work it out. The result will be good--God promised!

3. You are being conformed to the image of God.

> For whom He foreknew, He also predestined to become
> conformed to the image of His Son, that He might be the first-
> born among many brethren;
> Romans 8:29

You are being conformed to the image of the Son of God. This happens as you allow His Life to fill yours. That is power over temptation! That One inside of you is much greater than the one tempting you.

> You are from God, little children, and have overcome them;
> because greater is He who is in you than he who is in the
> world.
> I John 4:4.

4. Consciousness that God is on your side

> What then shall we say to these things? If God is for us, who is
> against us?
> Romans 8:31

By now, you know that you are not alone. God is on your side. He not only sees you as a winner and an overcomer, but He is also actively involved in making you that! What temptation could win against you and God?

5. Inexhaustible supply

> He who did not spare His own Son, but delivered Him up for us
> all, how will He not also with Him freely give us all things?
> Romans 8:32

God even gave His only Son to die for you. Don't you think He will give you everything you need to overcome the enemy in temptation?

6. Jesus pleading your cause

> ...who is the one who condemns? Christ Jesus is He who died,
> yes, rather who was raised, who is at the right hand of God,
> who also intercedes for us.
> Romans 8:34

Can you accept this? Jesus not only gave His life, but He is also at the right hand of God interceding for you! There is much positive strength, encouragement and power coming your way. Only resistance to God's will can block this provision from coming into your life.

F. YOU HAVE THE VICTORY.

"Yet amid all these things we are more than conquerors and gain a surpassing victory through Him who loves us" (Rom. 8:37, TAB). Paul had just listed a number of trials that they had come through, and with each trial there were opportunities for temptation, but he claimed overwhelming victory through them all. You can too!

G. YOU ARE LOVED.

You know that nothing will separate you from Christ's love. He loves you no matter how many times you have failed Him in the past. He loves you no matter how many trials have been coming your way. Satan would have you believe that if things are difficult, then surely God cannot love you as much as another brother or sister. Not true! Absolutely nothing can separate you from the love of God through Christ Jesus. God never cuts off His love or His strength when you are in time of trouble and need. God's love is one constant you can depend on forever!

> For I am convinced that neither death, nor life, nor angels, nor principalities, nor things present, nor things to come, nor powers, nor height, nor depth, nor any other created thing, shall be able to separate us from the love of God, which is in Christ Jesus our Lord.
> Romans 8:38-39

VI. SUMMATION

A. Temptations, trials and tests come to each believer. It is not wrong for them to come your way. It is wrong not to allow the Holy Spirit and His Word to overcome the situation through you!

B. Your response to trials should be several: determine in your heart that you will pass the test, quench the darts of Satan, and resist his luring temptation. Give a positive response to trials--meet them with the Word of God, assured that God in you will meet the crisis. Use your experience to grown strong in the Lord. When the trial is over, you have just proved once more that the Word works!

C. You overcome the fiery trials by allowing the fire of God's Word to cleanse your life so that there is nothing in you that will respond to the temptations of Satan, nothing that will prevent complete victory in testing times! Stay in God's cleansing fire and the dross in your life will be burned off. Rejoice that the Lord will put you over during a trial. Ask God to give you wisdom to know what steps to take; then take them!

D. During the trials, Satan comes with varied temptations. He may cause you to question God's Word concerning promises of His help. He may blind you to the condition of a promise. He may tempt you to give up, to disregard God's Word, or even accept a counterfeit provision; however, you are armed with the living Word of God and cannot only recognize his devices, but also defeat him overwhelmingly.

E. Your faith in Christ and in God's Word provides all you need to overcome temptation. You are freed from the power of sin and given the ability of the Holy Spirit to work in your life. The whole Trinity is working on your behalf. You have assurance of victory and a constant flow of love from your God. You need never fall into temptation for lack of support. God is on your side!

VII. ASSIGNMENTS

A. Listen to the tape carefully.

B. Complete the study guide questions.

C. Recommended reading: More Than Conquerors, by Terry Mize.

REFERENCES:

1. W. E. Vine, Expository Dictionary of New Testament Words, (Old Tappan, New Jersey, Fleming H. Revell Company, 1966).

2. James Strong, S.T., LL.D., The Exhaustive Concordance of the Bible (MaLean, Virginia, MacDonald Publishing Company).

STUDY GUIDE QUESTIONS

1. From the definitions, which words best describe the temptations mentioned in the following verses: Heb. 2:18; Matt. 4:1; Acts 5:9.

2. Name the tests of the Israelites in Exodus 15:25 and 16:4.

3.   Read I Peter 1:6,7 in several translations. Explain the phrase "proof of your faith" (NAS).

4.   List the three tasks you might have in responding to trials.

5.   Discuss briefly at least one positive response to trials. Give a Biblical example.

6.   How can you use a trial to grow?

7.   Study James 1:1-22. What can you learn about overcoming fiery trials in this passage?

8.   Name five types of temptations that Satan uses on us.

9.   Choose one of the above and give a Biblical way of dealing with it. Use at least three scriptures.

10.   Read Romans 8 carefully. Explain how each of the following verses help you overcome temptation. Romans 8:1,2;9,14;13;15-17;26,27;31;32;37;38,39.

7 Your Authority as a Believer

I. ADAM'S ORIGINAL AUTHORITY

A. GIVEN BY GOD

1. Man was created to rule the earth--all the earth.

> Then God said, "Let Us make man in Our image, according to Our likeness; and let them rule over the fish of the sea and over the birds of the sky and over the cattle and over all the earth, and over every creeping thing that creeps on the earth." And God created man in His own image, in the image of God He created him; male and female He created them. And God blessed them; and God said to them, "Be fruitful and multiply, and fill the earth, and subdue it; and rule over the fish of the sea and over the birds of the sky, and over every living thing that moves on the earth."
> Genesis 1:26-28

Adam was to replenish the earth and subdue it. Subdue comes from the Hebrew word "kabash" which means "to conquer, subjugate, bring into bondage, force, keep under, bring into subjection." If anything gets out of line, get it back in line, Adam!

2. God created man in His own image, after His likeness (Genesis 1:26). God is a triune being; man is a triune being, body, soul, and spirit. Man was created for the pleasure of God.

> "Worthy art Thou, our Lord and our God, to receive glory and honor and power; for Thou didst create all things, and because of Thy will they existed, and were created."
> Revelation 4:11

God created the animals, yet He formed man out of the existing earth and then breathed His Life into him. Man and woman had God's image, God's authority, God's wisdom. They had their identity in Him! When God created man and woman He said they were "very good."

3. God gave the earth to man.

> The heavens are the heavens of the Lord; But the earth He has given to the sons of men.
> Psalm 115:16

4. Man was made to have dominion.

> Thou dost make him to rule over the works of Thy hands; Thou
> hast put all things under his feet,...
> Psalm 8:6

> But one has testified somewhere, saying, "WHAT IS MAN, THAT
> THOU REMEMBEREST HIM? OR THE SON OF MAN, THAT THOU
> ART CONCERNED ABOUT HIM? THOU HAST MADE HIM FOR A
> LITTLE WHILE LOWER THAN ANGELS: THOU HAST APPOINTED
> HIM OVER THE WORKS OF THY HANDS: THOU HAST PUT ALL
> THINGS IN SUBJECTION UNDER HIS FEET."
> Hebrews 2:6-8

5. Adam was to guard the garden. The word "guard" comes from the Hebrew word
"shamar" which means to protect, hedge about, or guard."

> Then the Lord God took the man and put him into the garden of
> Eden to cultivate it and keep it.
> Genesis 2:15

Adam had everything going for him: a perfect home, a beautiful, unspoiled wife,
and a wonderful job taking care of a weedless garden! He had intelligence that
surpasses anything we know today. He named all the animals and then
remembered their names! He had perfect recall.

B. GIVEN UP BY MAN...

1. ...by acting independently of God. Satan could not stand the fact that God had
given Adam authority over the world and His creation. Authority is what he
wanted. So he planned to usurp that authority in order to become the "god of
this world." He went to Eve saying, "God knows that when you eat of that tree,
then you will be like God." But wait a minute. Hadn't God made Adam and Eve
in His image? Yes, Adam and Eve already had their authority, their power, their
position, their identity in God. Satan is questioning that identity! There are two
things that Satan wants to take from you: the authority of God's Word and your
identity in it. He wants to make you think that you are a nobody, that you don't
have the Life of God in you. He wants you to act independently of God as
though no authority belongs to you. When Satan acted independently of God and
wanted to have his own authority, he lost it all. Now he was enticing man to do
the same thing. Man's authority was in God--not apart from Him!

"How you have fallen from heaven, O star of the morning, son of the dawn! You have been cut down to the earth, You who have weakened the nations! But you said in your heart, 'I will ascend to heaven; I will raise my throne above the stars of God, And I will sit on the mount of assembly In the recesses of the north. I will ascend above the heights of the clouds; I will make myself like the Most High.' Nevertheless you will be thrust down to Sheol, To the recesses of the pit."
Isaiah 14:12-15

The word of the Lord came again to me saying, "Son of man, say to the leader of Tyre, 'Thus says the Lord God, "Because your heart is lifted up And you have said, 'I am a god, I sit in the seat of gods, In the heart of the seas'; Yet you are a man and not God, Although you make your heart like the heart of God--Behold, you are wiser than Daniel; There is no secret that is a match for you. By your wisdom and understanding You have acquired riches for yourself, And have acquired gold and silver for your treasuries. By your great wisdom, by your trade You have increased your riches, And your heart is lifted up because of your riches-- Therefore, thus says the Lord God, 'Because you have made your heart Like the heart of God, Therefore, behold, I will bring strangers upon you, The most ruthless of the nations. And they will draw their swords Against the beauty of your wisdom And defile your splendor. They will bring you down to the pit, And you will die the death of those who are slain In the heart of the seas. Will you still say, "I am a god," In the presence of your slayer, Although you are a man and not God, In the hands of those who would you? You will die the death of the uncircumcised By the hand of strangers, For I have spoken!' declares the Lord God!"'"
Again the word of the Lord came to me saying, "Son of man, take up a lamentation over the king of Tyre, and say to him, 'Thus says the Lord God, "You had the seal of perfection, Full of wisdom and perfect in beauty. You were in Eden, the garden of God; Every precious stone was your covering: The ruby, the topaz, and the diamond; The beryl, the onyx, and the jasper; The lapis lazuli, the turquoise, and the emerald, And the gold, the workmanship of your settings and sockets, Was in you. On the day that you were created They were prepared. You were the anointed cherub who covers, And I placed you there. You were on the holy mountain of God; You walked in the midst of the stones of fire. You were blameless in your

ways From the day you were created, Until unrighteousness was
found in you.   By the abundance of your trade You were
internally filled with violence, And you sinned; Therefore I
have cast you as profane From the mountain of God.   And I
have destroyed you, O covering cherub, From the midst of the
stones of fire.   Your heart was lifted up because of your
beauty; You corrupted your wisdom by reason of your
splendor.   I cast you to the ground; I put you before kings,
That they may see you.   By the multitude of your iniquities, In
the unrighteousness of your trade, You profaned your
sanctuaries.   Therefore I have brought fire from the midst of
you; It has consumed you, And I have turned you to ashes on
the earth In the eyes of all who see you.   All who know you
among the peoples Are appalled at you; You have become
terrified, And you will be no more."'"
Ezekiel 28:1-19

2.   ...by refusing to use the authority he had.   Adam was to "keep" the garden, to
guard and protect it.   One who spoke contrary to God's Word was inside.   Adam
should have used his authority to stop the serpent and warn his wife.   He was
there with her. By refusing to use his authority, he lost it!

When the woman saw that the tree was good for food, and that it
was a delight to the eyes, and that the tree was desirable to
make one wise, she took from its fruit and ate; and she gave
also to her husband with her, and he ate.
Genesis 3:6

3.   Adam and Eve lost four things:

a)   THEIR DOMINION   They gave up their dominion to Satan by disobeying God.
Jesus recognized that Satan had that authority over this world.   He did not
dispute Satan's right to give Him the kingdoms during the temptation in Luke
4:5-6, though He told him to leave and that God was the only one to be
worshipped.

And he led Him up and showed Him all the kingdoms of the
world in a moment of time.   And the devil said to Him, "I
will give You all this domain and its glory; for it has been
handed over to me, and I give it to whomever I wish."
Luke 4:5-6

b) THE TREE OF LIFE

> Then the Lord God said, "Behold, the man has become like
> one of Us, knowing good and evil; and now, lest he stretch
> out his hand, and take also from the tree of life, and eat,
> and live forever"--
> Genesis 3:22

They had to be kept from the tree of life lest they would eat of it and live
forever in their sin. They died spiritually as well as physically as a result of
their sin.

> Therefore, just as through one man sin entered into the
> world, and death through sin, and so death spread to all
> men, because all sinned--for until the Law sin was in the
> world; but sin is not imputed when there is no law.
> Nevertheless death reigned from Adam until Moses, even
> over those who had not sinned in the likeness of the offense
> of Adam, who is a type of Him who was to come.
> Romans 5:12-14

c) THEIR IMAGE OF GOD

> "You are of your father the devil, and you want to do the
> desires of your father. He was a murderer from the
> beginning, and does not stand in the truth, because there
> is no truth in him. Whenever he speaks a lie, he speaks
> from his own nature; for he is a liar, and the father of
> lies."
> John 8:44

Though he was created in the image of God, Adam had now taken on a
strange, evil nature: that of Satan. Jesus at one time said to a group of
Jews, "You are all of your father, the devil," signifying the general state of
man without true faith in God.

d) THEIR PERFECT ENVIRONMENT

> ...therefore the Lord God sent him out from the garden of
> Eden, to cultivate the ground from which he was taken. So
> He drove the man out; and at the east of the garden of Eden

> He stationed the cherubim, and the flaming sword which
> turned every direction, to guard the way to the tree of life.
> Genesis 3:23-24

Adam now had to cultivate a cursed ground and eat by the sweat of his brow.
They had to leave the constant presence of God. Now they worshipped Him
with sacrifices.

C. PROMISED BACK BY GOD

Satan is delighted. Now he has the authority over man, and he hates him. Instead
of ministering to God's creation (as he was created to do) he now has authority over
God's creation. God sees this and puts a curse on him. Then He says something
that really shakes Satan up. God promises that "the seed of the woman will bruise
the head of the serpent." The head is a symbol of authority.

> "And I will put enmity Between you and the woman, And between
> your seed and her seed; He shall bruise you on the head, And you
> shall bruise him on the heel."
> Genesis 3:15

> But I want you to understand that Christ is the head of every man,
> and the man is the head of a woman, and God is the head of Christ.
> I Corinthians 11:3

Satan's authority was to be crushed. A member of Adam's race would be born that
would be qualified to get that authority back. So Satan thought, "Oh, there is going
to be a Seed that will come from woman, that is really going to get me. I'd better get
the Seed first."

D. FOUGHT AGAINST BY SATAN

Satan didn't fully understand the promise of the Seed, but he began a long campaign
to destroy that promised Seed:

1. He saw that Abel's sacrifice was acceptable to God; therefore, he incited Cain to
    kill Abel, hoping to cut off the Seed.

2. When he heard about the covenant with Abraham and Abraham's seed, he knew
    that the seed of Abraham must be killed. Through circumstances, he stirred up
    Easu to kill Jacob, thinking he was the promised Seed. But Jacob stood up in his
    new found image as Israel (one who has prevailed with God and man) and found
    peace with his warning brother Esau. Whenever a man would rise up in God and
    find his image, he ruled his circumstances.

3. In trying to kill the Seed and not knowing who the Seed might be, he enticed the Pharaoh to order the murder of all Hebrew babies; however, two parents named Amram and Jochebed stood up in their image of authority and refused to have their baby thrown into the Nile. Their son, Moses, became the deliverer.

4. In the Promised Land he heard that the Seed was to come through the family of David. He attacked the family. Finally, a wicked woman named Jezebel caused the whole of Israel to follow after Baal. She arranged for her daughter to marry one from the family of David and become the queen of Judah. Her daughter, Athaliah, was as wicked as Jezebel, and when her husband died, she had her son and all his heirs killed. Now the Seed is destroyed--Satan thinks he has won. Ah, but there is one little grandson, Joash, hidden away by a faithful woman married to a priest. At the end of seven years, they brought him out, crowned him king, and killed Athaliah. Satan had come close to destroying all of David's seed, but had failed.

5. During the captivity, there was a decree made by the king, at the suggestion of Haman (yet inspired by Satan) to kill all the Jews in the land. But Queen Esther fasted and prayed for three days, went before the king, and saved the lives of the Jews! A Jewish queen stood in her image of authority and saved her nation.

6. In the New Testament, wise men came to Herod looking for a king. King Herod, stirred up by Satan to get the Seed, ordered the murder of all Jewish babies. But a man named Joseph stood up in his authority and obeyed God's voice to him in a dream. This baby Jesus was hidden in Egypt until King Herod died. Satan had missed again, and the Seed was not destroyed. Why? Because whenever men stand in their God given authority, Satan is defeated.

7. At Jesus' baptism, a voice came from the Father saying, "This is my beloved Son in whom I am well pleased." This must be the Seed! Now Satan attacks Jesus. In the temptation he seeks to get Jesus to bow and worship him and acquire his authority. Jesus refused to bow down; therefore He must be killed. Finally he succeeded in killing Jesus, but that was all part of the plan! Death could not hold Jesus. He arose to put the final touches on His plan to give man authority once more.

> Since then the children share in flesh and blood, He Himself likewise also partook of the same, that through death He might render powerless him who had the power of death, that is, the

devil; and might deliver those who through fear of death were subject to slavery all their lives.
Hebrews 2:14-15

E. RESTORED BY THE SEED

Jesus went into hell and took the keys of death and hell. He could not be kept by death because He had never sinned. He came up out of the grave and took the captive saints to heaven with Him. Jesus unlocked the power of death! He led captive a host of captives (Ephesians 4:8-9). Jesus not only defeated the power of death (Hebrews 2:14), but He also completely restored the authority that Satan had taken from man. He had released man again to reign.

...and the living One; and I was dead, and behold, I am alive forevermore, and I have the keys of death and of Hades.
Revelation 1:18

Therefore it says, "WHEN HE ASCENDED ON HIGH, HE LED CAPTIVE A HOST OF CAPTIVES, AND HE GAVE GIFTS TO MEN." (Now this expression, "He ascended," what does it mean except that He also had descended into the lower parts of the earth?
Ephesians 4:8-9

"Now there was a certain rich man, and he habitually dressed in purple and fine linen, gaily living in splendor every day. And a certain poor man named Lazarus was laid at his gate, covered with sores, and longing to be fed with the crumbs which were falling from the rich man's table; besides, even the dogs were coming and licking his sores. Now it came about that the poor man died and he was carried away by the angels to Abraham's bosom; and the rich man also died and was buried. And in Hades he lifted up his eyes, being in torment, and saw Abraham far away, and Lazarus in his bosom. And he cried out and said, 'Father Abraham, have mercy on me, and send Lazarus, that he may dip the tip of his finger in water and cool off my tongue; for I am in agony in this flame.' But Abraham said, 'Child, remember that during your life you received your good things, and likewise Lazarus bad things; but now he is being comforted here, and you are in agony. And besides all this, between us and you there is a great chasm fixed, in order that those who wish to come over from here to you may not be able, and that none may cross over from there to us.' And he said, 'Then I beg you, Father, that you send him to my father's house--warn them, lest they also come to this place of torment.' But Abraham

said, 'They have Moses and the prophets; let them hear them.' But he said, 'No, Father Abraham, but if someone goes to them from the dead, they will repent!' But he said to him, 'If they do not listen to Moses and the Prophets, neither will they be persuaded if someone rises from the dead.'"
Luke 16:19-31

...and the tombs were opened; and many bodies of the saints who had fallen asleep were raised; and coming out of the tombs after His resurrection they entered the holy city and appeared to many.
Matthew 27:52-53

When He had disarmed the rulers and authorities, He made a public display of them, having triumphed over them through Him.
Colossians 2:15

...which He brought about in Christ, when He raised Him from the dead, and seated Him at His right hand in the heavenly places, far above all rule and authority and power and dominion, and every name that is named, not only in this age, but also in the one to come. And He put all things in subjection under His feet, and (by grace you have been saved), and raised us up with Him, and seated us with Him in the heavenly places, in Christ Jesus, in order that in the ages to come He might show the surpassing riches of His grace in kindness toward us in Christ Jesus.
Ephesians 1:20-23

...even when we were dead in our transgressions, made us alive together with Christ (by grace you have been saved) and raised us up with Him, and seated us with Him in the heavenly places, in Christ Jesus, in order that in the ages to come He might show the surpassing riches of His grace in kindness toward us in Christ Jesus.
Ephesians 2:5-7

For if by the transgression of the one, death reigned through the one, much more those who receive the abundance of grace and of the gift of righteousness will reign in life through the One, Jesus Christ.
Romans 5:17

And just as we have borne the image of the earthy, we shall also

bear the image of the heavenly.
I Corinthians 15:49

II.   GOD SENDS A SECOND ADAM.

A. HE HAS A PERFECT NATURE.

1.   This second Adam was born of a virgin; the sin nature was not transferred to Him. He was born without death in Him. He had only the Life of God. He must stand as the original Adam, pure and righteous. He was truly man, born of a woman, but without the stain of sin.

> Therefore the Lord Himself will give you a sign: Behold, a virgin will be with child and bear a son, and she will call His name Immanuel.
> Isaiah 7:14

> "And behold, you will conceive in your womb, and bear a son, and you shall name Him Jesus. He will be great, and will be called the Son of the Most High; and the Lord God will give Him the throne of His father David; and He will reign over the house of Jacob forever; and His kingdom will have no end." And Mary said to the angel, "How can this be, since I am a virgin?" And the angel answered and said to her, "The Holy Spirit will come upon you, and the power of the Most High will overshadow you; and for that reason the holy offspring shall be called the Son of God.
> Luke 1:31-35

2.   This Adam was obedient in all things.

> And being found in appearance as a man, He humbled Himself by becoming obedient to the point of death, even death on a cross.
> Philippians 2:8

> For as through the one man's disobedience the many were made sinners, even so through the obedience of the One the many will be made righteous.
> Romans 5:19

He did only what the Father told Him; He was acting in complete harmony with the Father.

3. This Adam was strong--strong enough to undo the work of the devil, strong enough to get authority back for man.

B. HE HAS A DEFINED TASK...

1. ...to redeem man, to give him back what he originally had, to restore him to his former owner.

> But when the fulness of the time came, God sent forth His Son, born of a woman, born under the Law, in order that He might redeem those who were under the Law, that we might receive the adoption as sons.
> Galatians 4:4-5

2. ...to destroy the works of the devil. "...The reason the Son of God was made manifest (visible) was to undo (destroy, loosen, and dissolve) the works the devil has done" (I John 3:8 TAB). What are the works that Satan has done that Jesus is to destroy?

a) Sin: lawlessness, disobedience, carnality, error, apostasy, discord, "missing the mark" (Jesus came to loose you from the hold of sin.)

b) Sickness: Jesus bore your sicknesses and diseases on His own body so that you might be healed. Sickness was not from God. It came as a curse, the result of disobedience and sin.

> ...and while being reviled, He did not revile in return; while suffering, He uttered no threats, but kept entrusting Himself to Him who judges righteously;...
> I Peter 2:23

> And when evening had come, they brought to Him many who were demon-possessed; and He cast out the spirits with a word, and healed all who were ill.
> Matthew 8:16

> Surely our griefs He Himself bore, And our sorrows He carried; Yet we ourselves esteemed Him stricken, Smitten of God, and afflicted.
> Isaiah 53:4

c) Poverty: Satan seeks to impoverish his slaves, ruin them, or put their eyes on material gain only and by any means. God wants to give you power to gain wealth and then to acknowledge where it came from.

> "But you shall remember the Lord your God, for it is He who is giving you power to make wealth, that He may confirm His covenant which He swore to your fathers, as it is this day."
> Deuteronomy 8:18

> It is the blessing of the Lord that makes rich, And He adds no sorrow to it.
> Proverbs 10:22

> "For she does not know that it was I who gave her the grain, the new wine, and the oil, And lavished on her silver and gold, Which they used for Baal."
> Hosea 2:8

Jesus came and became poor that we might become rich. He was not poor spiritually, but He was poor in regard to this world's goods, and also in giving up the glory that He had with the Father. God gave us a firsthand example of how to prosper. He sowed His only Son and reaped millions!

d) Death: Death passed upon all men because of Adam's sin, but the New Adam conquered death and took the sting out of it. "The last Adam became a life-giving spirit."

> Therefore, just as through one man sin entered into the world, and death through sin, and so death spread to all men, because all sinned--
> Romans 5:12

> Since then the children share in flesh and blood, He Himself likewise also partook of the same, that through death He might render powerless him who had the power of death, that is, the devil; and might deliver those who through fear of death were subject to slavery all their lives.
> Hebrews 2:14-15

So also it is written, "The First MAN, Adam, BECAME A LIVING SOUL." The last Adam became a life-giving spirit.
I Corinthians 15:45

3.   ...to bind the strong man.

And He was casting out a demon, and it was dumb; and it came about that when the demon had gone out, the dumb man spoke; and the multitudes marveled. But some of them said, "He casts out demons by Beelzebul, the ruler of the demons." And others, to test Him, were demanding of Him a sign from heaven. But He knew their thoughts, and said to them, "Any kingdom divided against itself is laid waste; and a house divided against itself falls. And if Satan also is divided against himself, how shall his kingdom stand? For you say that I cast out demons by Beelzebul. And if I by Beelzebul cast out demons, by whom do your sons cast them out? Consequently they shall be your judges. But if I cast out demons by the finger of God, then the kingdom of God has come upon you. When a strong man, fully armed, guards his own homestead, his possessions are undisturbed; but when someone stronger than he attacks him and overpowers him, he takes away from him all his armor on which he had relied, and distributes his plunder. He who is not with Me is against Me; and he who does not gather with Me, scatters."
Luke 11:14-23

In order to bind the strong man, it takes one who is stronger. Jesus is the Stronger Man. Satan had for centuries bound his victims in sin, disease, poverty, and fear of death. The Jews, however, had a covenant with God, and when they exercised their covenant, they experienced freedom from the bondage of Satan. Now a new covenant is to be given. Jesus is anointed to announce the Good News. He is proclaiming release to the captives. The strong man is about to be bound!

"THE SPIRIT OF THE LORD IS UPON ME, BECAUSE HE ANOINTED ME TO PREACH THE GOSPEL TO THE POOR. HE HAS SENT ME TO PROCLAIM RELEASE TO THE CAPTIVES, AND RECOVERY OF SIGHT TO THE BLIND, TO SET FREE THOSE WHO ARE DOWN-TRODDEN, TO PROCLAIM THE FAVORABLE YEAR OF THE LORD."
Luke 4:18

4.   ...to spoil principalities and powers.

> When He had disarmed the rulers and authorities, He made a
> public display of them, having triumphed over them through
> Him.
> Colossians 2:15

Satan had armor, but it was spoiled by Jesus. He had power, but it was
conquered. Jesus made an open show of His victory over Satan. He spoiled
him--stripped off his power. Here are some of the powers that have been
stripped from him:

a) Principalities:

> For our struggle is not against flesh and blood, but against
> the powers, against the world forces of this darkness,
> against the spiritual forces of wickedness in the heavenly
> places.
> Ephesians 6:12

These are chief rulers of highest rank. Satan has high ranking powers, but
according to Ephesians 1:21, Jesus is far above all principalities and powers.
We are seated with Jesus above them too! These principalities are far below
you!

> ...far above all rule and authority and power and dominion,
> and every name that is named, not only in this age, but also
> in the one to come.
> Ephesians 1:21

b) Powers: These are authorities derived from Satan. But look at what Jesus
    gave us: "Behold, I have given you authority to tread upon serpents and
    scorpions, and over all the power of the enemy, and nothing shall injure you"
    (Luke 10:19).

c) World rulers of darkness: (Ephesians 6:12) We struggle against such
    rulers, but we have the victory and win. These are evil spirits that plague
    nations, like the one that Michael, the archangel, helped overcome when he
    hindered a messenger from going to Daniel.

> "But the prince of the kingdom of Persia was withstanding
> me for twenty-one days; then behold, Michael, one of the
> chief princes, came to help me, for I had been left there

with the kings of Persia."
Daniel 10:13

d) Spiritual wickedness in high places: meaning "high offices." We can bind the devil from bringing this kind of wickedness into our government and to our congressmen. Jesus has already bound the strong man!

5.   ...to destroy Satan--to paralyze him.

> Since then the children share in flesh and blood, He Himself likewise also partook of the same, that through death He might render powerless him who had the power of death, that is, the devil.
> Hebrews 2:14

By His death, Jesus destroyed him who had the power of death, even the devil. Satan's total destruction is sure.

> And the devil who deceived them was thrown into the lake of fire and brimstone...and...will be tormented day and night forever and ever.
> Revelation 20:10

And the devil who deceived them was thrown into the lake of fire and brimstone, where the beast and the false prophet are also; and they will be tormented day and night forever and ever.

C. HE HAS COMPLETE SUCCESS.

Jesus restored the four things that Adam and Eve lost:

1. He gave us back dominion, authority, and power.

a) He said, "All authority is given unto Me...go therefore..."

> And Jesus came up and spoke to them, saying, "All authority has been given to Me in heaven and on earth. Go therefore and make disciples of all the nations, baptizing them in the name of the Father and the Son and the Holy Spirit, teaching them to observe all that I commanded you; and lo, I am with you always, even to the end of the age."
> Matthew 28:18-20

    b) He gave us His Name, His power of attorney to do His kind of work.

> "And these signs will accompany those who have believed: in My name they will cast out demons, they will speak with new tongues; they will pick up serpents, and if they drink any deadly poison, it shall not hurt them; they will lay hands on the sick, and they will recover."
> Mark 16:17-18

> "Truly, truly, I say to you, he who believes in Me, the works that I do shall he do also; and greater works than these shall he do; because I go to the Father."
> John 14:12

    c) He sent His Holy Spirit to empower us.

> "But you shall receive power when the Holy Spirit has come upon you; and you shall be My witnesses both in Jerusalem, and in all Judea and Samaria, and even to the remotest part of the earth."
> Acts 1:8

2. He gave us the tree of life.

    a) He gave us eternal life.

> "Truly, truly, I say to you, he who hears My word, and believes Him who sent Me, has eternal life, and does not come into judgment, but has passed out of death into life."
> John 5:24

    b) He made us righteous, and "the fruit of the righteous is a tree of life" (Proverbs 11:30).

    c) He gives us the desires of our heart, and "desire fulfilled is a tree of life" (Proverbs 13:12).

3. He gave us back the image of God.

    a) "And put on the new self, which in the likeness of God has been created in righteousness and holiness of the truth" (Ephesians 4:24).

b) "...Being renewed to a true knowledge according to the image of the One who created him..." (Colossians 3:10).

c) "For whom He foreknew, He also predestined to become conformed to the image of His Son, that He might be the first-born among many brethren" (Romans 8:29).

d) "For we are His workmanship, created in Christ Jesus for good works..." (Ephesians 2:10).

4. He gave us the right to enter a perfect environment.

a) There will be no curse.

> And there shall no longer be any curse; and the throne of God and of the Lamb shall be in it, and His bond-servants shall serve Him.
> Revelation 22:3

b) There will be no death, mourning, crying, or pain.

> "...and He shall wipe away every tear from their eyes; and there shall no longer be any death; there shall no longer be any mourning, or crying, or pain; the first things have passed away."
> Revelation 21:4

c) There will be a new heaven and a new earth (Revelation 21:4).

d) There will be the tree of life again.

> ...in the middle of its street. And on either side of the river was the tree of life, bearing twelve kinds of fruit, yielding its fruit every month; and the leaves of the tree were for the healing of the nations.
> Revelation 22:2

e) God's physical presence will always be with us.

And I heard a loud voice from the throne, saying, "Behold, the tabernacle of God is among men, and He shall dwell among them, and they shall be His people, and God Himself shall be among them."
Revelation 21:3

And I saw no temple in it, for the Lord God, the Almighty, and the Lamb, are its temple.
Revelation 21:22

And the city has no need of the sun or of the moon to shine upon it, for the glory of God has illumined it, and its lamp is the Lamb.
Revelation 21:23

III. THE AUTHORITY OF JESUS

A. THE SOURCE OF HIS AUTHORITY

1. The Father gave Jesus His authority.

"For just as the Father has life in Himself, even so He gave to the Son also to have life in Himself; and He gave Him authority to execute judgment, because He is the Son of Man. Do not marvel at this; for an hour is coming, in which all who are in the tombs shall hear His voice, and shall come forth; those who did the good deeds to a resurrection of life, those who committed the evil deeds to a resurrection of judgment. I can do nothing on My own initiative. As I hear, I judge; and My judgment is just, because I do not seek My own will, but the will of Him who sent Me."
John 5:26-30

2. Jesus came in the Father's Name.

"I have come in My Father's name, and you do not receive Me; if another shall come in his own name, you will receive him."
John 5:43

3. Jesus is God. There is no greater authority! God came in the flesh.

God, after He spoke long ago to the fathers in the prophets in many portions and in many ways, in these last days has spoken

to us in His Son, whom He appointed heir of all things, through whom also He made the world. And He is the radiance of His glory and the exact representation of His nature, and upholds all things by the word of His power. When He had made purification of sins, He sat down at the right hand of the Majesty on high; having become as much better than the angels, as He has inherited a more excellent name than they.
Hebrews 1:1-4

4. He was given a Name that is above every name.

Therefore also God highly exalted Him, and bestowed on Him the name which is above every name, that at the name of Jesus EVERY KNEE SHOULD BOW, of those who are in heaven, and on earth, and under the earth,...
Philippians 2:9-10

"And she will bear a Son; and you shall call His name Jesus, for it is He who will save His people from their sins."
Matthew 1:21

"Therefore the Lord Himself will give you a sign: Behold, a virgin will be with child and bear a son, and she will call His name Immanuel."
Isaiah 7:14

B. THE POSITION OF HIS AUTHORITY

1. God exercises His power and authority from heavenly places. God occupies a very strong position of authority in heavenly places. He sits in the heavens. He is in control. His position of power is in the heavenlies.

"And all the inhabitants of the earth are accounted as nothing, But He does according to His will in the host of heaven And among the inhabitants of earth; And no one can ward off His hand Or say to Him, 'What hast Thou done?'"
Daniel 4:35

He who sits in the heavens laughs, The Lord scoffs at them.
Psalm 2:4

2. Jesus is seated in the heavenlies.

> ...far above all rule and authority and power and dominion, and
> every name that is named, not only in this age, but also in the
> one to come.
> Ephesians 1:21

Jesus is the Head, and we are the Body. We are not separated from the Body. He is seated in the heavenlies, and so are we. He is in the position of power, and so are we. When we see Him seated at the right hand of power, we see that He has some very special authority.

What kind of power and authority does He have at the right hand of the Father? We need to know because whatever He has, we have. We are part of the Body.

a) The enemy is going to be put under Jesus' feet.

> "The Lord says to my Lord: "Sit at My right hand, Until I
> make Thine enemies a footstool for Thy feet."
> Psalm 110:1

b) He is sitting at the right hand of power.

> Jesus said to him, "You have said it yourself; nevertheless I
> tell you, hereafter you shall see THE SON OF MAN SITTING
> AT THE RIGHT HAND OF POWER, AND COMING ON THE
> CLOUDS OF HEAVEN."
> Matthew 26:64

In warfare, the man in charge of his army gets on a high place so that he can look to see what his army is doing and what the enemy is doing. He observes and gives directions. Jesus is at the right hand of the Father. He is observing and giving directions. He has the position of power.

c) He sent the Holy Spirit of power.

> "Therefore having been exalted to the right hand of God,
> and having received from the Father the promise of the Holy
> Spirit, He has poured forth this which you both see and
> hear. For it was not David who ascended into heaven, but
> he himself says: 'THE LORD SAID TO MY LORD, "SIT AT
> MY RIGHT HAND, UNTIL I MAKE THINE ENEMIES A
> FOOTSTOOL FOR THY FEET."'"
> Acts 2:33-34

When Jesus sat down He did something that had not happened on the earth before. He gave the Holy Spirit to His believers. He now had the authority to do that. Any believer could receive the Holy Spirit whereas before only a few select ones had received Him.

d) He is interceding at the right hand of the Father.

> ...who is the one who condemns? Christ Jesus is He who died, yes, rather who was raised, who is at the right hand of God, who also intercedes for us.
> Romans 8:34

Jesus entered into a place of praying for His Body. He is holding them up, ever living to make intercession for them. Part of power is intercession. That is what Jesus entered into at the right hand of the Father.

> Hence, also, He is able to save forever those who draw near to God through Him, since He always lives to make intercession for them.
> Hebrews 7:25

e) All things are upheld by the Word of His power.

> And He is the radiance of His glory and the exact representation of His nature, and upholds all things by the word of His power. When He had made purification of sins, He sat down at the right hand of the Majesty on high;...
> Hebrews 1:3

f) He stood up to greet the first Christian martyr.

> But being full of the Holy Spirit, he gazed intently into heaven and saw the glory of God, and Jesus standing at the right hand of God; and he said, "Behold, I see the heavens opened up and the Son of Man standing at the right hand of God."
> Acts 7:55-56

Stephen was received by Jesus and was able to literally sit down with Him.

3. He has His people inscribed in the palm of His hands.

But Zion said, "The Lord has forsaken me, And the Lord has forgotten me." "Can a woman forget her nursing child, And have no compassion on the son of her womb? Even these may forget, but I will not forget you. Behold, I have inscribed you on the palms of My hands; Your walls are continually before Me."
Isaiah 49:14-16

This is a prophecy about how the people felt during the exile--forgotten of God. But God says, "I won't forget you. I have inscribed you in the palms of My hands. Your walls are continually before Me." When God sees us, He sees us inscribed on the hands of Jesus. During the exile, the walls of Jerusalem were down, but God didn't see them down. He saw a restored Jerusalem. When God looks at us and our broken personalities, He sees us whole, complete. We are being completed, and God sees our walls up--a finished product!

For I am confident of this very thing, that He who began a good work in you will perfect it until the day of Christ Jesus.
Philippians 1:6

Many times, during Bible days, people would draw out what they were going to do for the day on their hands, and then they would follow their plans. Jesus says, "I have your master plan on my hands. I have a perfect plan for your life and I see the walls all up." Just think of God's personal concern for you. He says that even the hairs of your head are numbered. He says that He even keeps a book on you.

For Thou didst form my inward parts; Thou didst weave me in my mother's womb. I will give thanks to Thee, for I am fearfully and wonderfully made; Wonderful are Thy works, And my soul knows it very well. My frame was not hidden from Thee, When I was made in secret, And skillfully wrought in the depths of the earth. Thine eyes have seen my unformed substance; And in Thy book they were all written, The days that were ordained for me, When as yet there was not one of them. How precious also are Thy thoughts to me, O God! How vast is the sum of them! If I should count them, they would outnumber the sand. When I awake, I am still with Thee.
Psalm 139:13-18

He talks about you before you are made, after you are made, and all the stages you are going to go through. God doesn't see the messes. He is aware of them, but He has faith that you are going to come out of them because you are complete in Christ.

> And we proclaim Him, admonishing every man and teaching
> every man with all wisdom, that we may present every man
> complete in Christ.
> Colossians 1:28

In the Old Testament, the priest carried the names of the tribes on a breastplate over the heart. But Jesus seems to carry our names on His hands. Why? Because the hand has to do with strength and power, and Jesus wants His Body to be strong, powerful, and living in authority. The nailprints in His hands give Him the right to hold up our names. He paid for our sins, therefore, we are righteous ones and are allowed a position of authority with Him.

4. He is confessing your name before the Father and the angels in heaven. Are you confessing Christ before men? Then your name is getting around in heaven! Jesus is the High Priest of your confession.

> "Everyone therefore who shall confess Me before men, I will also
> confess him before My Father who is in heaven. But whoever
> shall deny Me before men, I will also deny him before My Father
> who is in heaven."
> Matthew 10:32,33

> "And I say to you, everyone who confesses me before men, the
> Son of Man shall confess him also before the angels of God."
> Luke 12:8

IV. YOUR RESTORED AUTHORITY

A. YOU ARE SEATED WITH CHRIST.

1. Recognize your position.

> ...even when we were dead in our transgressions, made us
> alive together with Christ (by grace you have been saved), and
> raised us up with Him, and seated us with Him in the heavenly
> places, in Christ Jesus,...
> Ephesians 2:5-6

The Head has power in heaven, the Body has power on the earth. You are seated on the right hand of Jesus. What are you doing up there? You are watching your Head. Do as He does!

2.   Receive your blessings.

> Blessed be the God and Father of our Lord Jesus Christ, who
> has blessed us with every spiritual blessing in the heavenly
> places in Christ,...
> Ephesians 1:3

You are blessed with all spiritual blessing in heavenly places. You receive these blessings with an attitude of faith. You choose to look at these situations down here the way Jesus would see them from up there. Look at situations through the Word. If you stay in earthly places in your thinking, you don't get heavenly blessings.

What are you going to do with your situation? Sit down in heavenly places, or sit down here and gripe? Take your position of authority. "Set your mind on things above." Your treasury of heavenly blessings is above, but it is available for you to use down here!

> If then you have been raised up with Christ, keep seeking the
> things above, where Christ is, seated at the right hand of God.
> Set your mind on the things above, not on the things that are
> on earth.
> Colossians 3:1-2

3.   Remember that Christ is the Source of your treasures. In Christ are hidden all the treasures.

> ...in whom are hidden all the treasures of wisdom and
> knowledge.
> Colossians 2:3

Whatever you need is in Jesus. When you get up there in heavenly places and you look at all these treasures, something begins to happen to you. You watch Jesus. He is the Head. He wants to intercede for the Body. He is the Head. He wants to confess the Word. He is the Head. He wants to send power to the Body. He is the Head. He sends the Spirit to the Body. As you look at Jesus you begin to want to be like Him. Your nature changes to be like His. You begin to intercede. You want to see the Word work, to see the Spirit work. Then Psalm 37:4 begins to come true in your life. As you delight yourself in the Lord, your desire gets in line with the One in whom you are delighting, and you receive not only what you want, but what He wants! You are getting into heavenly places!

> Delight yourself in the Lord; And He will give you the desires
> of your heart.
> Psalm 37:4

B. JESUS WANTS YOU TO REIGN IN LIFE.

1. You are ruling and reigning through the One, Jesus Christ.

    > For if by the transgression of the one, death reigned through
    > the one, much more those who receive the abundance of grace
    > and of the gift of righteousness will reign in life through the
    > One, Jesus Christ.
    > Romans 5:17

    You are to be in charge of circumstances, not allowing them to be in charge of
    you. In Christ you are to be the ruling one. Don't allow the enemy to suffocate
    you with circumstances that stop the work of Jesus through you!

2. You are to reign in life. You are not going to reign, unless you stay in life by
    staying in the Word. A nasty attitude and words of revenge are not in life--they
    are in the realm of death. When you speak death words you are not reigning in
    life! Your attitude is wrong. You only rule as you stay in the Word, and keep
    your attitude in life. Make sure your spirit is clean and your mouth speaks life,
    then you will reign in life.

3. You are to crush Satan under your feet.

    > And the God of peace will soon crush Satan under your feet.
    > The grace of our Lord Jesus be with you.
    > Romans 16:20

    Because Jesus has crushed the devil, you are to do the same. God gave that
    power and authority to the Church. If you are not commanding Satan, he is
    commanding you.

4. You are to know your inheritance power.

    > ...that the God of our Lord Jesus Christ, the Father of glory,
    > may give to you a spirit of wisdom and of revelation in the
    > knowledge of Him. I pray that the eyes of your heart may be
    > enlightened, so that you may know what is the hope of His
    > calling, what are the riches of the glory of His inheritance in
    > the saints, and what is the surpassing greatness of His power

toward us who believe. These are in accordance with the working of the strength of His might...
Ephesians 1:17-19

What is the hope of your calling? God wants you to know it. The hope is that you will enter into your authority. What are the riches of the glory of His inheritance? God wants you to know that too! Your inheritance is power, authority over the devil. He also wants you to know what is the surpassing greatness of His power. He wants you to experience this power! But notice that it is for those who believe. If you don't believe that it will work, it won't work. But it is there, and you can have it. It is your inheritance, your calling. Be well acquainted with the power that you have within you as your inheritance, and then use it!

5. You are seated with Christ in heavenly places.

> ...which He brought about in Christ, when He raised Him from the dead, and seated Him at His right hand in the heavenly places, far above all rule and authority and power and dominion, and every name that is named, not only in this age. but also in the one to come. And He put all things in subjection under His feet, and gave Him as head over all things to the church, which is His body, the fulness of Him who fills all in all.
> Ephesians 1:20-23

> ...even when we were dead in our transgressions, made us alive together with Christ (by grace you have been saved), and raised us up with Him, and seated us with Him in the heavenly places, in Christ Jesus, in order that in the ages to come He might show the surpassing riches of His grace in kindness toward us in Christ Jesus,...
> Ephesians 2:5-7

God's purpose to seat us in heavenly places is so that we will take power and authority over the devil. God wants to show us the surpassing riches we have in Christ Jesus. We rule and reign with His Name.

> "Because he has loved Me, therefore I will deliver him; I will set him securely on high, because he has known My name."
> Psalm 91:14

6. You are a world overcomer.

>   For whatever is born of God overcomes the world; and this is
>   the victory that has overcome the world--our faith.
>   I John 5:4

You are not to allow the world to overcome you; you are to overcome the world. Affect the world wherever you go instead of letting the world affect and mold you.

7. You are greater than the enemy.

>   You are from God, little children, and have overcome them;
>   because greater is He who is in you than he who is in the
>   world.
>   I John 4:4

You overcome the influences and evil of the world because you have the Greater One inside you, and you bear His image. That image is always an image of authority!

C. JESUS GAVE YOU AUTHORITY IN FIVE AREAS.

1. You have authority over the evil influences of men. You have authority over people who rule and reign and shouldn't be there. Forgive these people but exercise authority over their evil.

2. You have authority over demonic forces.

>   "Behold, I have given you authority to tread upon serpents and
>   scorpions, and over all the power of the enemy, and nothing
>   shall injure you.
>   Luke 10:19

3. You have authority over afflictions, sickness, and disease.

>   Who shall separate us from the love of Christ? Shall
>   tribulations, or distress, or persecution, or famine, or
>   nakedness, or peril, or sword?
>   Romans 8:35

The love of Christ has power. Nothing will separate you from it. In all these things you are more than a conqueror because you are supposed to win. You are to take your authority over these situations. Satan wants to put all these things on you and separate you from the love and power of Jesus, but don't let him. You cannot be separated from His love. Don't let Satan separate you from the authority of His power either. Be a victor!

4. You have power over bad habits and wordly amusements (I John 5:4). The problems may be tremendous, but don't major on the problem. The Bible says our faith will overcome the world. That verse is still effective. Our faith still overcomes the world. You say the times are worse now than ever? God's power is as strong as ever! And so is your faith--it will overcome the world!

5. You have authority over circumstances.

> These things speak and exhort and reprove with all authority.
> Let no one disregard you.
> Titus 2:15

Don't let anyone look down on you. Take authority over the situation. When they spoke of Jesus, they said His Word had authority. Do you have His Word? Does it have authority? Then take His Word into the circumstances. You will have authority over them as Jesus did!

D. FOUR REASONS WHY THIS AUTHORITY BELONGS TO YOU

1. You have a body. Authority and dominion were given to the first humans that God made. This dominion still belongs to the human race--Jesus recovered it from Satan. Satan can do very little without a body. He seeks desperately for some bodies to do his evil deeds through.

> "When the unclean spirit goes out of a man, it passes through waterless places seeking rest, and not finding any, it says, 'I will return to my house from which I came.'"
> Luke 11:24

2. You have the Holy Spirit.

> Or do you not know that your body is a temple of the Holy Spirit who is in you, whom you have from God, and that you are not your own?
> I Corinthians 6:19

His anointing gives you power and authority. The Holy Spirit uses your body to do God's work. You are His temple. Allow Him to use you. Don't send Him to do the work!

140

3. You have the Name of Jesus.

    > But Peter said, "I do not possess silver and gold, but what I do
    > have I give to you. In the name of Jesus Christ the Nazarene--
    > walk!"
    > Acts 3:6

    You can use that Name as if it were your own.

4. You are one with God. Jesus is the Head and you have been placed into His
    Body. He is far above all power and authority. If you are one with Him, then
    you are far above the authorities and powers also. Jesus is not on earth
    physically, but you are, and you represent Him. You are not in heaven
    physically yet, but your Lord is, and He is representing you.

    > ...that they may all be one; even as Thou, Father, art in Me,
    > and I in Thee, that they also may be in Us; that the world may
    > believe that Thou didst send Me. And the glory which Thou
    > hast given Me I have given to them; that they may be one, just
    > as We are one; I in them, and Thou in Me, that they may be
    > perfected in unity, that the world may know that Thou didst
    > send Me, and didst love them, even as Thou didst love Me."
    > John 17:21-23

    Now you are Christ's body, and individually members of it.
    I Corinthians 12:27

E. JESUS SENDS YOU WITH AUTHORITY.

Jesus said to the Father, "As Thou didst send Me into the world, I also have sent
them into the world." We have already seen how Jesus was sent into the world. He
came with authority. He came in the Father's will with the Father's Word and in the
Father's Name. Jesus gave us His Name and sends us out to do His work.

Jesus came with a purpose: to destroy the works of the devil. He sends us with a
purpose: to teach the Word, to teach what He taught, to do the works that He did.
Go, as Jesus went, in authority, destroying the works of the enemy and establishing
a kingdom of righteousness!

V. YOUR AUTHORITY IN BATTLE

A. PUT ON YOUR FIGHTING CLOTHES.

There is a conflict when you start to enter into your position of authority, into heavenly places, because Satan is the prince of the power of the air. He is against anyone who wants to exercise authority.

You will not be able to sit down at the right hand with Jesus without a battle. Satan will do his best to keep you from knowing that you have power and authority over him. Ephesians 6:11-12 tells us that you there is a battle going on. God tells you to put on the full armor of God. There is a battle in high places.

> Put on the full armor of God, that you may be able to stand firm against the schemes of the devil. For our struggle is not against flesh and blood, but against the rulers, against the powers, against the world forces of this darkness, against the spiritual forces of wickedness in the heavenly places.
> Ephesians 6:11-12

There are seven pieces to the armor. Notice that God provides the armor, but you have to put it on. You put it on to withstand the evil day. That is, any day that Satan comes against you, anytime you have a trial! That is when you need to:

1. Gird your loins with truth.

> Stand firm therefore, HAVING GIRDED YOUR LOINS WITH TRUTH, And HAVING PUT ON THE BREASTPLATE OF RIGHTEOUSNESS,...
> Ephesians 6:14

Keep the Word in your mind. That is the first battle area. Truth will keep you in your position of authority.

2. Put on the breastplate of righteousness (Eph. 6:14). Righteousness has power. Say, "Look, you can't condemn me. I have the righteousness of God in Christ Jesus." When we first come to the Father, we are orphans because we have sinned, and we don't belong to His family; however, when we accept His Son, we put on His righteousness, and we are accepted like Jesus is accepted. We are one of the family, one of His sons. We have the breastplate of righteousness.

3. Shod your feet with the preparation of the gospel of peace.

    ...and having shod YOUR FEET WITH THE PREPARATION OF
    THE GOSPEL OF PEACE...
    Ephesians 6:15

    Your feet have to do with your walk, and that has to do with your will. You
    need to make sure that you are walking in the gospel of peace, that your will is
    to walk in the Word. The Word is not only to be in your mind, in your heart,
    but in your will.

4. Take the shield of faith.

    ...in addition to all, taking up the shield of faith with which
    you will be able to extinguish all the flaming missiles of the evil
    one...
    Ephesians 6:16

    This shield was shaped like a door. Small fiery darts dipped in burning tar were
    thrown to go over the shield aiming at people's eyes. But the shield of faith will
    put out those fiery darts! You can lift that shield in any direction and be
    protected from the enemy fire. It will work in any area of your life.

5. Take the helmet of salvation.

    ...and take THE HELMET OF SALVATION, and the sword of the
    spirit, which is the word of God...
    Ephesians 6:17

    This helmet is the hope of salvation. As long as you have hope, you won't fail.
    This hope will protect you.

    But since we are of the day, let us be sober, having put on the
    breastplate of faith and love, and as a helmet, the hope of
    salvation.
    I Thessalonians 5:8

6. Take the sword of the Spirit (Eph. 6:17). Put the Word in your spirit and it will
    come out to fight when you are attacked. There is nothing for your back
    because there is not retreat, no defeat in God. Being seated in heavenly places
    keeps you victorious.

7. Pray at all times.

> ...with all prayer and petition pray at all times in the Spirit,
> and with this in view, be on the alert with all perseverance and
> petition for all the saints,...
> Ephesians 6:18

You have the armor on, but what would the army be without a commander? We
say, "Father, I come to you in Jesus' Name. Would you please direct what I am
doing?" We also pray for the wounded saints, interceding for them. Seven
pieces of armor--it is the number of completion. Put it all on! Never take it off!
Always be ready for the evil day. If it doesn't come, you are ready to help
someone else!

B. STAND LIKE A CONQUEROR.

When you have done everything you know to do, stand! Stand like a conqueror.
The victory is already yours! You tell the enemy to get off your property, it has
been promised to you. You are the authority.

> Therefore, take up the full armor of God, that you may be able to
> resist in the evil day, and having done everything, to stand firm.
> Ephesians 6:13

VI. SUMMATION

A. God created the world for man's pleasure. He gave man dominion and authority over
His creation. Satan, however, got into the garden and tempted Adam and Eve to
disobey God, thereby giving their authority to him. That one, independent act of
Adam and Eve cost them their authority, the tree of life, their image of God, and
their perfect environment. But God always has an answer. He promised that a Seed
would come and bruise the serpent's head. This promise caused Satan to fight
against the Seed for centuries, trying to stop Him, and he finally did. He killed Him
on the cross. Then, with that final attack against the promised Seed, God fulfilled
the prophecy by crushing his head.

B. Jesus was the second Adam--a perfect, sinless man sent by God to redeem man from
the law of sin and to buy back the authority. Jesus came to destroy the works of
the devil, to undo the hold that sin, sickness, poverty, and death had on man. In
His death, He bound the strong man and spoiled the principalities and powers. Now
we are freed men, restored to have dominion and no longer slaves of Satan's works!

C. The authority of Jesus came from God Himself. He had His Father's Name and His Father's nature. Then when He had completed His work of redemption, He was given a Name and a position far above every name. He was given authority above everything! Now Jesus is seated in the heavenlies, at the right hand of power with God. He is interceding there for His Body on earth. He is directing His Body from a very effective viewpoint. He is upholding all things with His Word. The Jesus living within you is in command. He has rightful authority!

D. You are seated with Christ in the heavenlies. You are blessed with all spiritual blessings. Jesus wants you to reign in this life. He has provided all things for you to be totally victorious in this life, to live above the circumstances. You are equipped to influence your environment rather than be overcome by it!

E. Although authority belongs to you the moment you are born-again, you will not move in it automatically. Satan will fight. He does not give up an inch of ground without a battle. That is why God has given you a complete set of armor. Put on your fighting clothes, and then stand there like the conqueror you are!

VII. ASSIGNMENTS

A. Listen to the tape carefully and prayerfully.

B. Complete the study guide questions.

C. Recommended reading: Released to Reign, by Charles Trombley, and Authority in Three Worlds, by Charles Capps.

STUDY GUIDE QUESTIONS

1. Give three Scriptures that convince you that God gave authority and dominion to man.

2. How did Adam give up his authority?

3. List four things that Adam and Eve lost when they sinned.

4. Using a concordance or chain reference Bible, trace the promise of the Seed. Write down four promises concerning the Seed in the Old Testament. Look for Messianic promises.

5. Using Scripture, describe the nature of the second Adam.

6.   What was Jesus' task on earth? Give at least four definite things that He did.

7.   Jesus restored all four things that Adam had lost for the human race. Choose one of the four and explain how it has been restored to you personally.

8.   Give Biblical proof of Jesus' authority. Use at least four Scriptures.

9.   List four things that Jesus is doing at the right hand of God.

10. Study Isaiah 49:14-16. What does it mean to you in the light of this lesson?

11. Ephesians 1:3 says that you are blessed with all spiritual blessings. What is the key to receiving those blessings, to making them part of your everyday life here on earth?

12. Give four examples of the power you have to reign in life.

13. You have authority in the Name of Jesus. List five things you should do in that Name. Give Scripture.

14. Choose one piece of the armor that God has given you and find three more Scriptures that will help you to use that piece more effectively.

15. You are a conqueror! Make a list of victory verses. Write out as many as you wish.

8 Faith Gets Answers

I. FAITH IS PERSISTENT.

A. THE SYROPHENICIAN WOMAN

There are times when it seems like you have prayed in faith, but nothing is happening. You have confessed the Word, stood in agreement, done everything you know to do. These are times when you need the faith that will persist, that will continue in spite of what it looks like to others. You may be accused of not having faith. Forgive the accuser--you continue in faith. The Syrophenician woman is a perfect example of someone who persisted against the odds. She came to Jesus with great faith and a hopeless problem.

1. Notice that Jesus ignored her.

> But He did not answer her a word. And His disciples came to
> Him and kept asking Him, saying, "Send her away, for she is
> shouting out after us."
> Matthew 15:23

Have you ever felt, like this woman, that Jesus ignored you? It may have seemed that way, but Jesus knows all along what He is going to do. He wanted to help that woman, but He also wanted to teach another truth about faith. If you feel like you have been ignored, ask again. This woman did. Don't walk by sense knowledge. Exercise faith in God's Word.

2. The disciples wanted to send her away (Matt 15:23).

Imagine God's chosen ministers wanting to get rid of her! They seemingly had no compassion. She didn't fit the image of those to whom they ministered, and she was bothering them. Would you give up on God's healing if a pastor or evangelist was rough and abrupt towards you when you were in the healing line? This woman didn't! She knew why she was there. She refused to have her faith denied.

3. Jesus said He was sent to Israel, not to her.

> But He answered and said, "I was sent only to the lost sheep of
> the house of Israel."
> Matthew 15:24

That was a real shocker! Healing was for the Jews, but not for her. Have you ever felt that healing was for a certain select few, but not for you? Perhaps you have even been told that. This woman heard it, but she was determined to get help. She worshiped Jesus and "kept praying, 'Lord, help me!'"

4. Jesus said, "It is not right to take the children's bread and throw it to the little dogs" (Matt. 15:26, TAB).

Now she was likened to the little dogs! Was she going to walk away in disgust and hurt feelings? No, she didn't. She just replied with earnestness, "Yes, Lord, yet even the little pups eat the crumbs that fall from their (young) master's table" (Matt. 15:27, TAB).

5. She gets her answer.

> Then Jesus answered and said to her, "O woman, your faith is great; be it done for you as you wish." And her daughter was healed at once.
> Matthew 15:28

Jesus could wait no longer. "O woman, great is your faith! Be it done for you as you wish." Her daughter was cured from that moment. Faith is persistent.

B. THE BORROWING FRIEND

One day the disciples asked Jesus to teach them how to pray. Jesus taught them the "Lord's Prayer" and then continued with a little story. A man had an unexpected friend visit him, and he needed more bread. He went to another friend and asked to borrow three loaves. The trouble was that it was already midnight! "I cannot get up and give you anything." He said, "We are already in bed!"

Then Jesus added, "...although he will not get up and supply him anything because he is his friend, yet because of his shameless persistence and insistence, he will get up and give him as much as he needs. So I say to you, Ask and keep on asking, and it shall be given you; seek and keep on seeking, and you shall find; knock and keep on knocking, and the door shall be opened to you. For every one who asks and keeps on asking, receives, and he who seeks and keeps on seeking finds, and to him who knocks and keeps on knocking the door shall be opened..." (Luke 11:7-10, TAB).

This man had a persistent faith--and got results!

C. THE WIDOW AND THE UNJUST JUDGE

"Also Jesus told them a parable, to the effect that they ought always to pray and not to turn coward--faint, lose heart and give up" (Luke 18:1, TAB).

A widow went to a judge who did not fear nor respect God. She needed legal counsel and guidance. Even though this judge was unwilling to help her, she continued asking. Finally, he decided to help her or else she would be at his doorstep all the time. She was that persistent!

"Then the Lord said, Listen to what the unjust judge says! And will not our just God defend and protect and avenge His elect (His chosen Ones) who cry to Him day and night? Will He defer them and delay help on their behalf? I tell you, He will defend and protect and avenge them speedily. However, when the Son of man comes will he find (persistence in) the faith on the earth? (Luke 18:6-8, TAB). God is looking for persistence in our faith! Don't give up!

D. BLIND BARTIMAEUS

> And it came about that as He was approaching Jericho, a certain blind man was sitting by the road, begging. Now hearing a multitude going by, he began to inquire what this might be. And they told him that Jesus of Nazareth was passing by. And he called out, saying, "Jesus, Son of David, have mercy on me!" And those who led the way were sternly telling him to be quiet; but he kept crying out all the more, "Son of David, have mercy on me!" And Jesus stopped and commanded that he be brought to Him; and when he had come near, He questioned him, "What do you want Me to do for you?" And he said, "Lord, I want to regain my sight!" And Jesus said to him, "Receive your sight; your faith has made you well." And immediately he regained his sight, and began following Him, glorifying God; and when all the people saw it, they gave praise to God.
> Luke 18:35-43

Beside the road to Jericho sat a blind man, begging. His name was Bartimaeus. He heard a man passing by, but this man was different. It was Jesus of Nazareth, "the man that heals the sick and makes the blind to see." Quickly, he calls out, "Jesus, thou son of David, have mercy on me." People all around him tell him to be quiet. They are busy listening to the Master; they do not want a man's cries to interfere with the great teaching. But he persists. He wants his sight--and this man Jesus can give it to him. He keeps on shouting all the more, "You Son of David, have pity and mercy on me."

At last, Jesus calls for him. Bartimaeus throws off his cloak and runs to Jesus. Jesus asks, "What do you want me to do for you?" And the blind man said to Him, "Master, let me receive my sight." Jesus said to him, "Go your way! Your faith has healed you."

Bartimaeus was not discouraged when those around him tried to keep him quiet, to keep him from repeating his request to Jesus. He persisted and received his sight!

E. DANIEL PRAYED FOR TWENTY-ONE DAYS.

Daniel was burdened for his people. Three years had passed since the first group of Jews had gone back to Jerusalem. He knew they were under harassment from the surrounding enemies. He longed to understand the destiny of his people so he began to pray. He prayed and fasted for three weeks. Daniel was a man of prayer, and he was accustomed to getting results! God had always answered him, giving him wisdom, direction, protection. Now he had prayed three weeks. How long, Lord? Finally, the answer came! Notice that he didn't stop praying until He heard from God.

> Then behold, a hand touched me and set me trembling on my hands and knees. And he said to me, "O Daniel, man of high esteem, understand the words that I am about to tell you and stand upright, for I have now been sent to you." And when he had spoken this word to me, I stood up trembling. Then he said to me, "Do not be afraid, Daniel, for from the first day that you set your heart on understanding this and on humbling yourself before your God, your words were heard, and I have come in response to your words. But the prince of the kingdom of Persia was withstanding me for twenty-one days; then behold, Michael, one of the chief princes, came to help me, for I had been left there with the kings of Persia. Now I have come to give you an understanding of what will happen to your people in the latter days, for the vision pertains to the days yet future."
> Daniel 10:10-14

In this case, there was definite enemy interference, but that was not an area of defeat. God's princes fought Satan's and came through with an answer. On this side of the cross, you have the power and the authority over the powers of the air. These powers may delay your answers temporarily, but they need not defeat you. Keep on the armor of God, and you will be ever prepared. Be persistent and refuse defeat!

II.   FAITH INVESTIGATES WHEN ANSWERS DON'T COME.

    A. CONSIDER THESE QUESTIONS.

       1. Are you walking in love?

You have asked, been persistent, had faith, but still no visible results. Ask yourself, "Am I walking in love towards my brothers and sisters and the world around me?" Faith works by love. If your faith isn't working, check your love level.

> For in Christ Jesus neither circumcision nor uncircumcision means anything, but faith working through love.
> Galatians 5:6

> And if I have the gift of prophecy, and know all mysteries and all knowledge; and if I have all faith, so as to remove mountains, but do not have love, I am nothing.
> I Corinthians 13:2

       2. Have you been forgiving?

Matthew 6:14-15 tells us that if we do not forgive others, the Father will not forgive us. If we have sin in our hearts, our faith will not work for us. We will deal with this more extensively in another lesson, but if you are serious about wanting to know why your faith is not working, ask God to show you if there is unforgiveness in your heart.

> For if you forgive men for their transgressions, your heavenly Father will also forgive you. But if you do not forgive men, then your Father will not forgive your transgressions.
> Matthew 6:14-15

       3. Are you in envy or strife?

"For wherever there is jealousy (envy) and contention (rivalry and selfish ambition) there will also be confusion (unrest, disharmony, rebellion) and all sorts of evil and vile practices" (James 3:16, TAB). In that atmosphere, faith cannot grow and be productive. Envy and strife stifle faith. Root them out!

4. Are you acting in fear?

As we have already learned, fear is the opposing force to faith. When our actions are of fear, they are not of faith, and that is why answers are not coming. Rebuke the fears--they do not come from God.

> For God has not given us a spirit of timidity, but of power and
> love and discipline.
> II Timothy 1:7

5. Did you plant the right seed?

If you are waiting for abundance in harvesting people for the Lord, have you planted the Word in their hearts? Is there something growing?

Do you need finances? Have you given to others so that you might receive? Are you lonely and need friendship? Have you asked the Lord for friends? Have you planted the seeds of friendship in others? Sometimes there is a crop failure because nothing was planted! God's faith is a working faith that plants as well as reaps.

6. Are you asking according to faith or flesh?

Sometimes our motives for requests are not of faith, but only a desire of the flesh. We want something because it appeals to us, so we ask the Lord. He may give it to us, but He may also discern a fleshy motive there.

> So He gave them their request, But sent a wasting disease
> among them.
> Psalm 106:15

If He does, God, in His love, may not fulfill our requests. As He says in James 4:3, "You ask and do not receive, because you ask with wrong motives, so that you may spend it on your pleasures." You ask of God and yet fail to receive because you ask with wrong purpose and evil, selfish motives.

Your intention is (when you get what you desire) to spend it in sensual pleasures.

Or, your flesh may have an idea of the moment, and you pray for it. God doesn't answer. Why? Usually you soon know why--it was a whim of the moment. Elijah was a great man of faith, but at one point he prayed to die. That was the flesh, not faith. God didn't answer.

> But he himself went a day's journey into the wilderness, and came and sat down under a juniper tree; and he requested for himself that he might die, and said, "It is enough; now, O Lord, take my life, for I am not better than my fathers."
> I Kings 19:4

When we know that we are asking according to God's will, we can ask with confidence and faith. Check your motive!

7. Are you doubting?

Mark 11:23: "Truly, I tell you, whoever says to this mountain, 'Be lifted up and thrown into the sea!' and does not doubt at all in his heart, but believes that what he says will take place, it will be done for him" (TAB).

James 1:6-8: "Only it must be in faith that he asks, with no wavering--no hesitating, no doubting. For the one who wavers (hesitates, doubts) is like the billowing surge out at sea, that is blown hither and thither and tossed by the wind. For truly, let not such a person imagine that he will receive anything he asks for from the Lord, for being as he is a man of two minds--hesitating, dubious, irresolute--he is unstable and unreliable and uncertain about everything (he thinks, feels, decides)" (TAB).

When you are making your request, believe that God will answer you--believe while you are praying! "For this reason I am telling you, whatever you ask for in prayer, believe--trust and be confident--that it is granted to you, and you will get it" (Mark 11:24, TAB).

8. Are you substituting emotion for faith?

When we hear the testimony of others, we can get a spiritual high that blesses us. We soar to the mountain tops with someone else's experience. We are challenged to do the same thing they did so we excitedly make a similar request. Nothing happens! We are disappointed. What went wrong? Testimonies are meant to encourage us, but they can never take the place of going back to God's Word and getting His promise firsthand. Those testimonies should drive us right back to the Word to get His promise firsthand. Those testimonies should drive us right back to the Word--that is where faith comes from! Make sure you are asking with faith, not mere emotion. Be joyful with others for what God has done for them, praise God for His wonderful works; then get into the Word for your own food, blessing, and faith building!

9. Are you waiting for God?

Do you want to give up? Did the answer take longer than you had hoped? If you have passed the above checklist, keep your fighting clothes on, and trust God. Satan might be delaying the answer, but it is on its way!

"Wait for the Lord; Be strong, and let your heart take courage; Yes, wait for the Lord" (Ps. 27:14).

B. IF YOU NEED TO, REPENT.

If you did not pass the checklist, if the Lord revealed several wrong attitudes, then there is no substitute for repentance. Do not make positive confessions of the answer being on its way when your sin is blocking it. Get rid of the roadblock first; then confess the Word!

False prophets in Jeremiah's time were prophesying peace and prosperity, but it didn't work. God wanted them to repent of their disobedient ways. They refused. God had only one recourse--the curses of the law came upon them. They wanted the blessing, and God wanted to give them the blessing, but they would not repent. They chose the course their life was to follow.

That which came as the word of the Lord to Jeremiah in regard to the drought: "Judah mourns, And her gates languish. They sit on the ground in mourning, And the cry of Jerusalem has ascended. And their nobles have sent their servants for water; They have come to the cisterns and found no water. They have returned with their vessels empty; They have been put to shame and humiliated, And they cover their heads. Because the ground is cracked, For there has been no rain on the land; The farmers have been put to shame, They have covered their heads. For even the doe in the field has given birth only to abandon her young, Because there is no grass. And the wild donkeys stand on the bare heights; They pant for air like jackals, Their eyes fail For there is no vegetation. Although our iniquities testify against us, O Lord, act for Thy name's sake! Truly our apostasies have been many, We have sinned against Thee. Thou Hope of Israel, Its Savior in time of distress, Why art Thou like a stranger in the land Or like a traveler who has pitched his tent for the night? Why art Thou like a man dismayed, Like a mighty man who cannot save? Yet Thou art in our midst, O Lord, And we are called by Thy name; Do not forsake us!" Thus says the Lord to this people, "Even so they have loved to wander; they have not kept their feet in check. Therefore the Lord does

not accept them; now He will remember their iniquity and call their sins to account." So the Lord said to me, "Do not pray for the welfare of this people. When they fast, I am not going to listen to their cry; and when they offer burnt offering and grain offering, I am not going to accept them. Rather I am going to make an end of them by the sword, famine and pestilence." But, "Ah Lord God!" I said, "Look, the prophets are telling them, 'You will not see the sword nor will you have famine, But I will give you lasting peace in this place.'" Then the Lord said to me, "The prophets are prophesying falsehood in My name. I have neither sent them nor commanded them nor spoken to them; they are prophesying to you a false vision, divination, futility and the deception of their own minds. Therefore thus says the Lord concerning the prophets who are prophesying in My name, although it was not I who sent them-- yet they keep saying, 'There shall be no sword or famine in this land'--by sword and famine those prophets shall meet their end! The people also to whom they are prophesying will be thrown out into the streets of Jerusalem because of the famine and the sword; and there will be no one to bury them--neither them, nor their wives, nor their sons, nor their daughters--for I shall pour out their own wickedness on them."
Jeremiah 14:1-16

On the other hand, God gave Jonah the message of repentance to Nineveh. Though Jonah tried to avoid giving it, he finally preached to Nineveh. They repented fully and immediately, and God spared the city.

Be careful to repent when God points out sin in your life. Unconfessed sin is a faith-killer--you cannot afford to have it around!

C. FIND OUT IF GOD HAS A BETTER WAY.

James and John had ambitions of greatness. They wanted to sit on either side of Jesus in His Glory.

And James and John, the two sons of Zebedee, came up to Him, saying to Him, "Teacher, we want You to do for us whatever we ask of you." And He said to them, "What do you want Me to do for you?" And they said to Him, "Grant that we may sit in Your glory, one on Your right, and one on Your left." But Jesus said to them, "You do not know what you are asking for. Are you able to drink the cup that I drink, or to be bapized with the baptism with which I am baptized?" And they said to Him, "We are able." And Jesus

said to them, "The cup that I drink you shall drink; and you shall be baptized with the baptism with which I am baptized. But to sit on My right or on My left, this is not Mine to give, but it is for those for whom it has been prepared." And hearing this, the ten began to feel indignant with James and John. And calling them to Himself, Jesus said to them, "You know that those who are recognized as rulers of the Gentiles lord it over them; and their great men exercise authority over them. But is it not so among you, but whoever wishes to becomes great among you shall be your servant; and whoever wishes to be first among you shall be slave of all. For even the Son of Man did not come to be served, but to serve, and to give His life a ransom for many."
Mark 10:35-45

They asked Jesus to grant them this request. Jesus said He could not--it wasn't something He could give; however, He did not belittle their ambition. He showed them the right way to be great. He said, "Whoever wishes to be great among you shall be your servant."

Your stand in faith might be the highest you know, but God is the Creator God--He has a hundred ways to meet your need. He might be pointing you to a higher way-- one which might go unnoticed if your answer comes exactly as you request. Ask God if He has a better plan, a higher level of faith to which He is leading you. Ask Him if He is about to do "exceeding abundantly beyond all" that you have asked.

Now to Him who is able to do exceeding abundantly beyond all that we ask or think, according to the power that works within us, to Him be the glory in the church and in Christ Jesus to all generations forever and ever. Amen
Ephesians 3:20

D. COMPARE YOUR REQUEST WITH GOD'S PLAN FOR YOUR LIFE.

Do you know what God's specific call on your life is? Obey that call, and put your faith in line with that call. If God has called you to work with youth on Saturday nights, then don't pray for a job that will conflict with that. God is able to give you one that leaves you free to do the work He called you to do. God wants your life to harmonize. He will not answer prayers that are inconsistent with His revealed will for your life.

III.   FAITH IS COMMITTED.

In some ways we have dealt with this in every lesson, but let us take some time to really spell out commitment. What are you committed to? Will you walk in faith as long as the path is smooth--or will you follow Christ all the way? Are you committed to a faith-teaching or to a faith-God? God will not let you down. A teaching or a formula might, but God and His Word are true. They will never fail. The world is upheld by His Word.

> And He is the radiance of His glory and the exact representation of His
> nature, and upholds all things by the word of His power. When He had
> made purification of sins, He sat down at the right hand of the Majesty
> on high;
> Hebrews 1:3

If His Word failed, the earth would be on a chaotic course; however, it is not. It is still in the exact course that the Lord put it in. Someday soon, He will alter that and, by His Word, create a new heaven and a new earth. Until then, it will continue.

> But according to His promise we are looking for new heavens and a new
> earth, in which righteousness dwells.
> II Peter 3:13

All of us must pray the prayer of commitment. "Lord, Thy will be done on earth, as it is in heaven." That means that you are praying for God's will to be done in your life. God's will is done on earth through people! Will you do God's will and follow His revelation through the Word to your spirit no matter what? Will you work at the job and in the situation God has placed you, no matter what? You have authority and power to be a channel of God's love and transforming power wherever you are. It may not always be easy. Will you do His will when it is difficult, when others don't understand, when there is opposition from those you thought to be friends? Are you so committed to your faith in God that nothing can stop you from following Him fully?

Commitment is exemplified well by the three Hebrews who were thrown into the fiery furnace. As the king was pronouncing his judgment over them, they said, "If it be so, our God whom we serve is able to deliver us from the furnace of the blazing fire; and He will deliver us out of your hand, O king. But even if He does not, let it be known to you, O king, that we are not going to serve your gods or worship the golden image that you have set up" (Dan. 3:17-18). Their faith was so committed to God that they were willing to die for Him! They would worship no other God!

Commitment is a decision to dedicate and consecrate yourself to God and His ways. Commitment is not a feeling. It is a decision from which there is no retreat--a decision to swim "upstream" all the way rather than conform to the world's flow, with the crowd's "downstream" mentality. "Swimming upstream" requires faith. Floating downstream requires no action at all. Be a committed person of faith--that pleases God!

> And without faith it is impossible to please Him, for he who comes to God must believe that He is, and that He is a rewarder of those who seek Him.
> Hebrews 11:6

IV. SUMMATION

A. There are numerous examples in the Bible of people who were persistent in their prayers. They would not give up until they had heard from God. At times your faith will get instant answers. At other times you will need to be persistent. Ask, seek, knock until you have God's answer to your situation.

B. You may be puzzled as you see others get answers to their faith, but yours does not seem to be fruitful. Check your motives, your walk with others, your fear and strife level. Make sure there are no roadblocks that you have put up that prevent God from answering your prayers. When God shows you areas in your life that need to be changed, do so. Be repentant and obedient. Your faith will get answers.

C. No matter what happens--which person, teacher, or system has failed you--God never has and never will fail you! You can completely trust and put your faith in Him. Commit yourself to Him totally and unconditionally. Committed faith pleases God and gets answers.

V. ASSIGNMENTS

A. Listen to the tape carefully.

B. Complete the study guide questions.

C. Recommended reading: Can Your Faith Fail? by Charles Capps. Praying Beyond God's Ability, by Dr. Roy Hicks.

STUDY GUIDE QUESTIONS

1. Besides the illustrations given in the lesson, find three more that indicate to you that the God-kind of faith is persistent.

2. Why does not walking in love with others hinder your faith? Give at least three Scriptures.

3. Read the following verses, then summarize the Bible's teaching on forgiveness: Matthew 18:21-35; Matthew 6:14; Mark 11:25,26; Luke 17:3-4; Ephesians 4:32.

4. How does envy and strife stifle faith?

5. Read Romans 14:23 in several translations. Write out its meaning in your own words.

6. How is planting the right seeds related to getting answers to our faith? Give Scripture.

7. Explain the difference between asking in faith and asking according to the flesh.

8. What should Christians do with their doubts? How can we ask without wavering and doubting?

9. Find Scriptures that will help you ask according to the Word and not your emotions.

10. Give three Scriptures that will help you, or someone else, to wait for God and not be impatient when faith answers are not instantaneous.

11. Find five verses that you could pray as a total commitment of your faith in God and in His Word. Pray these with a decision to never retreat from this commitment.

9 Faith in Action

INTRODUCTION

Hebrews 11 is truly a parade of the heroes of faith. We read of them and are encouraged, not only by their faith, but also because we have read their lives and know they are people like you and me. God used ordinary people. Some failed the Lord at times, others had blatant weaknesses in some area of their lives, yet God looked at their faith in Him and accomplished tremendous things through them. The letter to the Hebrews was written especially to the Jews--people who had difficulty believing what they could not, or had not seen. This review of the faith of their great men is to demonstrate that the faith God requires is nothing new to the Jewish people. It is the same faith that has motivated the Jewish race from its beginning.

I. ABEL--ATONING FAITH

> By faith Abel offered to God a better sacrifice than Cain, through which he obtained the testimony that he was righteous, God testifying about his gifts, and through faith, though he is dead, he still speaks.
> Hebrews 11:4

Abel recognized that he was sinful and believed God to have told him the true way of atonement--to offer a blood sacrifice. He did not come his own way, as Cain did. He came God's way, demonstrating that he, in himself, had no righteousness of his own. Even then, he knew from God that "without the shedding of blood there is no remission of sin." He threw himself at the mercy of God. Cain came with the fruit of his own hands, gave a thank offering, but there was no recognition of his own sin, of his need of atonement. Abel showed us that faith does it God's way! Both Abel and Cain had the hearing of faith: "Without the shedding of blood there is no remission of sins." Abel brought a blood sacrifice. Cain's sacrifice was from the earth which was cursed. His sacrifice was also his own self efforts. He was religious. He wanted to offer a sacrifice, but it was a bloodless one. Faith obeys God's Word.

II. ENOCH--PLEASING FAITH

> By faith Enoch was taken up so that he should not see death; And he was not found because God took him up; for he obtained the witness that before his being taken up he was pleasing to God. And without faith it is impossible to please Him, for he who comes to God must believe that He is, and that He is a rewarder of those who seek Him.
> Hebrews 11:5-6

In Genesis 5 we read eight times "and he died." In verses 21-24 we have a notable exception: "And Enoch lived sixty-five years, and became the father of Methuselah. Then Enoch walked with God three hundred years after he became the father of Methuselah, and he had other sons and daughters. So all the days of Enoch were three hundred and sixty-five years. And Enoch walked with God; and he was not, for God took him." Enoch, the seventh from Adam, died not. He was translated without seeing death. Less than 100 words are recorded about him, yet they are powerful words.

Enoch was one of the two men who "walked with God." There is no fault recorded about him. He is the only one, outside of Jesus, of whom it is written, "He pleased God," and he is one of the two who missed death!

The days of Enoch were flagrantly wicked.

> And about these also Enoch, in the seventh generation from Adam, prophesied, saying, "Behold, the Lord came with many thousands of His holy ones, to execute judgment upon all, and to convict all the ungodly of all their ungodly deeds which they have done in an ungodly way, and of all the harsh things which ungodly sinners have spoken against Him."
> Jude 14-15

He was a preacher of righteousness and prophesied Christ's second coming. In spite of the sin of his time, Enoch walked with God. His walk shows reconciliation because "How can two walk together except they be agreed?" (Amos 3:3). Enoch agreed with God. He pleased God. How did he do that? It was his faith, for "without faith it is impossible to please him."

Enoch walked with God for 300 years. He didn't start until he was sixty-five. Enoch began after the birth of his first son. He called him Methuselah which means, "When this child dies the deluge shall come." I'm certain that Enoch and his wife took meticulous care of their young son. Methuselah lived the longest of all men, because God in His great mercy did not want to send the deluge (flood). The year Methuselah died the flood came. Growing faith takes you into growing steps of blessing. Enoch went from faith to faith. After 300 years of daily walking in faith with God, he reached the apex of this faith--translation. He never tasted death!

Enoch enjoyed a continuous fellowship with God. Nothing, not even death, interrupted that friendship. This pleasing walk of faith is available to you too!

III.   NOAH--DELIVERING FAITH

> By faith Noah, being warned by God about things not yet seen, in reverence prepared an ark for the salvation of his household, by which

he condemned the world, and became an heir of the righteousness
which is according to faith.
Hebrews 11:7

A. NOAH FOUND GRACE.

Noah also lived in a wicked generation; however, he found grace in the eyes of the
Lord.

> Then the Lord saw that the wickedness of man was great on the
> earth, and that every intent of the thoughts of his heart was only
> evil continually. And the Lord was sorry that He had made man on
> the earth, and He was grieved in His heart. And the Lord said, "I
> will blot out man whom I have created from the face of the land,
> from man to animals to creeping things and to birds of the sky; for
> I am sorry that I have made them."
> Genesis 6:5-7

> But Noah found favor in the eyes of the Lord.
> Genesis 6:8

He was a man of different character. "Noah was a righteous man, blameless in his
time; Noah walked with God" (Genesis 6:9). This man was just and walked with God,
just as his great grandfather, Enoch, had done!

B. NOAH ACTED ON FAITH.

"By faith Noah, being warned by God about things not yet seen, in reverence
prepared an ark for the salvation of his household, by which he condemned the world
and became an heir of the righteousness which is according to faith" (Hebrews 11:7).

1. The ground of his faith was in God's Word--"being warned by God."

2. The sphere of his faith--"things not yet seen." They had never seen rain, it
    was unknown.

3. Character of his faith--"moved with fear"

4. Evidence of his faith--"prepared the ark"

5. Witness of his faith--"by which he condemned the world"

6. Issue of his faith--"for the saving of his household"

7. Reward of his faith--"he became an heir of righteousness which is according to faith."

Noah acted on the Word of an invisible God, doing what seemed foolish to the casual bystander. He built a boat five hundred miles from the nearest body of water. He built it in enormous dimensions and then filled it with animals. He did what God said. He believed that God was telling them the truth when He warned of a great flood of judgment coming upon the earth. Noah had no visible signs of the flood until after he was shut inside the ark. For at least one hundred years Noah built the ark to the exact specifications of his Lord. His faith delivered him from destruction with the rest of mankind. Acting on the Word of God delivers us from His judgment!

C. THE ARK WAS GOD'S PROVISION.

God gave Noah the design for the ark, with instructions as to materials, size and construction. Noah was to cover it inside and out with pitch. (The word for pitch is "kapher" which means "to make an atonement.") This ark was to be totally waterproof--a refuge from divine judgment. Into this ark, man was invited to come. It was an invitation from God Himself and included Noah's whole household.

> Then the Lord said to Noah, "Enter the ark, you and all your household; for you alone I have seen to be righteous before Me in this time."
> Genesis 7:1

It was an invitation to absolute safety! Noah "entered as God had commanded him; and the Lord closed it behind him" (Genesis 7:16). For one whole year that ark was God's provision of safety for Noah and his family. Noah's faith brought him through the greatest upheaval that his world has ever known. God provided the way to go through. No matter what is happening to the world around you, nor what will happen, your God is able to provide a way of escape, a place of safety! Have faith in your God!

D. THE RAINBOW WAS GOD'S AGREEMENT.

> "Now behold, I Myself do establish My covenant with you, and with your descendants after you; and with every living creature that is with you, the birds, the cattle, and every beast of the earth with you; of all that comes out of the ark, even every beast of the earth. And I establish My covenant with you; and all flesh shall

163

never again be cut off by the water of the flood, neither shall there again be a flood to destroy the earth." And God said, "This is the sign of the covenant which I am making between Me and you and every living creature that is with you, for all successive generations; I set My bow in the cloud, and it shall be a sign of a covenant between Me and the earth. And it shall come about, when I bring a cloud over the earth, that the bow shall be seen in the cloud, and I will remember My covenant, which is between Me and you and every living creature of all flesh; and never again shall the water become a flood to destroy all flesh. When the bow is in the cloud, then I will look upon it, to remember the everlasting covenant between God and every living creature of all flesh that is on the earth." And God said to Noah, "This is the sign of the covenant which I have established between Me and all flesh that is on the earth."
Genesis 9:9-17

Whenever Noah looked up into the clouds and saw a rainbow, he remembered God's covenant with him, His covenant to never again destroy the earth with water. Sometimes he saw the bow, other times he didn't, but the agreement was still intact. God made a covenant with you and me. It was made with Christ's blood. Whether we see visible signs of this agreement or not, it is always binding. God will never break His part of the covenant made with mankind through the blood of Jesus Christ.

1. God took the initiative for the covenant. "I set my bow in the cloud." He took the initiative with the New Covenant. "For God so loved the world that He gave His Son."

2. The bow was set in the clouds upon God's smelling a sweet savor from a sacrifice. His covenant with us was established when He saw the sacrifice of His Son. His death made the way clear for us.

> And the Lord smelled the soothing aroma; and the Lord said to Himself, "I will never again curse the ground on account of man, for the intent of man's heart is evil from his youth; and I will never again destroy every living thing, as I have done. While the earth remains, seedtime and harvest, and cold and heat, and summer and winter, and day and night shall not cease."
> Genesis 8:21-22

...how much more will the blood of Christ, who through the eternal Spirit offered Himself without blemish to God, cleanse your conscience from dead works to serve the living God? And for this reason He is the mediator of a new covenant, in order that since a death has taken place for the redemption of the transgressions that were committed under the first covenant, those who have been called may receive the promise of the eternal inheritance. For where a covenant is, there must of necessity be the death of the one who made it.
Hebrews 9:14-16

3. The bow is security against the deluge of God's wrath. Acceptance of Christ is also security against God's wrath.

> For this is like the days of Noah to Me; when I swore that the waters of Noah should not flood the earth again, so I have sworn that I will not be angry with you, nor will I rebuke you."
> Isaiah 54:9

> He who believes in the Son has eternal life; but he who does not obey the Son shall not see life, but the wrath of God abides on him."
> John 3:36

4. The sun gives being to the rainbow. Christ, the sun of righteousness, **gives** being to the covenant of grace (Heb. 9:15).

5. The arch of the rainbow is high, reaching to the heavens. The ends stoop **and** reach the earth. The great covenant Head is in heaven, yet through the gos**pel** he reaches down to men.

> But the righteousness based on faith speaks thus, "DO NOT SAY IN YOUR HEART, 'WHO WILL ASCEND INTO HEAVEN?' (that is, to bring Christ down), or 'WHO WILL DESCEND INTO THE ABYSS' (that is, to bring Christ up from the dead)." But what does it say? "THE WORD IS NEAR YOU, IN YOUR MOUTH AND IN YOUR HEART"--that is, the word of faith which we are preaching.
> Romans 10:6-8

6. God's bow is extensive, reaching from one end of heaven to the other. His covenant of grace is wide in its reach, stretching back to eternity past **and** reaching forward to eternity future.

7. The bow promises refreshing rain. The bow that encircles the throne gives us the assurance of the rain of the Spirit.

> As the appearance of the rainbow in the clouds on a rainy day, so was the appearance of the surrounding radiance. Such was the appearance of the likeness of the glory of the Lord. And when I saw it, I fell on my face and heard a voice speaking.
> Ezekiel 1:28

> And He who was sitting was like a jasper stone and a sardius in appearance; and there was a rainbow around the throne, like an emerald in appearance.
> Revelation 4:3

> So rejoice, O sons of Zion, And be glad in the Lord your God; For He has given you the early rain for your vindication. And he has poured down for you the rain, The early and latter rain as before.
> Joel 2:23

> "And it will come about after this That I will pour out My Spirit on all mankind; And your sons and daughters will prophesy, Your old men will dream dreams, Your young men will see visions."
> Joel 2:28

8. The rainbow is not always in sight. Noah walked by faith, and so must we. "The just shall live by faith."

> ...for we walk by faith, not by sight--...
> II Corinthians 5:7

IV. ABRAHAM--OBEDIENT FAITH

By faith Abraham, when he was called, obeyed by going out to a place which he was to receive for an inheritance; and he went out, not knowing where he was going. By faith he lived as an alien in the land of promise, as in a foreign land, dwelling in tents with Isaac and Jacob, fellow heirs of the same promise; for he was looking for the city which has foundations, whose architect and builder is God. By faith even Sarah herself received ability to conceive, even beyond the proper time of life, since she considered Him faithful who had promised; therefore, also, there was born of one man, and him as good

as dead at that, as many descendants AS THE STARS OF HEAVEN IN NUMBER, AND INNUMBERABLE AS THE SAND WHICH IS BY THE SEASHORE. All these died in faith, without receiving the promises, but having seen them and having welcomed them from a distance, and having confessed that they were strangers and exiles on the earth. For those who say such things make it clear that they are seeking a country of their own. And indeed if they had been thinking of that country from which they went out, they would have had opportunity to return. But as it is, they desire a better country, that is a heavenly one. Therefore God is not ashamed to be called their God; for He has prepared a city for them.
Hebrews 11:8-16

"Abram" means "father of altitude." "Abraham" means "father of a multitude." We have already studied much about Abrahm's faith from Romans 4. He was a man who followed God obediently without knowing where he was going. He left all his spiritual inheritance. Abraham trusted God from the very beginning. He answered God's call on his life, followed His directions to a new land, and Canaan as a sojourner, ready to move on if God should call. His eyes were not on his earthly inheritance, though that was extensive, but on the heavenly. He was looking towards his permanent dwelling place. Abraham reveals that living in the altitude of God's Word brings a multitude of results.

V. SARAH--REJUVENATING FAITH (Hebrews 11:11-12)

Sarah received faith to conceive a child in her old age. It was physically impossible for her to bear children, yet, on God's Word, she did. Sarah believed the Word, though she faltered in her faith at one point and gave her maid to Abraham. She must have repented; all that is mentioned here is her faith. She had faith to bear a son from whose family line came the Messiah! Sarah received strength. Strength here, is the Greek word "dunamus" which means "miracle working power." Faith in God's Word brings miracle working power in your body.

VI. ABRAHAM--PROVEN FAITH

By faith Abraham, when he was tested, offered up Isaac; and he who had received the promises was offering up his only begotten son; it was he to whom it was said, "In Isaac your descendants shall be called." He considered that God is able to raise men even from the dead; from which he also received him back as a type.
Hebrews 11:17-19

Since Abraham is often referred to as the father of faith, he bears mentioning again. When he came up against a test, he passed with a high grade. God asked him to sacrifice his only son, Isaac. Abraham had such faith in God's Word that he quietly did what God required, not understanding this strange command, but knowing that somehow God would again raise Isaac from the dead. He knew that God would come through so he followed instructions. By his actions, he proved his faith and trust in God.

Even when you receive difficult commands from the Lord, it is a blessing to obey. You may not understand the "why" of the instruction, but many of God's choicest blessings go by when we say "no" to the Lord because we are unwilling to take the risk involved in being obedient. It may seem like a risk, but it really isn't. Your obedience to God brings a sure return every time! Abraham was willing to give up one son, and his descendents became as the sands of the sea. He was given back his own son with a numberless return! In his experience, Abraham met Jehovah-Jireh, the God who sees ahead and makes provision for every trial.

VII.   ISAAC, JACOB, AND JOSEPH--FORWARD LOOKING FAITH

> By faith Isaac blessed Jacob and Esau, even regarding things to come. By faith Jacob, as he was dying, blessed each of the sons of Joseph, and worshipped, leaning on the top of his staff. By faith Joseph, when he was dying, made mention of the exodus of the sons of Israel, and gave orders concerning his bones.
> Hebrews 11:20-22

These men had just a glimpse of what God had planned for Israel. Isaac knew of the covenant that God had made with his father Abraham, and believed that God would keep His Word. He blessed Jacob concerning things to come. He blessed him with material blessings. To Esau, Isaac gave a prophetic message of servanthood as well as material blessings.

> Then he came to his father and said, "My father." And he said, "Here I am. Who are you, my son?" And Jacob said to his father, "I am Esau your first-born; I have done as you told me. Get up, please, sit and eat of my game, that you may bless me."
> Genesis 27:18-19

Jacob had faith that one day Joseph and his descendents would go back to the land of Canaan. He blessed Joseph's children with the double portion and said, "By you Israel shall pronounce blessing saying, 'May God make you like Ephraim and Manasseh.'"

> And he blessed them that day, saying, "By you Israel shall pronounce blessing, saying, 'May God make you like Ephraim and Manasseh!'" Thus he put Ephraim before Manasseh. Then Israel said to Joseph, "Behold, I am about to die, but God will be with you, and bring you

back to the land of your fathers. And I give you one portion more than your brothers, which I took from the hand of the Amorite with my sword and my bow."
Genesis 48:20-22

Joseph also saw the day when the sons of Israel would go back to Canaan. He gave instructions concerning his bones--he wanted them buried in the Promised Land! In Exodus we read that they carried Joseph's bones when they left Egypt. When they arrived in the Promised Land, Joshua tells us that they buried Joseph's bones in Shechem. Can you imagine--they had carried his bones for forty years! In Matthew 27;52-53, I believe that after the resurrection, among the saints who appeared upon the streets of Jerusalem was Joseph. His bones had now been resurrected. What a faith!

...and the tombs were opened; and many bodies of the saints who had fallen asleep were raised; and coming out of the tombs after His resurrection they entered the holy city and appeared to many.
Matthew 27:52-53

VIII.   AMRAM AND JOCHEBED--COURAGEOUS PARENTAL FAITH

By faith Moses, when he was born, was hidden for three months by his parents, because they saw he was a beautiful child; and they were not afraid of the king's edict.
Hebrews 11:23

Moses' parents had tremendous faith. They fearlessly disobeyed the Pharoah, knowing it was not God's will to kill their male children. They dared to obey God and save their son. The midwives of the day also feared God, disobeying the king of Egypt, but saving the men alive. God blessed and rewarded them for their faith in Him and He gave them houses.

But the midwives feared God, and did not do as the king of Egypt had commanded them, but let the boys live. So the king of Egypt called for the midwives and said to them, "Why have you done this thing, and let the boys live?" And the midwives said to Pharaoh, "Because the Hebrew women are not as the Egyptian women; for they are vigorous, and they give birth before the midwife can get to them." So God was good to the midwives, and the people multiplied, and became very mighty. And it came about because the midwives feared God, that He established households for them.
Exodus 1:17-21

To have this kind of faith, Amram and Jochebed must have heard from God, for faith comes from hearing the word of God. Amram means "the people is exalted." He was not seeing that in actuality, but his son was to be part of a divine plan that would exalt his people. Jochebed means, "Jehovah is glorious." These parents saw only slavery and evil coming from the earthly ruler, but they looked beyond that to Jehovah and knew He was glorious. That is the truth they wanted embossed on their children.

IX. MOSES--LEADERSHIP FAITH

> By faith Moses, when he had grown up, refused to be called the son of Pharoah's daughter; choosing rather to endure ill-treatment with the people of God, than to enjoy the passing pleasures of sin; considering the reproach of Christ greater riches than the treasures of Egypt; for he was looking to the reward. By faith he left Egypt, not fearing the wrath of the king; for he endured, as seeing Him who is unseen. By faith he kept the Passover and the sprinkling of the blood, so that he who destroyed the first-born might not touch them. By faith they passed through the Red Sea as though they were passing through dry land; and the Egyptians, when they attempted it, were drowned.
> Hebrews 11:24-29

There is more about Moses than any other individual in the eleventh chapter of Hebrews. His name means, "drawn out" in God's mighty plan to be a prophet, priest and king. His life shows tremendous contrast. He was the baby of slaves in Egypt, placed in an ark and sent down the Nile River in order to rescue him from the plan of a wicked Pharoah to kill all male babies. The daughter of Pharoah rescued him, "drew him out" of the waters and raised him as her own son. He became the leader--even of Pharoah's army. How interesting that the Pharoah who was trying to wipe out the Israelites would give food, lodging, and education to the very man who would bring about what he was trying to prevent!

> "And Moses was educated in all the learning of the Egyptians, and he was a man of power in words and deeds."
> Acts 7:22

Moses made decisions of faith which totally changed history:

A. BY FAITH HE TURNED DOWN THE THRONE.

1. He refused to be called the son of Pharaoh's daughter. When Moses grew up he knew that he was to be the one who would deliver Israel from Egypt. This word must have come from God, for he had the faith to refuse the throne, an unlikely

decision for one who had been raised a prince of Egypt! His brethren, however, did not see him as the deliverer. As yet, he was going in his own strength. But his faith was working in one area: he knew which choice he didn't want. He refused to be called the son of an Egyptian princess because he knew the true honor of being a son of Abraham, the father of the faithful!

> "But when he was approaching the age of forty, it entered his mind to visit his brethren, the sons of Israel. And when he saw one of them being treated unjustly, he defended him and took vengeance for the oppressed by striking down the Egyptian. And he supposed that his brethren understood that God was granting them deliverance through him; but they did not understand. And on the following day he appeared to them as they were fighting together, and he tried to reconcile them in peace, saying, 'Men, you are brethren, why do you injure one another?' But the one who was injuring his neighbor pushed him away, saying, 'WHO MADE YOU A RULER AND JUDGE OVER US? YOU DO NOT MEAN TO KILL ME AS YOU KILLED THE EGYPTIAN YESTERDAY DO YOU?'"
> Acts 7:23-28

2. He chose to suffer slavery with his own people. Because of his own fleshly enemy, he tried to be a leader and avenge his brother in his own strength. He had to flee Egypt.

> So he looked this way and that, and when he saw there was no one around, he struck down the Egyptian and hid him in the sand. And he went out the next day, and behold, two Hebrews were fighting with each other; and he said to the offender, "Why are you striking your companion?" But he said, "Who made you a prince or a judge over us? Are you intending to kill me, as you killed the Egyptian?" Then Moses was afraid, and said, "Surely the matter has become known." When Pharaoh heard of his matter, he tried to kill Moses. But Moses fled from the presence of Pharaoh and settled in the land of Midian; and he sat down by a well.
> Exodus 2:12-15

He saw the affliction of his brethren, and after "looking this way and that" he slew the Egyptian. He was looking to the energy of the flesh; walking by what he saw, rather than by what he knew to be right. His identification with the people, however, made his choice clear: he would rather be a godly slave than a heathen king. He would rather suffer with the people of God than enjoy the pleasures of sin. He knew all about the pleasures that were available to him at the palace--perhaps even future pharaoh of Egypt-- but he resolutely refused them!

3. He considered the reproaches of Christ greater riches. Moses had a revelation of the coming Messiah. He knew that suffering with Him, whatever that would cost, was greater riches than all the treasure of Egypt. In Christ there are true treasures that cannot in any way be compared with the glitter that the world might offer.

4. He was looking for a reward. Moses knew as he obeyed the voice of God to his heart, there was a reward. This reward was totally unseen. He followed in faith with great respect for what God would give him, rather than looking to the temporal riches that the Pharaoh could offer him. It will help you to live the faith life diligently if you have respect for God's reward. Look to Him, not men. That will keep your faith alive and not disappointed! Keep your eyes on God's goals.

B. BY FAITH HE FORSOOK EGYPT.

1. He left Egypt a wanted man. The first time Moses left Egypt he was the most wanted man alive. He had just killed a man. He did not leave in faith; he left in fear. His picture was in every post office. He fled to the desert of Midian. The leader of armies became the keeper of a flock. He who was educated in court was now dwelling in a desert.

    Where was God in all this? Was his plan to lead His people out foiled? Would He "draw out" another man? Would He scrap plan one and begin plan two? Would He give Moses a second chance?

2. He meets his God. God's love is unconditional. He allows His "drawn out," "drawn through" Moses to sweat it out in a desert. Moses finds a wife there (Zipporah), and a marvelous father-in-law. Moses keeps sheep for his father-in-law for forty years. At the end of this time, he approaches Mt. Horeb with his sheep. Mt Horeb means, "fresh inspiration," and here it is that he meets the God of second chances. He is attracted to a bush that is burning, but not consumed. He comes aside, and an angel appears out of the midst of the fire. Our God is a consuming fire. In Exodus 3:5 He expresses His holiness to Moses: "Do not come near here. Remove your sandals from your feet, for the place on which you are standing is holy ground." In verse 6 He shows His covenant relationship: "I am the God of your father, the God of Abraham, the God of Isaac, and the God of Jacob." In verse 7 He expresses His compassion: "I have surely seen the affliction of My people who are in Egypt, and have given heed to

their cry because of their taskmasters, for I am aware of their sufferings."
Then in verse 8 He declares His purpose: "So I have come down to deliver them
from the power of the Egyptians, and to bring them up from that land to a good
and spacious land...."

3. God calls Moses. Exodus 3:10 says, "Therefore, come now, and I will send you
to Pharaoh, so that you may bring My people, the sons of Israel, out of Egypt."
After all these years, God still wanted Moses to do the job!

4. Moses' reaction

   a) The reaction of Moses at 80 is totally different that at 40. Moses said,
   "Who am I," instead of, "Don't you know who I am?" . But God assured him
   that He would go with him, that he was being sent by God and would return
   to that very mountain and worship God.

   > But Moses said to God, "Who am I, that I should go to
   > Pharaoh, and that I should bring the sons of Israel out of
   > Egypt?"
   > Exodus 3:11

   b) Moses' reaction is still a negative one. "When they ask me who sent me,
   what shall I say?" . How powerful God will be, whatever His people need.
   Don't limit Him with one name!

   > Then Moses said to God, "Behold, I am going to the sons of
   > Israel, and I shall say to them, 'The God of your fathers
   > has sent me to you.' Now they may say to me, 'What is His
   > name?' What shall I say to them?"
   > Exodus 3:13

   > And God said to Moses, "I AM WHO I AM"; and He said,
   > "Thus you shall say to the sons of Israel, 'I AM has sent me
   > to you.'"
   > Exodus 3:14

   c) God said that Moses was to go to the elders of Israel and to the king of
   Egypt, but Moses had another argument: "They will not hear me." Moses
   was timid, hestitant, fearful, unbelieving, rebellious--yet God used him!

5. God gave him signs--the first recorded signs in history.

a) He gave him a rod. A rod means support. Whatever is in your hand can be power for good or evil. When Moses threw the rod on the ground, it became a serpent. Picking it up by the tail, it became a rod again. It was a sign for the people.

> And the Lord said to him, "What is that in your hand?" And he said, "A staff." Then He said, "Throw it on the ground." So he threw it on the ground, and it became a serpent; and Moses fled from it. But the Lord said to Moses, "Stretch out your hand and grasp it by its tail"--so he stretched out his hand and caught it, and it became a staff in his hand--...
> Exodus 4:2-4

b) The leprous hand

> And the Lord furthermore said to him, "Now put your hand into your bosom." So he put his hand into his bosom, and when he took it out, behold, his hand was leprous like snow. Then He said, "Put your hand into your bosom again." So he put his hand into his bosom again and when he took it out of his bosom, behold, it was restored like the rest of his flesh. "And it shall come about that if they will not believe you or heed the witness of the first sign, they may believe the witness of the last sign."
> Exodus 4:6-8

This time Moses was to put his hand inside his cloak. It turned leprous. When he put his hand back inside once more it was restored. God said, "And it shall be that if they will not believe you or heed the witness of the first sign, they may believe the witness of the last sign."

Moses is to learn the marvelous power of God. The hand speaks of energy. Sin in your heart can make your hand leprous. Leprosy is used as a type of sin. The hand does not change the heart, but the heart changes the hand.

6. Moses had one final excuse--his lack of eloquence. God is angry at this excuse, but sends Aaron to be his mouth piece. Now Moses can go. The men who sought his life are dead. Moses took what he had: he took his rod, and he took the Word of God. What you have may be simple, but if it is accompanied by the Word, it will be powerful!

So Moses took his wife and his sons and mounted them on a
donkey, and he returned to the land of Egypt. Moses also took
the staff of God in his hand.
Exodus 4:20

7. God used Moses to bring judgment upon Egypt. Moses asked Pharaoh to let His
people go. The answer was continuously no, and each negative answer brought a
plague upon Egypt, a judgment upon one of the heathen gods of the land.
Finally, after the death of the first-born, Pharaoh let the people go, and they
went out with great wealth.

8. This time Moses left Egypt by faith, not fear. After witnessing the great series
of miracles that God did in Egypt, Moses left with over a million people. Even
though the king was fearfully angry with him, Moses left with faith. He knew his
God! Moses moved with power!

C. THROUGH FAITH HE KEPT THE PASSOVER.

By faith he kept the Passover and the sprinkling of the blood, so
that he who destroyed the first-born might not touch them.
Hebrews 11:28

1. It predicted the "Lamb of God."

a) "Behold the Lamb of God which taketh away the sin of the world." Jesus was
marked out for death before He was slain.

The next day he saw Jesus coming to him, and said,
"Behold, the Lamb of God who takes away the sin of the
world!"
John 1:29

...but with precious blood, as of a lamb unblemished and
spotless, the blood of Christ. For He was foreknown before
the foundation of the world, but has appeared in these last
times for the sake of you...
I Peter 1:19-20

b) The lamb was to be without blemish. Jesus was without blemish or spot.

c) It had to be a male of the first year. It was to die in the fullness of its
strength. Christ died in the prime of His manhood.

'And when a man offers a sacrifice of peace offerings to the Lord to fulfill a special vow, or for a freewill offering, of the herd or of the flock, it must be perfect to be accepted; there shall be no defect in it. Those that are blind or fractured or maimed or having a running sore or eczema or scabs, you shall not offer to the Lord, nor make of them an offering by fire on the altar to the Lord.'
Leviticus 22:21-22

I say, "O my God, do not take me away in the midst of my days, Thy years are throughout all generations."
Psalm 102:24

Notice Exodus 12:3-5:   In vs. 3 it is a lamb.
                               In vs. 4 it is the lamb.
                               In vs. 5 it is your lamb.

"Speak to all the congregation of Israel, saying, 'On the tenth of this month they are each one to take a lamb for themselves, according to their fathers' households, a lamb for each household. Now if the household is too small for a lamb, then he and his neighbor nearest to his house are to take one according to the number of persons in them; according to what each man should eat, you are to divide the lamb. Your lamb shall be an unblemished male a year old; you may take it from the sheep or from the goats.'
Exodus 12:3-5

Jesus loved me, and gave himself for me.

"I have been crucified with Christ; and it is no longer I who live, but Christ lives in me; and the life which I now live in the flesh I live by faith in the Son of God, who loved me, and delivered Himself up for me."
Galatians 2:20

2. It was for the whole assembly. The whole assembly was to kill the lamb. Christ died for the whole world. Christ died at the very time in Jerusalem that the pascal lambs were being slain in the temple.

> 'And you shall keep it until the fourteenth day of the same
> month, then the whole assembly of the congregation of Israel is
> to kill it at twilight.'
> Exodus 12:6

3. It was to feed them. They were to eat the lamb, all of it.

> 'And they shall eat the flesh that same night, roasted with fire,
> and they shall eat it with unleavened bread and bitter herbs.
> Do not eat any of it raw or boiled at all with water, but rather
> roasted with fire, both its head and its legs along with its
> entrails. And you shall not leave any of it over until morning,
> but whatever is left of it until morning, you shall burn with
> fire.'
> Exodus 12:8-10

The lamb is God's person and His food, "the bread of life." It takes death to
have the food of life. They ate the Passover with unleavened bread (leaven
being a type of sin) and bitter herbs (which are a type of repentance). Each
family was to eat the whole lamb, or else have another family eat with them.
Nothing must be left. We must have the whole Jesus--not have Him in parts. We
have Him completely. Nothing is lacking, neither do we leave out any part of
Him! After feeding on the lamb, they left Egypt strong and healthy. Feed on the
Lamb of God, and you will grow and be in health!

4. The lamb was roasted with fire. They had to feed on what had been subjected to
   fire (Exodus 12:9). Christ also had to experience death and the fire of God's
   judgment. Fire prepared the food for the Israelites. The fire of God's wrath on
   Jesus took care of our sins, and now He is our food, our bread of life.

5. They dressed for action.

> 'Now you shall eat it in this manner: with your loins girded,
> your sandals on your feet, and your staff in your hand; and
> you shall eat it in haste-- it is the Lord's Passover.'
> Exodus 12:11

a) Their loins were girded. Our loins are to be girded with truth. Ungirded
   garments could entangle the feet, be a hinderance to life, or be a weight.

> ...fixing our eyes on Jesus, the author and perfecter of
> faith, who for the joy set before Him endured the cross,

177

despising the shame, and has sat down at the right hand of
the throne of God.
Hebrews 12:2

b) Their shoes were on their feet. These shoes did not wear out, and their feet
did not swell. We are to have our feet shod with the preparation of peace.

"And I have led you forty years in the wilderness; your
clothes have not worn out on you, and your sandal has not
worn out on your foot."
Deuteronomy 29:5

"Your clothing did not wear out on you, nor did your foot
swell these forty years."
Deuteronomy 8:4

c) Their staff was in their hand. The staff was a sign of their pilgrimage. We
are also pigrims on this earth. Our citizenship is in heaven. The staff was
also to show them that they were to lean on something outside of themselves.
Psalm 23:4 tells us it is the rod and the staff of our shepherd that is our
comfort.

For our citizenship is in heaven, from which also we eagerly
wait for a Savior, the Lord Jesus Christ;...
Philippians 3:20

Even though I walk through the valley of the shadow of
death, I fear no evil; for Thou are with me; Thy rod and
Thy staff, they comfort me.
Psalm 23:4

d) They were to eat in haste; be ready to depart. We are to be ever ready to
depart from this place, ever looking for the return of our Savior!

6. They put the blood on the doorpost. The lamb was slain at the door. The blood
was put on the lintel and side posts. Now there was blood in four places. This
was a true type of Christ's atoning death for us. Christ had blood on his head
from the thorns, on his side, and hands and feet.

"And you shall take a bunch of hyssop and dip it in the blood
which is in the basin, and apply some of the blood this is in the

basin to the lintel and the two doorposts; and none of you shall
go outside the door of his house until morning."
Exodus 12:22

7. The blood saved them.

"For the Lord will pass through to smite the Egyptians; and
when He sees the blood on the lintel and on the two doorposts,
the Lord will pass over the door and will not allow the destroyer
to come in to your houses to smite you."
Exodus 12:23

The Lord did not just pass over them when He saw the blood, but He stood on
guard to protect them from the destroyer. The Lord still does the same. The
blood of Jesus not only saves us from His judgment, but also from the darts and
onslaughts of the enemy.

8. The Passover led to freedom and a new beginning. Notice that Moses had never
done this type of thing before. He knew that sacrificial blood atoned for their
sin, but the Passover was new to him. By faith, he obeyed God and led the
people in the Passover. It was the last meal they were to have as slaves. They
went out free and wealthy, strong and healthy. Our new life begins with the
Lamb of God. He takes away our sins, and gives us a new beginning. "...old
things are passed away, behold all things are become new" (II Cor. 5:17).

D. BY FAITH THEY PASSED THROUGH THE RED SEA.

By faith they passed through the Red Sea as though they were
passing through dry land; and the Egyptians, when they attempted
it, were drowned.
Hebrews 11:29

They were leaving the place of slavery and poverty. They were under a new Lord,
but the old one didn't give up easily. Pharaoh had fought long and hard to keep the
Israelites, and now he repents of his decision to finally let them go. He is angered
by their leaving, by the many deaths in Egypt, by the loss of free labor. He is
determined to bring them back. Satan seldom gives up his slaves of sin without a
fight. But the people move on in faith, and God comes through again. He opens the
Red Sea, and they cross over into safety from their enemies! Stepping out in faith
in a hard place (they were in a hard place: the sea was before them, the army
behind them) will be rewarded. The Lord is still your deliverer!

X. YOU--FAITH FOR EVERY OCCASION

Studying this list of men, you can see that God gives faith for every situation in every age. He is your source of faith. You need never run out. God's kind of faith will cover every circumstance which you will ever face. God will never call you to a place or a work without equipping you fully to be successful there. According to the rest of the chapter, some received the faith to do the impossible, others to go through torturous ridicule--but they were all commended for their faith! God will meet you where you are with His kind of faith. Receive His faith and be a channel for its use. Faith can only be increased as it is used. Put your faith into action!

XI. SUMMATION

A. Your faith and walk with God can please Him. He wants to have a continuous, unbroken fellowship with His children. Like Enoch, you can agree with God, and spend your lifetime walking in harmony with Him.

B. Doing things God's way, even when we don't understand it, will always bring a blessing. Faith delivered Noah and his whole household during an age when the rest of the world was in rebellion against God. Abraham proved his faith and trust in God when he dared to obey God and sacrifice his son. He had learned early in his faith walk that God is true to His Word.

C. Isaac, Jacob and Joseph blessed their children, believing that God would keep the promises He had made to their father Abraham. We know that God will fulfill all of His promises. This should definitely influence the way we speak to our children.

D. Moses' parents were full of faith to believe that God had a future for their son who was condemned to die by the Pharaoh. No matter how hopeless it may seem for your son or daughter, have faith that God can redeem your present circumstances and turn them around for a blessing.

E. Moses learned to know His God step by step as he followed Him in obedience. He did not have the Word written down as we do; he had to daily listen to God's voice, and be obedient. That was the greatest qualification for an effective leader in those days, and it still is today!

F. Remember, there is nothing that your God cannot do through you. Your faith in Him need never fail. He is the source for the faith necessary for every situation.

XII. ASSIGNMENTS

    A. Listen to the tape prayerfully.

    B. Complete the study guide questions.

    C. Recommended reading: We've Come This Far by Faith, by Carolyn Wilde.

STUDY GUIDE QUESTIONS

1. We all want faith that pleases God. Using a concordance, find four ways that faith will act. What does the Word say pleases God?

2. Besides the wrath of God in eternity, from what else does your faith in God deliver you? Name two things.

3. The ark was God's provision for Noah's deliverance. What is your provision? What delivers you during hard times?

4. Find three Scriptures that emphasize the importance of obedient faith.

5. Give four Scriptures that promise rejuvenating faith, or strength for your whole life.

6. Share a test or a trial that you have been through lately. How was your faith tested, and what Scriptures did you use to overcome the trial or pass the test? Has God ever asked you to do a difficult thing? What was your response?

7. The most basic forward look of faith that we have as a body of believers is the soon coming of Christ. How should our faith be acting as we look forward to this blessed event? What does Scripture say?

8. Parents have great responsibilites for their children, and each must be carried out in faith. Name at least four parental responsibilities mentioned in the Bible which require both faith and faithfulness.

9. What 3 choices did Moses make by faith according to Hebrews 11:24-26?

10. In Exodus 3:5-8, God reveals Himself to Moses. This was the God he was to follow for the rest of his life by faith. List four things that God revealed to Moses.

11. When God called Moses, some very common excuses came from Moses' mouth. What were they (Exodus 3:10-15)? What would God's Word say to you, should you use the same excuses?

12.   Not everyone is called to be a leader of a nation, or even of a large group of people; however, each one of us is a leader in some capacity. God wants you to be the best! You may be the leader at your job, in your neighborhood, at your church, or just in your family. Study the leadership qualities of I Timothy 3,4. List as many as you can. Now ask God to develop you in the leadership area that He has given you. Someone is looking to you for guidance in some measure!

10 Faith and Fellowship with God

I. GOD DESIRES OUR FELLOWSHIP.

A. GREAT MEN WALKED WITH GOD.

1. Enoch walked with God. He had fellowship with Him on such an intimate level that God recorded this experience as "walking with God." He agreed with God, for "...how can two walk together except they agree" (Amos 3:3). Enoch put friendship and fellowship with God above other things.

> Then Enoch walked with God three hundred years after he became the father of Methuselah, and he had other sons and daughters. So all the days of Enoch were three hundred and sixty-five years.
> Genesis 5:22-23

2. Some years later a descendant, Noah, did the same things. He walked with God in spite of the fact that his whole generation was going in another direction. Noah maintained fellowship with God to such an extent that God shared His plans with him. God told him how disappointed He was in man and how He planned to destroy all mankind with a flood. Noah trusted God's Word. His fellowship with God had taught him to listen to God. He received information as to how to save all his household from destruction. Noah did not hesitate to obey. His fellowship with God had built faith in him. He believed God unreservedly.

3. Moses had a great desire to know God. He knew the Name of God. He spent time talking to God as a friend would talk to a friend, but the great longing of his heart was to really know the ways of God--to know Him. He cried to God, "If I have found favor in Thy sight, let me know Thy ways that I may know Thee." God replied, "MY presence will go with you." He would be with Moses all the time. They could have constant fellowship and communion.

> Thus the Lord used to speak to Moses face to face, just as a man speaks to his friend. When Moses returned to the camp, his servant Joshua, the son of Nun, a young man, would not depart from the tent. Then Moses said to the Lord, "See, Thou dost say to me, 'Bring up this people!' But Thou Thyself has not let me know whom Thou wilt send with me. Moreover, Thou hast said, 'I have known you by name; and you have also found favor in My sight. Now therefore, I pray Thee, if I have found favor in Thy sight, let me know Thy ways, that I may know

Thee, so that I may find favor in Thy sight. Consider too, that this nation is Thy people.
Exodus 33:11-13

4. Paul's longing was to "know Christ." He urged others to walk according to the pattern that he had set.

But whatever things were gain to me, those things I have counted as loss for the sake of Christ. More than that, I count all things to be loss in view of the surpassing value of knowing Christ Jesus my Lord, for whom I have suffered the loss of all things, and count them but rubbish in order that I may gain Christ, and may be found in Him, not having a righteousness of my own derived from the Law, but that which is through faith in Christ, the righteousness which comes from God on the basis of faith, that I may know Him, and the power of His resurrection and the fellowship of His sufferings, being conformed to His death;
Philippians 3:7-10

Brethren, join in following my example, and observe those who walk according to the pattern you have in us.
Philippians 3:17

B. GOD INITIATES FELLOWSHIP WITH MEN.

1. He came to dwell in the meeting tent.

"And I will consecrate the tent of meeting and the altar; I will also consecrate Aaron and his sons to minister as priests to Me. And I will dwell among the sons of Israel and will be their God. And they shall know that I am the Lord their God who brought them out of the land of Egypt, that I might dwell among them; I am the Lord their God."
Exodus 29:44-46

2. Later, God again said to the Israelites, "I will make My dwelling among you, and My soul will not reject you. I will also walk among you and be your God, and you shall be My people."

3. After the Babylonian captivity, during the restoration of Jerusalem and the temple, God gave them another assurance of His desire to dwell with them: "Sing for joy and be glad, O daughter of Zion; for behold I am coming and I will dwell in your midst" (Zech. 2:10).

4. Jesus announced God's plan for the New Covenant believers: "If anyone loves Me, he will keep My word; and My Father will love him, and We will come to him, and make Our abode with him" (John 14:23).

5. We are the temple of the living God. He said, "I will dwell in them and walk among them; And I will be their God, and they shall be My people" (II Cor. 6:16).

6. When man went his own way, it was always God who initiated a way for man to come back. He provided the sacrifice for Adam and Eve, He made a covenant with Abraham, He gave the law to the people of Israel, and finally, "God so loved the world that He gave His only begotten Son" (John 3:16). God desires your fellowship so much that He even gave His perfect, and only, Son.

> God is faithful, through whom you were called into fellowship
> with His Son, Jesus Christ our Lord.
> I Corinthians 1:9

II.   FELLOWSHIP WITH GOD IS CONDITIONAL.

A. IF YOU WILL TAKE HEED TO THE LAW

1. If you will obey "...all these blessings will come..."

> "Now it shall be, if you will diligently obey the Lord your God, being careful to do all His commandments which I command you today, the Lord your God will set you high above all the nations of the earth. And all these blessings shall come upon you and overtake you, if you will obey the Lord your God."
> Deuteronomy 28:1-2

2. "If you will walk in My statutes...then I shall give you..."

> "If you walk in My statutes and keep My commandments so as to carry them out, then I shall give you rains in their season, so that the land will yield its produce and the trees of the field will bear their fruit."
> Leviticus 26:3-4

3. "If you will walk in My statutes...I will also walk among you and be your God and you shall be My people" (Lev. 26:12).

B. IF YOU WALK IN THE LIGHT

Jesus is the light of the world. We are to walk in that light. If we continue to walk in darkness, we do not have fellowship with God nor with one another.

> And this is the message we have heard from Him and announce to you, that God is light, and in Him there is not darkness at all. If we say that we have fellowship with Him and yet walk in the darkness, we lie and do not practice the truth; but if we walk in the light as He Himself is in the light, we have fellowship with one another, and the blood of Jesus His Son cleanses us from all sin.
> I John 1:5-7

> Again therefore Jesus spoke to them, saying, "I am the light of the world; he who follows Me shall not walk in the darkness, but shall have the light of life."
> John 8:12

There is a condition to fellowship--walk in the Light. Walk where He is, where God's Word leads you!

C. IF YOU KEEP HIS COMMANDMENTS

We are right back to what was written in Deuteronomy. Our fellowship is still dependent upon our obedience to the Word of God. If we know to do the right thing, we are to do it. Obey the Word that was given to you. The Word says that we are liars if we say we know God and yet do not keep His Word.

> ...and He himself is the propitiation for our sins; and not for ours only, but also for those of the whole world. And by this we know that we have come to know Him, if we keep His commandments. The one who says, "I have come to know Him," and does not keep His commandments, is a liar, and the truth is not in him; but whoever keeps His word, in him the love of God has truly been perfected. By this we know that we are in Him: the one who says he abides in Him ought himself to walk in the same manner as He walked.
> I John 2:2-6

And the one who keeps His commandments abides in Him, and He in
him. And we know by this that He abides in us, by the Spirit
whom He has given us.
I John 3:24

III. FELLOWSHIP WITH GOD HAS POWERFUL RESULTS.

A. PHYSICAL PROSPERITY

The blessings of Deuteronomy 28:1-14 was a result of fellowship with God. Having a
relationship was vital--they were His covenant people. But as covenant people they
were to maintain their fellowship through obedience to the law. The result was
fantastic. God would be their guide, their healer, their protector, their life-giver,
their need-supplier. All that they needed was theirs as a result of simple obedience;
however, as one reads the Old Testament, it is clear that God did not want blind
obedience--He wanted love and fellowship. The obedience was merely a sign of the
love and fellowship that existed between God and man.

"Because He loved your fathers, therefore He chose their
descendants after them. And He personally brought you from
Egypt by His great Power."
Deuteronomy 4:37

"And you shall love the Lord your God with all your heart and with
all your soul and with all your might."
Deuteronomy 6:5

"And now, Israel, what does the Lord your God require from you,
but to fear the Lord your God, to walk in all His ways and love
Him, and to serve the Lord your God with all your heart and with
all your soul, and to keep the Lord's commandments and His
statutes which I am commanding you today for your good? Behold,
to the Lord your God belong heaven and the highest heavens, the
earth and all that is in it. Yet on your fathers did the Lord set His
affection to love them, and He chose their descendants after them,
even you above all peoples, as it is this day. Circumcise then your
heart, and stiffen your neck no more."
Deuteronomy 10:12-16

B. FRUIT-BEARING

As you have fellowship with God and "actualize" the abiding of the Lord in your life,
you will bear fruit. In other words, as the presence of Christ in your life is more

and more real to you, it affects everything you do: your efforts are fruitful; you accomplish what you set out to do; you have the energy to fulfill what God wants of you (John 15:4,5,16); you learn to let Jesus live His life through you!

> "Abide in Me, and I in you. As the branch cannot bear fruit of itself, unless it abides in the vine, so neither can you, unless you abide in Me. I am the vine, you are the branches; he who abides in Me, and I in him, he bears much fruit; for apart from Me you can do nothing."
> John 15:4-5

> "You did not choose Me, but I chose you, and appointed you, that you should go and bear fruit, and that your fruit should remain, that whatever you ask of the Father in My name, He may give to you."
> John 15:16

C. ANSWERED PRAYER

> "If you abide in Me, and my words abide in you, ask whatever you wish and it shall be done for you."
> John 15:7

Your power in prayer is directly related to your fellowship with God. It is not a "you be good and I will reward you" syndrome. It is a Life Principle throughout the Word. From our walk and communion and knowledge of God come the power for answered prayer.

> ...that the God of our Lord Jesus Christ, the Father of glory, may give to you a spirit of wisdom and of revelation in the knowledge of Him. I pray that the eyes of your heart may be enlightened, so that you may know what is the hope of His calling, what are the riches of the glory of His inheritance in the saints.
> Ephesians 1:17-18

> For this reason also, since the day we heard of it, we have not ceased to pray for you and to ask that you may be filled with knowledge of His will in all spiritual wisdom and understanding, so that you may walk in a manner worthy of the Lord, to please Him in all respects, bearing fruit in every good work and increasing in the knowledge of God;...
> Colossians 1:9-10

Grace and peace be multiplied to you in the knowledge of God and of Jesus our Lord; seeing that His divine power has granted to us everything pertaining to life and godliness, through the true knowledge of Him who called us by His own glory and excellence.
II Peter 1:2-3

As we come to know our God better, we begin to understand His ways--the method He would choose to solve a problem. The more we know Him, the more God-like our prayers become. When our prayers are in line with His will in all situations, there is no doubt as to its being answered.

D. UNITY OF THE BELIEVERS

Our fellowship with God will bring us into line with His thinking, also into unity with others of the Body of Christ. We all have the mind of Christ as believers, yet it is this constant fellowship with Him that teaches us how to express His mind in our daily life. As each member of the body expresses His thoughts, clashes between us are diminished.

"I do not ask in behalf of these alone, but for those also who believe in Me through their word; that they may all be one; even as Thou, Father, art in me, and I in Thee, that they also may be in Us; that the world may believe that Thou didst send Me. "And the glory which Thou hast given Me I have given to them; that they may be one, just as We are one: I in them, and Thou in Me, that they may be perfected in unity, that the world may know that Thou didst send me, and didst love them, even as Thou didst love Me."
John 17:20-23

E. LOVE PERFECTED IN BELIEVERS

Constant communion with God means constantly obeying Him, which results in walking as He walked, living with the love of God perfected in us.

"...and I have made Thy name know to them, and will make it know; that the love wherewith Thou didst love Me may be in them, and I in them."
John 17:26

"By this is My Father glorified, that you bear much fruit, and so prove to be My disciples."
John 15:8

...the one who says he abides in Him ought himself to walk in the
same manner as He walked.
I John 2:6

F. CONFIDENCE

When you are in continual fellowship with your Lord, you will have confidence at the
day of His coming, looking forward every day to His appearing. You will not be
ashamed, because His coming will only be one more step in your friendship with God.
Your love for Him will have perfected your actions and attitudes, and there will be
no fear of Him, no fear of judgment.

And now, little children, abide in Him, so that when He appears,
we may have confidence and not shrink away from Him in shame at
His coming.
I John 2:28

By this, love is perfected with us, that we may have confidence in
the day of judgment; because as He is, so also are we in this world.
I John 4:17

And this is the confidence which we have before Him, that if we ask
anything according to His will, He hears us. And if we know that
He hears us in whatever we ask, we know that we have the
requests which we have asked from Him.
I John 5:14-15

This fellowship produces a confidence that your prayers are answered--that anything
you ask of Him according to His will, He hears you and you have your request.

IV.   THE TRAGEDY OF BROKEN FELLOWSHIP

A. UNCONFESSED SIN BREAKS FELLOWSHIP

"If I regard wickedness in my heart, the Lord will not hear."
Psalm 66:18

"Behold, the Lord's hand is not so short that it cannot save;
neither is His ear so dull that it cannot hear. But your iniquities
have made a separation between you and your God, and your sins
have hidden His face from you, so that He does not hear."
Isaiah 59:1-2

Fellowship is a two-way conversation. If your sins are unconfessed, there is a wall between you and God. He does not hear you. You may pray with what you call faith, but your prayer gets you nowhere. Sin has stopped communication between you and your God.

"If we say that we have fellowship with Him and yet walk in the
darkness, we lie and do not practice the truth."
I John 1:6

B. PRAYERS ARE NOT ANSWERED

David sinned with Bathsheba. For many months he regarded this iniquity in his heard without repentance. Psalm 32:3-4 explains how he felt during this time. God had to send Nathan, the prophet, to him to expose the gravity of his sin with Bathsheba. His prayer for the healing of his infant son was not heart because he had kept silent about his sin (II Samuel 12:12-18). For the better part of the year, David's fellowship with God had been broken. His prayers were not answered, and he felt like a sick man.

If you are troubled with lack of answered prayer, make sure there is no cause for broken fellowship with your Lord.

C. FAITH IS IMPAIRED

The Source of our faith is God and His Word. If our fellowship with the Source is broken, the supply of faith is also affected. We know that the Source is within us, but He cannot work through us when sin is in the way. Sin stops your faith from working in your life.

V. RESTORED FELLOWSHIP IS INSTANTLY AVAILABLE.

A. SEARCH AND TRY YOUR WAYS.

1. Stay ahead of the accuser.

   Listen to the voice of the Holy Spirit. Receive His examination and conviction, and then the devil will have no opportunity to accuse and condemn you.

   Let us examine and probe our ways, And let us return to the
   Lord.
   Lamentations 3:40

I considered my ways, And turned my feet to Thy testimonies.
Psalm 119:59

Search me, O God, and know my heart; Try me and know my
anxious thoughts; And see if there be any hurtful way in me,
And lead me in the everlasting way.
Psalm 139:23-24

2. Watch out for enemy tricks.

There are two tricks of the enemy that we should be aware of in examining
ourselves. First, he would have us drag out everything we ever did and brood
over the wrongs of our life, sending us into a pit of despair and self-pity, or, he
would have us so busy with our affairs that we barely notice when we have
sinned--a kind of hardening of the heart. We think we need no examination.
Both are enemy lies. Your fellowship with the Lord will make you sensitive to
grieving the Holy Spirit. You will know when you have sinned, confess what you
are convicted of, and then leave it with the Lord. Receive your forgiveness, and
don't allow a hardness to come over you.

> "And they shall not teach again, each man his neighbor and
> each man his brother, saying, 'Know the Lord,' for they shall
> all know Me, from the least of them to the greatest of them,"
> declares the Lord, "for I will forgive their iniquity, and their
> sin I will remember no more."
> Jeremiah 31:34

3. Be truly repentant (Psalm 51).

When God convicts of a sin, don't cover it up with an excuse or put it off on
someone else. Call it sin and not by another name. If you have, for instance,
been lax in your prayer life, acknowledge your sin and ask forgiveness. God
says for us to "pray always." If He has shown you that you have not been
praying as He said, then your sin is disobedience to His revealed will for your
life. You cannot say to God, "But, you know how busy I have been." You can
say, "I have been disobedient; I have put other things ahead of my fellowship
with you. Forgive my sin."

Repentance involves both a turning from sin and a turning to God. It is not just
a repetition of the things done--not just a verbal recitation of offenses--it is a
life-changing process.

B. ACCEPT FORGIVENESS.

The Word says that "if we say we have no sin, we are deceiving ourselves, and the truth is not in us. If we confess our sins, He is faithful and righteous to forgive us our sins and to cleanse us from all unrighteousness" (I John 1:8-9).

> "My little children, I write you these thing so that you may not violate God's law and sin; but if any one should sin, we have an Advocate (One who will intercede for us) with the Father; (it is) Jesus Christ (the all) righteous--upright, just, Who conforms to the Father's will in every purpose, thought and action."
> I John 2:1 TAB

The ways to restored fellowship is to accept the responsibility of sinning, repent, confess it to God, and trust Him to forgive us completely. Jesus intercedes on our behalf. There is not unwillingness whatsoever on God's part to cleanse us thoroughly and continually. We accept this cleansing by faith in God's Word.

C. FORGIVE AS YOU HAVE BEEN FORGIVEN.

Mark 11:23-26 teaches us some great faith principles concerning asking in faith. But notice that right along with this truth is that of forgiveness. Your faith will not work if you do not forgive. In fact, your forgiveness hinges on you forgiving others (vs. 26). Christians are to search their own hearts for sins against God, and along with that, release the offenses of others towards them.

> "Truly I say to you, whoever says to this mountain, 'Be taken up and cast into the sea, and does not doubt in his heart, but believes that what he says is going to happen, it shall be granted him. Therefore I say to you, all things for which you pray and ask, believe that you have received them, and they shall be granted you. And whenever you stand praying, forgive, if you have anything against anyone; so that your Father also who is in heaven may forgive you your transgressions. But if you do not forgive, neither will your Father who is in heaven forgive your transgressions."
> Mark 11:23-26

If you have an unforgiving spirit towards anyone, it will cause your faith prayers to be ineffectual! Remember the parable Jesus taught in Matthew 18.

D. LIVE IN FORGIVENESS.

Each day your fellowship with God is growing more precious. Your time with Him becomes the number one priority in your life. You are walking in the light of His Word. He shows you treasures from His Word and reveals His plans for your life-- gives you a vision of the work He plans to do through you. It is the Life of Christ that meets the needs of others through you. When you are offended--someone sins against you--the Life within you responds as Jesus did: "Father, forgive them." You instantly forgive them too, No bitterness has a chance to take hold in your life. There is no fertile ground for the enemy to plant seeds of hate, fear, or doubt, nothing to keep the faith within you from growing, nothing to feed fantasies of revenge. The minute you realize that someone has sinned against you, ask God to teach you to respond with, "I forgive them. I release my judgment against them. I turn the situation to you, Lord." Each time you do this, you have robbed Satan of a victory and put out one of his darts.

If you find it difficult to forgive someone, picture Jesus standing beside you with the nail prints in his hands saying, "I forgave you." You will realize afresh the extent of God's forgiveness of your sins. It puts a new light on you forgiving others.

VI. SUMMATION

A. Man was created to have fellowship with God. Since the first day God made man, He also provided a way for man to communicate, to fellowship, with God.

B. This fellowship with a Holy God means we come to Him--His way. There are conditions to this friendship. He provides the means--our task is to abide by them.

C. God is powerful, and friendship with Him has wonderful results. Our fellowship with Him is actually our abiding in Him, our dependence upon Him for everything we have, are, and need. His reponse is to supply everything.

D. Sin can break that wonderful fellowship and cause our prayers to be unanswered and our faith to fail. We are powerless unless properly connected to God.

E. But hallelujah! God makes provision even for the broken connections. All we do is repent and confess our sin. He immediately cleanses us and restores us completely to fellowship with Him. God wants to teach us all to live in forgivenss and repentance--to have nothing between us and our God, nor between us and our brothers. Be strong in your fellowship with God. It will make you strong in your faith in God!

VII. ASSIGNMENTS

A. Listen to the tape carefully.

B. Complete the study guide questions.

C. Suggested reading: <u>Living in Instant Forgiveness</u>, by Paul & Mary Birt.
<u>Prayer That Moves Mountains</u>, by Gordon Lindsay.

STUDY GUIDE QUESTIONS

1. As you fellowship with God, you will come to know Him better. Do a study on "knowing Christ" or "knowing God," using a concordance or study Bible.

2. Fellowship depends on our walking in the Word, or walking in the light. Find as many Scriptures as you can that explain what this means. Describe the Life that is "walking in the light."

3. Study I John 1 and 2. List all the qualities of a Christian that would, in some way, be a result of fellowship with God.

4. Study Psalm 51 and list the steps that David went through in his confession prayer to God. What specific things did he ask God to do for him?

5. What do you think the Word teaches about restitution in connection with asking forgiveness (Lev. 5:15,16; Luke 19:8,9)?

6. How can we handle the fear of being hurt again when we constantly forgive a person for the same offense over and over?

11 Faith for Prosperity

I. GOD WANTS YOUR SOUL TO PROSPER.

"Beloved, I pray that in all respects you may prosper and be in good health, just as your soul prospers.
III John 2

A. BY RENEWING YOUR MIND

"A prosperous soul is one in which the mind is renewed, the will conformed, the emotions controlled, and the thinking faculties selective of that which it thinks." That is what Jerry Savelle says in Prosperity of the Soul. According to the Word, that is it! A prosperous soul encompasses your entire being--the real you inside your body.

The best way to renew your mind is to replace your thoughts with God's thoughts. His thoughts are so much higher that yours, and they will be effective. When God made you a new creature, He also included your mind. He gave you Christ's mind. "But we have the mind of Christ, the Messiah, and do hold the thoughts (feelings and purposes) of His heart" (I Corinthians 2:16, TAB). The way to experience having the mind of Christ is to have your mind filled with His Word! You are commanded to renew your mind. When you do, your soul will prosper!

"For My thoughts are not your thoughts, Neither are your ways My ways," declares the Lord. "For as the heavens are higher than the earth, So are My ways higher than your ways, And My thoughts than your thoughts. For as the rain and the snow come down from heaven, And do not return there without watering the earth, And making it bear and sprout, And furnishing seed to the sower and bread to the eater; So shall My word be which goes forth from My mouth; It shall not return to Me empty, Without accomplishing what I desire, And without succeeding in the matter for which I sent it."
Isaiah 55:8-11

Therefore if any man is in Christ, he is a new creature; the old things passed away; behold, new things have come.
II Corinthians 5:17

And do not be conformed to this world, but be transformed by the renewing of your mind, that you may prove what the will of God is, that which is good and acceptable and perfect.
Romans 12:2

B. BY CONFORMING YOUR WILL

You are constantly making choices to do things your way, the world's way, or God's way. You face hundreds of decisions each day. You always make one--you always choose. Is it conformed to God's will? You are warned not to be conformed to the world (Romans 12:2) and told that you "have need of steadfast patience and endurance, so that you might fully accomplish the will of God and thus receive and carry away (and enjoy to the full) what is promised" (Hebrews 10:36).

Yet, we know that we have help in willing to do His will. Philippians 2:13 says, "...It is God Who is all the while effectually at work in you--energizing and creating in you the power and desire--both to will and to work for His good pleasure and satisfaction and delight" (TAB). He gives you the will to conform to His will. Yield to Him, and prosper your soul!

C. BY CONTROLLING YOUR EMOTIONS

There are times when the emotions seek to rule your life. Fear, anxiety, anger, or nervousness would like to control. Each one seeks to be in the driver's seat of your life. When this happens, you tend to seem unproductive--not prosperous. With the strength of Christ, you can claim the fruit of the spirit to control your life. You already have all these qualities resident within you in Christ. It is a matter of switching control from your emotions to His emotions. We are to be controlled by love, joy, peace, etc. No destroying emotions can overcome us when we actively allow the fruit of the spirit to control our souls.

> But the fruit of the Spirit is love, joy, peace, patience, kindness,
> goodness, faithfulness, gentleness, self-control; against such
> things there is not law.
> Galatians 5:22-23

The fruit of the spirit is what the presence of the Holy spirit accomplishes in our lives! Look at that list again--the possessor of those qualities is a prosperous soul!

D. BY ACCEPTING THE BLESSINGS THAT ARE ALREADY YOURS

Ephesians 1:17-18 says that there is already a very wealthy inheritance in you. When you got saved, there was a wealthy inheritance given you. You have riches in His inheritance! You need to know this. It will put you over and give you supernatural ability to prosper.

> ...that the God of our Lord Jesus Christ, the Father of glory, may
> give to you a spirit of wisdom and of revelation in the knowledge of

Him. I pray that the eyes of your heart may be enlightened, so that you may know what is the hope of His calling, what are the riches of the glory of His inheritance in the saints,...
Ephesians 1:17-18

Paul says in Ephesians 1:3 that you are blessed with all spiritual blessings: You are seated in the heavenlies with Him.

Blessed be the God and Father of our Lord Jesus Christ, who has blessed us with every spiritual blessing in the heavenly places in Christ,...
Ephesians 1:3

...and raised us up with Him, and seated us with Him in the heavenly places in Christ Jesus,...
Ephesians 2:6

...which He brought about in Christ, when He raised Him from the dead, and seated Him at His right hand in the heavenly places,...
Ephesians 1:20

Can you imagine anyone seated in the heavenlies, blessed with all spiritual blessings, not prospering in their soul?

II.   GOD WANTS YOU TO PROSPER MATERIALLY.

III John 2 says, "Beloved, I pray that in all respects you may prosper and be in good health, just as your soul prospers."

A. DOES GOD LIKE RICH MEN?

Abraham was very, very wealthy. God blessed him in all things. Job was also a very wealthy man. God really complimented him when He said, "You are perfect, Job. You are righteous; you flee evil." Yet he was a very rich man. Other rich men were Jacob, Isaac and Isaiah.

God spoke to Solomon when He came unto him in the night and said, "Solomon, what would you like to have?" He said, " I want to be rich in wisdom." Solomon didn't say that he wanted wealth. He said that he wanted wisdom. God said, "All right, you are going to be rich in wisdom; however, because you asked for wisdom, and because you have believed, I am also going to bless you financially." Solomon became a very wealthy man (II Samuel 1:7-12).

Yes, God does love rich men!

Proverbs 10:22 says, "It is the blessing of the Lord that makes rich, And He adds no sorrow to it." God wants riches to come from Him. Go to Him believing He is the Source. He wants you to be rich, to prosper in every area of your life.

There is a right and wrong to everything. Staying in God's Word keeps you doing what is right in God's eye. We can't ignore the fact that there were some rich men in the Bible that God didn't like at all--that is, He certainly didn't like what they were doing! Jesus told a parable about a rich man in Luke 12:16-21. His land brought forth plentifully, and he pulled down his old barns and built bigger ones. He gathered in the crops and dwelt on his riches. But God said unto him, "You fool! This very night they (that is, the messengers of God) demand your soul of you; and all the things that you have prepared, whose will they be" (TAB)? God called him a fool. He was rich, but he was a rich fool. Why? Because he stored up his wealth to enjoy by himself. He did not count God as his source! He could not take riches to heaven, and he didn't plant anywhere in the work of the Gospel. We do not want to be called rich fools.

> And He told them a parable, saying, "The land of a certain rich man was very productive. And he began reasoning to himself, saying, 'What shall I do, since I have no place to store my crops?' And he said, 'This is what I will do: I will tear down my barns and build larger ones, and there ' will store all my grain and my goods. And I will say to my soul, "Soul, you have many goods laid up for many years to come; take your ease, eat, drink and be merry."' But God said to him, 'You fool! This very night your soul is required of you; and now who will own what you have prepared?' So is the man who lays up treasure for himself, and is not rich toward God."
> Luke 12:16-21

How different the story of the disciples is! They sold everything they had and followed Jesus. Because of this, Jesus told them, "You will receive a 100 fold return in this life."

B. GOD MADE SOME POWERFUL PROSPERITY PROMISES.

1. God gives His people the power to get wealth.

> "But you shall remember the Lord your God, for it is He who is giving you power to make wealth, that He may confirm His

covenant which He swore to your fathers as it is this day."
Deuteronomy 8:18

2. He said that He would cause the remnant of his people to possess all things.

'For there will be peace of the seed: the vine will yield its fruit,
the land will yield its produce, and the heavens will give their
dew; and I will cause the remnant of this people to inherit all
these things.'
Zechariah 8:12

3. He said that the wealth of the sinner is laid up for the righteous.

A good man leaves an inheritance to his children's children,
And the wealth of the sinner is stored up for the righteous.
Proverbs 13:22

4. The returning exiles knew that the God of heaven would prosper them.

So I answered them and said to them, "The God of heaven will
give us success; therefore we His servants will arise and build,
but you have no portion, right, or memorial in Jerusalem."
Nehemiah 2:20

5. God wanted the Israelites to abound in prosperity.

"And the Lord will make you abound in prosperity, in the
offspring of your body and in the offspring of your beast and
in the produce of your ground, in the land which the Lord
swore to your fathers to give you."
Deuteronomy 28:11

6. It is your Heavenly Father's pleasure to give you these things (Matthew 6:24-
32).

Let them shout for joy and rejoice, who favor my vindication;
And let them say continually, "The Lord be magnified, Who
delights in the prosperity of His servant."
Psalm 35:27

7. God wants to give you sufficiently all things.

"And God is able to make all grace (every favor and earthly blessing) come to you in abundance, so that you may always and under all circumstances and whatever the need, be self-sufficient--possessing enough to require no aid or support and furnished in abundance for every good work and charitable donation."
II Corinthians 9:8, TAB

C. GOD SHOWS YOU THE KEYS TO PROSPERITY.

1. BE OBEDIENT.

"Therefore keep the words of this covenant, and do them, that you may deal wisely and prosper in all that you do."
Deuteronomy 29:9, TAB

2. PUT GOD FIRST.

"But seek for (aim at and strive after) first of all His kingdom, and His righteousness (His way of doing and being right), and then all these things taken together will be given you besides."
Matthews 6:33, TAB

No good thing is withheld from those who walk uprightly. The rich man in the parable was called a fool because he had laid up treasure for himself, yet was not rich toward God. Be rich toward God. How? Read the Word, tithe, pray, preach, act upon the Word, pray in the Spirit, and obey the Word.

For the Lord God is a sun and shield; The Lord gives grace and glory; No good thing does He withhold from those who walk uprightly.
Psalm 84:11

"So is the man who lays up treasure for himself, and is not rich toward God."
Luke 12:21

3. BE DILIGENT IN WHATEVER YOU DO.

"He becomes poor who works with a slack and idle hand, but the hand of the diligent makes rich."
Proverbs 10:4, TAB

People say, "I want to be rich," but they don't want to work. Still others have said, "I want to do something for God. I want a big ministry." Yet, they are never available to do anything in the ministry. It doesn't work! If you are going to have a good church, a good ministry, or a positive life style, you are going to have to fast, pray, and be in the Word. You can't be slothful in any way.

Slothful people are called sluggards in the Bible. Isn't that a terrible word? A slothful person sleeps-in every day and is late to work. Yet, he wonders why he doesn't make progress.

> "As the door turns on its hinges, so does the lazy man (move not from his place) upon his bed."
> Proverbs 26:14, TAB

The sluggard always makes excuses about why he doesn't succeed.

> "The sluggard says, there is a lion in the way! A lion is in the streets."
> Proverbs 26:13, TAB

We come up against many lions today--icy streets, sunny days which are ready to be enjoyed, and many more excuses to stay home. Will the lion win or will you win? If you want to be rich, be diligent, and be a good worker. Being lazy will never make you rich.

4. GO BY THE WORD--GET RICHES BY GOD'S WISDOM

Wisdom speaks in Proverbs:

> "Riches and honor are with me, enduring wealth, and righteousness..."
> Proverbs 8:18, TAB

> "Length of days in her right hand, and in her left hand are riches and honor."
> Proverbs 3:16, TAB

The wisdom of God will show you how to get rich. Remember the Lord, and ask for His wisdom. He will give you the wisdom to get wealth.

"I walk in the way of righteousness, In the midst of the paths of justice, To endow those who love me with wealth, That I may fill their treasuries."
Proverbs 8:20-21

5.   HAVE THE RIGHT ATTITUDE TOWARD GOD.

a)   Blessed is the man that trusteth in Him..will not want any good thing.

> O taste and see that the Lord is good; How blessed is the man who takes refuge in Him! O fear the Lord, you His saints; For to those who fear Him, there is not want. The young lions do lack and suffer hunger; But they who seek the Lord shall not be in want of any good thing.
> Psalm 34:8-10

b)   The man that delights in the Lord, his seed shall be blessed. Riches and wealth are in his house.

> Praise the Lord! How blessed is the man who fears the Lord, Who greatly delights in His commandments. His descendants will be mighty on earth; The generation of the upright will be blessed. Wealth and riches are in his house, And his righteousness endures forever.
> Psalm 112:1-3

c)   Fear of the Lord brings riches, honor, and life.

> The reward of humility and the fear of the Lord Are riches, honor and life.
> Proverbs 22:4

d)   In the house of the righteous is much treasure.

> Much wealth is in the house of the righteous, But trouble is in the income of the wicked.
> Proverbs 15:6

e)   As long as Uzziah sought the Lord, God prospered him.

> And he continued to seek God in the days of Zechariah, who
> had understanding through the vision of God; and as long
> as he sought the Lord, God prospered him.
> II Chronicles 26:5

6. MEDITATE ON THE WORD.

> But his delight is in the law of the Lord, And in His law he
> meditates day and night. And he will be like a tree firmly
> planted by streams of water, Which yields its fruit in its
> season, And its leaf does not wither; And in whatever he does,
> he prospers.
> Psalm 1:2-3

The happy man of this Psalm meditates in the law (Word) day and night, and
everything he does prospers!

7. TITHE, GIVE, AND TAKE CARE OF GOD'S HOUSE.

a) God promised to open the windows of heaven and pour out a blessing for
those who would tithe.

> "Bring the whole tithe into the storehouse, so that there
> may be food in My house, and test Me now in this," says the
> Lord of hosts, "if I will not open for you the windows of
> heaven, and pour out for you a blessing until it overflows."
> Malachi 3:10

b) Take care of God's house. In Haggai 1:6,9 God says that His house was left
in disrepair. It was left out; therefore, His people did not prosper.

> "You have sown much, but harvest little; you eat, but there
> is not enough to be satisfied; you drink, but there is not
> enough to become drunk; you put on clothing, but no one is
> warm enough; and he who earns, earns wages to put into a
> purse with holes."
> Haggai 1:6

> "You look for much, but behold, it comes to little; when you
> bring it home, I blow it away. Why? Because of My house

which lies desolate, while each of you runs to his own house."
Haggai 1:9

c) Give to the poor, and you will not lack.

He who gives to the poor will never want, But he who shuts his eyes will have many curses.
Proverbs 28:27

D. HE WOULD LIKE TO ELIMINATE POVERTY.

1. BY GIVING PROMISES, AND MORE PROMISES

a) Seek the kingdom; then all these things will be added.

"But seek first His kingdom and His righteousness; and all these things shall be added unto you."
Matthew 6:33

b) There shall be no poor among you.

"However, there shall be no poor among you, since the Lord will surely bless you in the land which the Lord your God is giving you as an inheritance to possess, if only you listen obediently to the voice of the Lord your God, to observe carefully all this commandment which I am commanding you today."
Deuteronomy 15:4-5

c) Your needs shall be supplied according to His riches.

And my God shall supply all your needs according to His riches in glory in Christ Jesus.
Philippians 4:19

d) Jesus was anointed to preach the gospel to the poor.

"The Spirit of the Lord is upon Me, because He anointed Me to preach the gospel to the poor. He has sent Me to proclaim release to the captives, and recovery of sight to

the blind, to set free those who are downtrodden, to proclaim the favorable year of the Lord."
Luke 4:18

e) Christ became poor that you might become rich.

For you know the grace of our Lord Jesus Christ, that though He was rich, yet for your sake He became poor, that you through His poverty might become rich.
II Corinthians 8:9

2. BY TELLING US THE CAUSE OF POVERTY

a) Refusing instruction

Poverty and shame will come to him who neglects discipline, But he who regards reproof will be honored.
Proverbs 13:18

b) Being lazy.

Do not love sleep, lest you become poor; Open your eyes, and you will be satisfied with food. "Bad, bad," says the buyer; But when he goes his way, then he boasts.
Proverbs 20:13-14

c) Wickedness

A good man leaves an inheritance to his children's children, And the wealth of the sinner is stored up for the righteous. Abundant food is in the fallow ground of the poor, But it is swept away by injustice.
Proverbs 13:22-23

d) Selfishness

There is one who scatters, yet increases all the more, And there is one who withholds what is justly due, but it results only in want.
Proverbs 11:24

3. BY DELIVERING THE POOR WHEN THEY COME TO HIM

    a) He delivers the poor when they cry.

        For he will deliver the needy when he cries for help, The
        afflicted also, and him who has no helper. He will have
        compassion on the poor and needy, And the lives of the
        needy he will save.
        Psalm 72:12-13

    b) He satisfies the poor with bread.

        "I will abundantly bless her provision; I will satisfy her
        needy with bread."
        Psalm 132:15

    c) He lifts them up.

        "He raises the poor from the dust, he lifts the needy from
        the ash heap To make them sit with nobles, And inherit a
        seat of honor; For the pillars of the earth are the Lord's,
        And He set the world on them."
        I Samuel 2:8

    d) He raises the poor and needy from affliction.

        But He sets the needy securely on high away from affliction,
        And makes his families like a flock.
        Psalm 107:41

E. HE PROSPERS YOU FOR A PURPOSE.

God prospers you because he takes pleasure in doing so, but also to use you to be a
financial blessing to others. God uses man's hands to do His work on earth;
therefore, if He is going to bless one man, He is most likely going to use another man
to do so. In essence, we become channels for the riches of God. We receive, and
then we give to the work of God, to other brethren. Then we receive back--
probably from people--and have enough to give again. Jesus said, "Freely ye have
received, freely give" (Matthew 10:8).

III. WARNINGS CONCERNING RICHES

A. LABOR NOT TO BE RICH.

> Do not weary yourself to gain wealth, Cease from your
> consideration of it.
> Proverbs 23:4

Don't make being rich your prime goal because where your treasure is, there your
heart will be also.

Do not use your own wisdom to get money because then your heart will dwell on
money instead of establishing the covenant of God. "He who makes haste to be rich
(at any cost) shall not be unpunished..." (Proverbs 28:20,TAB).

B. RICHES BY GREED ARE NOT WORTH IT.

> "An inheritance hastily gotten (by greedy, unjust means) at the
> beginning, in the end will not be blessed."
> Proverbs 20:21,TAB

> "Wealth (not earned) but won in haste, or unjustly, or from the
> production of things for vain or detrimental use, (such riches) will
> dwindle away; but he who gathers little by little will increase
> them."
> Proverbs 13:11,TAB

C. BEWARE OF CRAVING, COVETING, AND LOVING MONEY.

> "But those who crave to be rich fall into temptation and a snare,
> and into many foolish (useless, godless) and hurtful desires that
> plunge men into ruin and destruction and miserable perishing. For
> the love of money is a root of all evils; it is through this craving
> that some have been led astray, and have wandered from the faith
> and pierced themselves through with many acute (mental) pangs."
> I Timothy 6:9,TAB

> "And He said to them, Guard yourselves and keep free from all
> coveteousness--the immoderate desire for wealth, the greedy
> longing to have more;   for a man's life does not consist and is not

derived from possessing overflowing abundance, or that which is over and above his needs."
Luke 12:15, TAB

D. CHOOSE THE RIGHT PLACE TO LAY UP YOUR TREASURES.

"Do not gather and heap up and store for yourselves treasures on earth, where moth and rust and worm consume and destroy, and where thieves break through and steal; But gather and heap up and gather up and store for yourselves treasures in heaven, where neither moth nor rust nor worm consume and destroy, and where thieves do not break through and steal; For where your treasure is, there will your heart be also."
Matthew 6:19-21, TAB

"Trust and rely confidently not on extortion and oppression, and do not vainly hope in robbery; if riches increase, set not your heart on them."
Psalm 62:10, TAB

"God will likewise break you down and destroy you for ever;...See, this is the man who made not God his strength--his stronghold and high tower; but trusted and confidently relied on the abundance of his riches, seeking refuge and security for himself through his wickedness. But I am like a green olive tree in the house of God; I trust and confidently rely on the loving-kindness and mercy of God for ever and ever."
Psalm 52:5,7,8, TAB

"As for the rich in this world, charge them not to be proud and arrogant and contemptuous of others, nor to set their hopes on uncertain riches but on God, Who richly and ceaselessly provides us with everything for (our) enjoyment."
I Timothy 6:17, TAB

IV. THE LAW OF GIVING

A. GOD GIVES ABUNDANTLY.

1. He created the world with abundance, and it was fruitful.

Then God said, "Let the waters teem with swarms of living

creatures, and let birds fly above the earth in the open expanse
of the heavens."
Genesis 1:20

And God created the great sea monsters, and every living
creature that moves, with which the waters swarmed after their
kind, and every winged bird after its kind; and God saw that it
was good. And God blessed them saying, "Be fruitful and
multiply, and fill the waters in the seas, and let birds multiply
on the earth."
Genesis 1:21-22

2. Christ came to give abundant life.

"The thief comes only to steal, and kill, and destroy; I came
that they might have life, and might have it abundantly."
John 10:10

3. God's children relish and feast in the abundance of His house.

How precious is Thy loving-kindness, O God! And the children
of men take refuge in the shadow of Thy wings. They drink
their fill of the abundance of Thy house; And Thou dost give
them to drink of the river of Thy delights. For with Thee is
the fountain of life; in Thy light we see light.
Psalm 36:7-9

4. The early church increased abundantly.

...praising God, and having favor with all the people, And the
Lord was adding to their number day by day those who were
being saved.
Acts 2:47

So then, those who had received his word were baptized; and
there were added that day about three thousand souls.
Acts 2:41

5. God gives abundance of grace.

For if by the transgression of the one, death reigned through
the one, much more those who receive the abundance of grace

and of the gift of righteousness will reign in life through the One, Jesus Christ.
Romans 5:17

...and the grace of our Lord was more than abundant, with the faith and love which are found in Christ Jesus.
I Timothy 1:14

6. God gives unlimited strength.

I can do all things through Him who strengthens me.
Philippians 4:13

7. We are _more_ than conquerors.

But in all these things we overwhelmingly conquer through Him who loved us.
Romans 8:37

8. God is abundant in mercy.

Blessed be the God and Father of our Lord Jesus Christ, who according to His great mercy has caused us to be born again to a living hope through the resurrection of Jesus Christ from the dead,...
I Peter 1:3

If we confess our sins, he is faithful and righteous to forgive us our sins and to cleanse us from all unrighteousness.
I John 1:9

B. WE ARE TO GIVE GENEROUSLY.

1. "There are those who (generously) scatter abroad, and yet increase more; there are those who withhold more than is fitting or what is justly due, but it tends only to want. The liberal person shall be enriched, and he who waters shall himself be watered" (Proverbs 11:24,25, TAB).

2. "He who has pity on the poor lends to the Lord, and that which he has given He will repay to him" (Proverbs 19:17, TAB).

3. "He covets greedily all the day long, but the (uncompromisingly) righteous gives and does not withhold" (Proverbs 21:26, TAB).

4. "He who has a bountiful eye shall be blessed, for he gives of his bread to the poor" (Proverbs 22:9, TAB).

5. Give and it shall be given to you, and all your needs will be supplied.

> "Give, and it will be given to you; good measure, pressed down, shaken together, running over, they will pour into your lap. for by your standard of measure it will be measured to you in return."
> Luke 6:38

> Now this I say, he who sows sparingly shall also reap sparingly; and he who sows bountifully shall also reap bountifully. Let each one do just as he has purposed in his heart; not grudgingly or under compulsion; for God loves a cheerful giver. And God is able to make all grace abound to you, that always having all sufficiency in everything, you may have an abundance for every good deed; as it is written, "HE SCATTERED ABROAD, HE GAVE TO THE POOR, HIS RIGHTEOUSNESS ABIDES FOREVER." Now He who supplies seed to the sower and bread for food, will supply and multiply your seed for sowing and increase the harvest of your righteousness.
> II Corinthians 9:6-10

C. GIVING TO GOD'S CHILDREN IS GIVING TO GOD.

When we are giving of our time, love, or goods to others we are doing it unto God. Jesus makes this teaching very clear, and our motivation should always be beyond the immediate, seeing ourselves not only acting on behalf of the Lord, but also doing it unto Him, which is really what is taking place.

> "And the King will answer and say to them, 'Truly I say to you, to the extent that you did it to one of these brothers of Mine, even the least of them, you did it to Me.' Then He will also say to those on His left, 'Depart from Me, accursed ones, into the eternal fire which has been prepared for the devil and his angels; for I was hungry, and you gave Me nothing to eat; I was thirsty, and you gave Me nothing to drink; I was a stranger, and you did not invite Me in; naked, and you did not clothe Me; sick, and in prison, and you did not visit Me.' Then they themselves also will answer, saying, 'Lord, when did we see You hungry, or thirsty, or a stranger, or naked, or sick, or in prison, and did not take care of

You?' Then He will answer them, saying, "Truly I say to you, to the extent that you did not do it to one of the least of these, you did not do it to Me.'"
Matthew 25:40-45

D. WE ARE TO GIVE BY FAITH.

1. The widow who gave her last meal gave it by faith. She saw no source for another meal, yet she perceived that the man of God needed to be fed first. By faith she fed him. She gave her last. Then, by faith, they all ate until the end of the drought. If you have only your last to give, trust God. He can make the last little bit multiply to supply your need for months (I Kings 17:9-16).

2. Another widow, in Jesus' day, gave out of her poverty by faith. She gave all she had. Jesus especially noticed her gift and said, "This poor widow has put in more than all of them (the rich people)." When you only have a little, give anyway. The size of the gift is of no importance. It is the attitude with which it is given. Give by faith, whether your gift be great or small!

And He looked up and saw the rich putting their gifts into the treasury. And He saw a certain poor widow putting in two small copper coins. And He said, 'Truly I say to you, this poor widow put in more than all of them; for they all out of their surplus put into the offering; but she out of her poverty put in all that she had to live on."
Luke 21:1-4

V. GOD WANTS YOUR BODY TO PROSPER.

"Beloved, I pray that in all respects you may prosper and be in good health, just as your soul prospers."
III John 2

A. THERE ARE MANY PROMISES TO THE OLD TESTAMENT BELIEVERS FOR HEALING.

1. God brought the Israelites, a hard-working slave nation, out of Egypt totally strong and healthy. That should say much for His will for His people.

Then He brought them out with silver and gold; And among His tribes there was not one who stumbled.
Psalm 105:37

2. He promised to take away all diseases from His people--that is a promise of divine health. This is what God desired for His beloved Israel.

    "And the Lord will remove from you all sickness; and He will not put on you any of the harmful diseases of Egypt which you have known, but He will lay them on all who hate you."
    Deuteronomy 7:15

3. He promised that no evil plague would even come near His people. No matter what plague or flu is rampant in town, it does not need to come near the house of the righteous. It was God's will then to route it away from His children, and He has not changed in this respect.

    No evil will befall you, Nor will any plague come near your tent.
    Psalm 91:10

4. Even after His people have sinned, rebelled, and reaped the consequences of their waywardness, God is merciful and promises to restore health and heal their wounds.

    "For I will restore you to health And I will heal you of your wounds," declares the Lord, "Because they have called you an outcast, saying: 'It is Zion no one cares for her.'"
    Jeremiah 30:17

5. He promises His people a glorious, prosperous future.

    "Behold, I will bring to it health and healing, and I will heal them; and I will reveal to them an abundance of peace and truth."
    Jeremiah 33:6

B. THE CROSS PROVIDED FOR PHYSICAL HEALING

1. After eating the Passover Lamb, the Israelites went out totally healed and strong. That lamb was a type of Christ, the Passover Lamb. When we partake of His body, we are to be healed and strong. When we do it unworthily, it is a cause of weakness and sickenss.

    Let a man (thoroughly) examine himself, and (only) when he has done so should he eat of the bread and drink of the cup. For any one who eats and drinks without discriminating and recognizing with the appreciation that (it is Christ's) body,

214

eats and drinks of a sentence--a verdict of judgment--upon himself, That (careless and unworthy participation) is the reason many of you are weak and sickly, and quite enough of you are fallen into the sleep of death.
I Corinthians 11:28-39, TAB

2. Isaiah prophesied, "Surely He has borne our griefs--sickness, weakness, and distress--carried our sorrows and pain (of punishment). Yet we ignorantly considered him stricken, smitten and afflicted by God (as if by leprosy)" (Isaiah 53:4, TAB).

...in order that what was spoken through Isaiah the prophet might be fulfilled, saying, "HE HIMSELF TOOK OUR INFIRMITIES, AND CARRIED AWAY OUR DISEASES."
Matthew 8:17

C. CHRIST ASSOCIATED THE PREACHING OF THE GOSPEL WITH HEALING THE SICK.

When Jesus went about preaching, He looked at the bodies of people as well as their soul. He was concerned with the prosperity of the whole person. Whenever He preached the Gospel, He also healed the sick and delivered the mentally tormented.

1. "Whenever you go into a town and they receive and accept and welcome you, eat what is set before you; And heal the sick in it and say to them, The kingdom of God has come close to you" (Luke 10:8-9, TAB).

2. "And He went about all Galilee, teaching in their synagogues and preaching the good news (Gospel) of the kingdom and healing every disease and every weakness and infirmity among the people" (Matthew 4:23, TAB).

3. "And these attesting signs accompany those who believe; in My name they will drive out demons; they will speak with new languages; They will pick up serpents, and (even) if they drink anything deadly, it will not hurt them; they will lay their hands on the sick, and they will get well" (Mark 16:17-18, TAB).

D. GOD TELLS US WHAT TO DO IF WE ARE SICK.

"Is there any one among you sick? He should call the church elders--the spiritual guides. And they should pray over him, anointing him with oil in the Lord's name. And the prayer (that is)

of faith will save him that is sick, and the Lord will restore him;
and if he has committed sins, he will be forgiven."
James 5:14-15, TAB

God indicates many times in His Word that He would have us be prosperous in our body, to be healthy, He never indicates that we are to bear up under sickness with a grim and determinate patience. Where sickness is concerned, Jesus healed it whenever there was faith present. His Word gives us instructions to ask for healing, rather than ask for patience to bear it!

E.   RIGHT SPEAKING LEADS TO PROSPERITY OF BODY.

   1.   "There are those who speak rashly like the piercing of a sword, but the tongue of the wise brings healing" (Proverbs 12:18, TAB).

   2.   "Pleasant words are as a honeycomb, sweet to the mind and healing to the body" (Proverbs 16:24, TAB).

VI.   SUMMATION

A.   It is most important for your soul to prosper. As it does, you will be walking in the wisdom of your Lord, thinking His kind of thoughts, living in His kind of faith. Renew your mind by allowing the Word to dominate it. Conform your will by making the quality decision to choose God's way. Control your emotions by remembering that Jesus is the Source of your life, and His spirit has positive emotional fruit for every negative feeling that comes your way. Live in the soul prosperity that belongs to you!

B.   God wants His children to prosper materially. It gives Him pleasure to see us with all our needs met and much left over to give to others. The Word shows us keys to material prosperity, many promises to stand on, and reasons for poverty if it overtakes us. God promised to supply your needs according to His riches... that is a bountiful supply!

C.   Though God wants us prospering, He warns us not to labor for riches, not to make riches our prime goal. We are to be so taken up with the Giver, that the gifts He gives are secondary. We realize that all our wealth comes from Him. He gives us the wisdom to gain wealth and the wisdom to spend it. God cannot bless a craving, coveting, or even greedy attitude toward money.

D.   Of primary importance to prosperity is the law of giving. We give to receive. God would not have us hoard what He gives us, looking out for our own interests and jealously guarding our possessions. His greatest blessings are for the generous of heart who realize that everything comes from God and who are cheerfully sharing their goods with others.

E. Your body also belongs to God. It is the temple of the Holy Spirit. That Holy Spirit quickens your mortal body. It should be healthy. God wants you to be healthy. Christ paid the price for your health on the cross and included physical healing with His preaching of the Gospel. Believe God's Word concerning health, and learn to prosper in your body!

VII. ASSIGNMENTS

A. Listen to the tape prayerfully.

B. Complete the study guide questions.

C. Recommended reading: Prosperity of the Soul, by Jerry Savelle. The Laws of the Spirit, by Bob Buess.

REFERENCES

1. Savelle, Jerry, Prosperity of the Soul, Harrison House, Tulsa, 1979.

STUDY GUIDE QUESTIONS

1. Using your concordance, do a topical study on your will. How many ways or Scriptures can you find that will help you to conform your will in order to prosper your soul?

2. You have already been blessed with all spiritual blessings. List as many of those blessings as you can. Give Scriptures where possible.

3. Write out three prosperity promises from the Word, making them faith prayers for your needs or for the prosperity of another.

4. What are seven keys to prosperity? (You may have others besides those listed in the lesson.)

5. Find those Scriptures that you could give to a person that thought God was the Author of his poverty, perhaps to humble him, or whatever reason.

6. Give four Scriptural warnings concerning riches.

7.   How can you specifically lay up treasures in heaven?

8.   Find some Scriptural ways to deal with a poor "freeloader."

9.   Find four giving examples in the Word--that is, of people giving generously to others.

10.   Now find four rewards for generous giving.

11.   What does "giving by faith" mean to you? Do you have an example to share from your life?

12.   We have studied healing several times in the course of these lessons. Think about what you believe concerning divine health. Now write out what you believe the Scriptures teach about living in health. How can you be continuously healthy? Do you have any questions about divine health that you would like to ask your Pastor?

12 Can God Change the Will?

I. WHAT CAN OR SHOULD WE DO WITH ANOTHER'S WILL?

Your prayers will many times be in direct contrast to another's will in a situation. You pray for the restoration of a marriage when one or the other partner seems set on giving it up and going into another marriage. Can you pray with faith, knowing that a person's will must be changed to answer your prayer?

You are praying for the restoration of a rebellious child. He makes decisions against the Word. He lives out of God's will and consistently tells you that he does not want to live for God. You keep praying. Can you pray with faith for God to change the person's will?

Someone you love very much is against the Baptism of the Holy Spirit. They study, they preach, and teach against what you believe. They are not even willing to discuss it. You are praying in faith that they receive the Baptism of the Holy Spirit, but they are not willing. Will God answer your prayer?

Numerous examples could be given. You are faced with them every day. Do you say, "Well, I prayed in faith; now it is up to that individual and God. My part is over"? How long does intercession last? If your prayer is not answered, you can easily blame it on the other's unwillingness to yield to God. He had a free will in the situation and chose to go against God. If it is answered, you feel God honored your prayer of faith.

Where are we in this? Does God override the free will of another in answering our prayer? Is it right to pray "over someone's head" in order for them to change their will concerning the Word? Is there ever a time when God says, "That's enough. They have had ample opportunity. Don't pray for them anymore"? Is this a special case when you are released from praying for a person?

Another question: If your prayer is not answered the way you prayed, whose fault is it? Does there have to be a fault? Do we need to attach blame somewhere when things didn't turn out the way we confessed or prayed? Is there any room at all for unanswered questions?

Everyone asks themselves these questions at one time or another. Let us look into God's Word and see if He has already answered them. First, let us look at how God has chosen to work.

II.   GOD HAS CHOSEN TO WORK THROUGH THE CHURCH.

A.   CHRIST DIED FOR THE CHURCH.

When Christ died on the cross, God the Father put all the sin of the world on Him. Not only the sin in an abstract sense, but also the sinner was put on Him. We died with Him. When the sin of the whole world was upon Jesus Christ, the Holy Spirit left Him. He could not be present with all that sin. The Father also turned His face from Jesus. Jesus' perfect, human spirit had been made sin. He was separated from His Father, and He was spiritually dead.

For if we have become united with Him in the likeness of His death, certainly we shall be also in the likeness of His resurrection, knowing this, that our old self was crucified with Him, that our body of sin might be done away with, that we should no longer be slaves to sin; for he who has died is freed from sin.
Romans 6:5-7

And about the ninth hour Jesus cried out with a loud voice, saying, "Eli, Eli, Lama Sabachthani?" that is, "My God, my God, Why hast Thou forsaken Me?"
Matthew 27:46

He made Him who knew no sin to be sin on our behalf, that we might become the righteousness of God in Him.
II Corinthians 5:21

Jesus took your spiritual death, your punishment for sin, for you. It was not just physical death, but it was spiritual death as well. Psalm 88 is a description of the agony of that death. The Father, however, made that spirit alive, and Jesus became a reborn spirit. He was the first begotten of the dead. That reborn, quickened spirit of Jesus stripped Satan; He skinned him! He damaged him in such a way as to make him useless.

For Christ also died for sins once for all, the just for the unjust, in order that He might bring us to God, having been put to death in the flesh, but made alive in the spirit.
I Peter 3:18

...and from Jesus Christ, the faithful witness, the firstborn of the dead, and the ruler of the kings of the earth.   To Him who loves

us, and released us from our sins by His blood,...
Revelation 1:5

When He had disarmed the rulers and authorities, He made a public
display of them, having triumphed over them through Him.
Colossians 2:15

Death could hold the Son of God no longer. His spirit returned to His body, and He
was resurrected. He went to the Heavenly Father to present His atoning blood. His
sacrifice was accepted!

"And God raised Him up again, putting an end to the agony of
death, since it was impossible for Him to be held in its power."
Acts 2:24

But when Christ appeared as a high priest of the good things to
come, He entered through the greater and more perfect tabernacle,
not made with hands, that is to say, not of this creation; and not
through the blood of goats and calves, but through His own blood,
He entered the holy place once for all, having obtained eternal
redemption.
Hebrews 9:11-12

B. CHRIST GAVE THE CHURCH HIS AUTHORITY.

When redemption had been accomplished, God gave the Lord Jesus a Name above
every name, seated Him at His right hand, and put all things under His feet. All
authority was given to Him.

...which He brought about in Christ, when He raised Him from the
dead, and seated Him at HIs right hand in the heavenly places, far
above all rule and authority and power and dominion, and every
name that is named, not only in this age, but also in the one to
come. And He put all things in subjection under His feet, and gave
Him as head over all things to the church, which is His body, the
fulness of Him who fills all in all.
Ephesians 1:20-23

Just before Jesus left this earth, He said, "All power and authority is given unto
Me." Then He said, "Go, in My name... teach all nations, baptize them in My
Name." Jesus gave His authority to the Church. He said to the Father, "As You
have sent me, so send I them into the world" (John 17:18). Jesus came with
authority and sends us to do our work with authority also.

Jesus gave us His Name, His power of attorney, to use while here on earth.

> "And these signs will accompany those who have believed: in My
> name they will cast out demons, they will speak with new tongues;
> they will pick up serpents, and if they drink any deadly poison, it
> shall not hurt them; they will lay hands on the sick, and they will
> recover."
> Mark 16:17-18

We are also seated in the heavenlies with all the power that Jesus has given to the church. We are seated with Him in the heavenlies, but we are working down here. Jesus is seated in the heavenlies, but working down here through His Body, the Church.

> But God, being rich in mercy, because of His great love with
> which He loved us, even when we were dead in our transgressions,
> made us alive together with Christ (by grace you have been
> saved), and raised us up with Him, and seated us with Him in the
> heavenly places, in Christ Jesus,...
> Ephesians 2:4-6

C. CHRIST, THE HEAD, FUNCTIONS THROUGH HIS BODY, THE CHURCH.

God has been clear in His Word as to what His will is. He has given the Church the authority and power to do His will. Now He waits for the Church to do her part.

We, as the Body of Christ, cannot function without the Head; however, what we sometimes do not understand is that the Head has chosen not to work without the body. The Word says that the branches cannot bear fruit except they abide in the vine, and yet, the vine without the branches cannot bear fruit either. God is using you and others of the Body of Christ to accomplish His work on earth.

III.   WHAT IS YOUR GOD-DELEGATED JOB?

A. TO BIND AND LOOSE

> "And I tell you, you are Peter...and on this rock...I will build My
> church, and the gates of Hades (the powers of the infernal region)
> shall not overpower it--or be strong to its detriment, or hold out
> against it. And I will give you the keys of the kingdom of heaven,
> and whatever you bind--that is, declare to be improper and
> unlawful--on earth must be already bound in heaven; and whatever

you loose on earth--declare lawful--must be what is already loosed
in heaven."
Matthew 16:18-19, TAB

We are to bind and loose on earth what was bound and loosed in heaven. When Jesus
stripped Satan, He bound all his authority. The problem is that Satan pretends that
he didn't get the message, and he proceeds with guerilla warfare against the saints.
That is why we have the armor. Satan has no legal right to get us, but he is trying
to render us useless, if possible. Yet Jesus said that the gates of Hell will <u>not</u>
prevail against us. Instead of Satan taking over our territory, we are to take over
his territory.

Satan's gates will not prevail--will not hold up against our offensive. When we agree
to loose a person bound by Satan, Jesus said that Hell could not prevail against us.
If Hell cannot prevail against us, why should a person's will stand against us?

B. TO INTERCEDE

1. God Promises to answer.

   a. Matthew 7:7-8 says, "Ask, and IT SHALL BE DONE." It does not say, "If
       the person is willing." It says, "It shall be done for him" (the person who is
       asking).

          "Ask, and it shall be given to you; seek, and you shall
          find; knock, and it shall be opened to you. For everyone
          who asks receives, and he who seeks finds, and to him who
          knocks it shall be opened."
          Matthew 7:7-8

   b. John 14:13-14: "If you ask <u>anything</u> in My name IT SHALL BE DONE."

          "And whatever you ask in My name, that will I do, that the
          Father may be glorified in the Son. If you ask Me anything
          in My name, I will do it."
          John 14:13-14

   c. I John 5:14-15 says that if we ask anything according to His will, we KNOW
       THAT WE HAVE IT.

> And this is the confidence which we have before Him, that,
> if we ask anything according to His will, He hears us.   And
> if we know that He hears us in whatever we ask, we know
> that we have the requests which we have asked from Him.
> I John 5:14-15

d. Matthew 9:29: "According to your faith be it unto you." WE KNOW THAT WE HAVE IT.

> Then He touched their eyes, saying, "Be it done to you
> according to your faith."
> Matthew 9:29

e. Matthew 21:22: Ask, believing, and YOU SHALL RECEIVE.

f. Mark 11:24: "All things that you ask, believe that you receive them and THEY SHALL BE GRANTED YOU."

g. Mark 9:23: "All things are POSSIBLE to HIM THAT BELIEVES."

2. God looks for men to intercede.

a. Ezekiel 22:30-31: "I searched for a man to stand in the gap." God is looking for men to intercede on behalf of others. For some reason God does not exercise His divine will and save them when there is no one to intercede.

b. I Timothy 2:1: "I urge that prayers, petitions, and intercessions be made for all men." God urges us to intercede as if the results depended more on our faithfulness in prayer than on their will.

c. James 5:16,17: "The faithful prayer of a righteous man availeth much."

> Therefore, confess your sins to one another, and pray for
> one another so that you may be healed. The effective
> prayer of a righteous man can accomplish much. Elijah was
> a man with a nature like ours, and he prayed earnestly that
> it might not rain; and it did not rain on the earth for three
> years and six months.
> James 5:16,17

C. TO TREAD UPON THE POWER OF THE ENEMY

> "Behold! I have given you authority and power to trample upon serpents and scorpions, and (physical and mental strength and ability) over all the power that the enemy possesses, and nothing shall in any way harm you."
> Luke 10:19, TAB

Let's piece together from the various gospels Jesus' last conversation with His disciples.

> "All authority in heaven and on earth has been given to me, Therefore go and make disciples of all nations, baptizing them in the name of the Father, and of the Son and of the Holy Spirit, and teaching them to obey everything I have commanded you. And surely I will be with you always, to the very end of the age."
> Matthew 28:18-20, NIV

> "And these signs will accompany those who believe; In my name they will drive out demons; they will speak in new tongues; they will pick up snakes with their hands and when they drink deadly poison, it will not hurt them at all; they will place their hands on sick people, and they will get well."
> Mark 16:17-18, NIV

> "I am going to send you what My Father has promised; but stay in the city until you have been clothed with power from on high."
> Luke 24:49, NIV

> "But you will receive power when the Holy Spirit comes on you; and you will be my witnesses in Jerusalem, and in all Judea and Samaria, and to the ends of the earth."
> Acts 1:8, NIV

> "After the Lord Jesus had spoken to them, he was taken up into heaven and he sat at the right hand of God. Then the disciples went out and preached everywhere, and the Lord worked with them and confirmed his word by the signs that accompanied it."
> Mark 16:19-20, NIV

You, as part of the Lord's Body, have both the authority and the power to tread upon the enemy. Obviously it is against his will; nevertheless, his will has no control in the matter. You have been given the power to do so. Go ahead and use it!

D. NOT TO MAKE ALTERNATE PLANS IN CASE GOD DOESN'T COME THROUGH

Many times we pray with what we call faith, but all the time half of our being is making alternate plans--"In case God does not come through on this one." That is double-mindedness. If we do not know God's will on a matter, then we pray for enlightenment and wisdom, guidance and clear counsel. When we know God's revealed will, we pray without hesitation, without doubt, and in complete faith, knowing that we receive our petition. Jesus said, "Ask, and ye shall receive."

E. TO GET YOUR WILL TO BELIEVE THAT GOD WILL ANSWER YOUR PRAYER

This whole series of lesson is designed to do just that. Faith is agreeing with God and then acting like it. God said He would answer the prayer of faith. Do you believe it? Is your prayer of faith conditional on the will of someone else? The Word of God does not say so. The Word does say that if you believe, you will receive. WILL TO BELIEVE!

F. TO BE LIGHT AND SALT

Jesus said that we are light to this world.

> "You are the salt of the earth; but if the salt has become tasteless, how will it be made salty again? It is good for nothing anymore, except to be thrown out and trampled under foot by men. You are the light of the world. A city set on a hill cannot be hidden."
> Matthew 5:13-14

Light causes the darkness to flee. The darkness does not have a choice. Salt overcomes the tendency to disintegrate and decay. We, as the salt of the earth, are overcoming the decay of the world. The world would already be totally destroyed with its own filth and rottenness if it were not for the salt of the earth. We are hindering that total destruction because of our very nature, not because it is the will of the world. It is our faith that overcomes the world--regardless of what the world wills or thinks!

If light refuses to shine whenever a person of darkness refuses to receive it, then our light is dependent on its object and not its Source. Your light Source is inextinguishable!

G. TO LOOK TO GOD FOR ENCOURAGEMENT

Remember that your faith is in God and in His Word. When you have been faithful in your intercession for another, then rest. Trust God to do His Work. If, on occasion, a person's will has not changed, leave that to God too. God loves that person more than you do and knows just how to deal with him. If you have unanswered questions in a situation, remember Deuteronomy 29:29: "The secret things belong to the Lord our God, but the things revealed belong to us and to our sons forever, that we may observe all the words of this law." Your task is to observe the revealed things and trust God with those things that have not been revealed to you.

IV. GOVERNING THE SPIRITS BEHIND THE WILL

A. TWO SOURCES OF WISDOM AND INFORMATION

Men listen to two sources of wisdom and information: God or the devil.

> Who among you is wise and understanding? Let him show by his good behavior his deeds in the gentleness of wisdom. But if you have bitter jealousy and selfish ambition in your heart, do not be arrogant and so lie against the truth. This wisdom is not that which comes down from above, but is earthly, natural, demonic. For where jealousy and selfish ambition exist, there is disorder and every evil thing. But the wisdom from above is first pure, then peaceable, gentle, reasonable, full of mercy and good fruits, unwavering, without hypocrisy. And the seed whose fruit is righteousness is sown in peace by those who make peace.
> James 3:13-18

There really is no other source. One source produces life and faith. The other eventually produces death, fear, and a host of other by-products. Our job is to govern the spirits that motivate the will. We know that God is willing to give the right information.

> The Lord is not slow about His promise, as some count slowness, but is patient toward you, not wishing for any to perish but for all to come to repentance.
> II Peter 3:9

He wants to draw all men unto Himself; He wants all to come to repentance. The problem is that there is a hindering force, a spirit that snatches God's Word from hearts, that brings confusion and blindness to their minds.

...in whose case the god of this world has blinded the minds of the
unbelieving, that they might not see the light of the gospel of the
glory of Christ, who is the image of God.
II Corinthians 4:4

We have power over that spirit and influence. Now we must use it. In Jesus' Name
we bind those powers (already bound in heaven) on earth and specifically those
powers operating in relation to the person for which we are praying. Ask the Father
to draw the person to Himself. This is His will. We pray in faith and believe that we
receive.

"No one can come to Me, unless the Father who sent Me draws him;
and I will raise him up on the last day."
John 6:44

B. DEVILS ARE SUBJECT TO US IN THE NAME OF JESUS.

"And the seventy returned with joy, saying, 'Lord, even the
demons are subject to us in Your name.'"
Luke 10:17

On the subject of casting out demons Jesus said, "Nothing shall be impossible to you
if you believe" (Matthew 17:20).

And He said to them, "Because of the littleness of your faith; for
truly I say to you, if you have faith as a mustard seed, you shall
say to this mountain, 'Move from here to there,' and it shall move;
and nothing shall be impossible to you."
Matthew 17:20

The demoniac of Gadara was possessed by a legion of spirits, yet they could not stop
him from running to Jesus. Jesus has power over the devil in a man's mind, and He
can shut the devil's mouth!

C. IN CHRIST THERE IS FREEDOM FROM THAT WHICH WARS AGAINST THE WILL.

In Romans chapter seven there is a description of a man who is doing many things
contrary to his will. It is a constant war, he says, doing that which he does not will
to do and not doing that which he wills to do. It is the flesh against the spirit. Do
you not believe that there are many in the world even among our loved ones who are
in this state? In their innermost being they do will to serve the Lord, but they are
bound. There is an answer. Jesus Christ sets us free from the law of sin and
death--the influence that seeks to keep men doing what they really do not want to

do. Christ sets us free from the evil influence governing our will. We need to declare that freedom, and pray that people will see their choice to be free.

> Thanks be to God through Jesus Christ our Lord! So then, on the one hand I myself with my mind am serving the law of God, but on the other, with my flesh the law of sin.
> Romans 7:25

> For the law of the Spirit of life in Christ Jesus has set you free from the law of sin and of death. For what the Law could not do, weak as it was through the flesh, God did: sending His own Son in the likeness of sinful flesh and as an offering for sin, He condemned sin in the flesh,...
> Romans 8:2-3

D. USE GOD'S MIGHTY WEAPONS.

1. We have spiritual weapons: "The truth is that, although of course we lead normal human lives, the battle we are fighting is on the spiritual level. The very weapons we use are not those of human warfare, but powerful in God's warfare for the destruction of the enemy's strongholds. Our battle is to bring down every deceptive fantasy and every imposing defense that men erect against the true knowledge of God. We even fight to capture every thought until it acknowledges the authority of Christ.

   > "Once we are sure of your obedience, we shall not shrink from dealing with those who refuse to obey."
   > II Corinthians 10:3-6, Phillips

How are we going to deal with those who refuse to obey? With spiritual weapons! They are mighty for the tearing down of the enemy's strongholds!

Many times our problem is that we are fighting with human, emotional, and psychological weapons. They do not work, and we think that God has not answered our prayers. That is not the case. We have argued, tried to convince, maybe even coerced someone to listen to our message. All the time we needed to bind the enemy and intercede in faith, allowing the Father to draw them, prepare the soil of their hearts for the good seed; then plant the Word. Again, allow the Lord to cause the seed to grow, and DO NOT GIVE UP! If you have given up, then the enemy has won by out waiting you.

229

2. Our spiritual weapons <u>will</u> stand against the devil's schemes.

> Finally, be strong in the Lord, and in the strength of His might. Put on the full armor of God, that you may be able to stand firm against the schemes of the devil. For our struggle is not against flesh and blood, but against the rulers, against the powers, against the world forces of this darkness, against the spiritual forces of wickedness in the heavenly places. Therefore, take up the full armor of God, that you may be able to resist in the evil day, and having done everything, to stand firm.
> Ephesians 6:10-13

V. GOD CAN CHANGE REBELS.

A. HE CHANGES THE HEART.

1. "When you ascended on high, you led captives in your train; you received gifts from men, even from the rebellious--that you O Lord God, might dwell there" (Psalm 68:18, NIV).

2. "For seven days they celebrated with joy the Feast of Unleavened Bread, because the Lord had filled them with joy by changing the attitude of the king of Assyria, so that he assisted them in the work on the house of God, the God of Israel" (Ezra 6:22, NIV).

3. "The king's heart is in the hand of the Lord; he directs it like a watercourse wherever he pleases" (Proverbs 21:1, NIV).

B. HE LETS THEM SEE THE RESULT OF THEIR REBELLION.

1. Jonah was determined to run away from God. His will was set. God was also determined to give the city of Ninevah a chance to repent. (I wonder who was praying for Ninevah?) He gave Jonah the command to go. Jonah refused and went the other way. Now, one of God's ways with His servants is that He makes it difficult to disobey. He let Jonah see the result of his rebellion. Being thrown overboard, then being swallowed by a large fish, was quite a price to pay for rebellion. He finally repented and went and preached. There was a mighty revival in Ninevah! This city also received a warning of what would happen if they continued in their rebellion against the God of heaven--destruction!

God prepared a large fish to keep Jonah from continuing in his rebellion. He can prepare a "fish" for your loved ones too!

2. In the book of Judges, we read over and over again how the people of Israel rebelled against God and went their own way. They "did what was right in their own eyes." Did God make them change their ways? Not exactly, but He sure showed them the results of their rebellion! Enemy nations came time and time again and oppressed the children of Israel. They would change their minds and cry out to God again, and God would deliver them--everytime.

3. If the person you are praying for is worse off now than before, it might be that God is just showing them the results of their rebellion, and the next step is the turning of their will to God. Keep trusting the God to whom you are praying! Don't be discouraged by the circumstances.

C. SOMETIMES HE MAKES A DRAMATIC VISIT.

Paul is an excellent example of this. He was a religious fanatic if the Bible ever describes one! He had totally rejected Jesus in favor of the old traditions of Judaism. He was so adamant in having his will set against Jesus that he went about persecuting Christians and even killing them.

> Now Saul, still breathing threats and murder against the disciples of the Lord, went to the high priest, and asked for letters from him to the synagogues at Damascus, so that if he found any belonging to the Way, both men and women, he might bring them bound to Jerusalem.
> Acts 9:1-2

One day, on his way to persecute more Christians, he was stopped by a great light from heaven, and Jesus Himself made a visit to Saul. That very hour Saul became a new creature in Christ. He made a choice then to follow Him. His will had made a complete turn! Do you have any Sauls in your family?

Who prayed for Paul? We don't know for sure, but it wouldn't be hard to imagine that all of the Christian community was united in prayer for this railing persecutor!

D. HE CHANGED YOU, DIDN'T HE?

When we get right down to it, we were all rebels against the Lord, and He drew us and brought us to the cross and made us new creatures. If He did it for us, is there anyone He cannot change? Jesus said, "Only have faith, all things are possible with God."

...in which you formerly walked according to the course of this world, according to the prince of the power of the air, of the spirit that is now working in the sons of disobedience.
Ephesians 2:2

VI. YOUR HARVEST DOES NOT DEPEND UPON SOMEONE ELSE'S WILL.

A. DO NOT BE WEARY IN WELL DOING.

"And let us not lose heart and grow weary and faint in acting nobly and doing right, for in due time and at the appointed season we shall reap, if we do not loosen and relax our courage and faint."
Galatians 6:9, TAB

B. DON'T LET THE DEVIL DEVOUR YOUR HARVEST.

"For this reason I am telling you, whatever you ask for in prayer, believe--trust and be confident--that it is granted to you, and you will (get it)."
Mark 11:24, TAB

C. JOIN THE SPIRIT IN SAYING "COME."

"The (Holy) Spirit and the bride the church, the true Christians say, Come! And let him who is listening say, Come! And let every one come who is thirsty who is painfully conscious of his need of those things by which the soul is refreshed, supported and strengthened; and whoever earnestly desires to do it, let him come and take and appropriate (drink) the Water of Life without cost."
Revelation 22:17, TAB

It takes both the Spirit and the Bride to give the invitation. You are part of the Bride. The Father has chosen to use the Bride, as well as the Spirit, to give the invitation.

D. DON'T PUT A DATE ON HARVEST TIME.

If you set a date for someone to get saved and turn his life over to God, then there is a time when you want to give up after the deadline is past. God does not want you to give up; therefore, do not set a time for your harvest. Plant, water, and let the Lord of the harvest decide when harvest time is to come. It may not be your turn to harvest. It may be someone else's time. Do not give up! Keep planting the seed, using your weapons, and interceding until harvest time does come, and your "rebel" is in the Body of Christ.

E. REMEMBER THAT THE WORD WILL NOT COME BACK VOID.

It is not your effort; it is your faith that brings answered prayer. You cannot use your will to overcome others. Do not allow Satan to get you weary and tired and continuing in fleshly effort. It is the power of God that will break down the strongholds.

Using His power does not take any of your own. He is the Source. Depend and trust your God and His Word to do the work, not your methods.

Let God handle another's free will. Faithfully perform the task God gave to you, and trust Him to honor His Word. He knows how to handle people's will.

VII. SUMMATION

A. God has chosen to use you, as part of the Body of Christ, to accomplish His will on earth. You have both the authority and power of Christ to do this.

B. Your job, then, is to find out what God's will is and do it. He would have you bind the enemy and loosen his grip on people. Intercede on their behalf. Use your faith to bring people to salvation and victory in Jesus. Keep looking to your Source to overcome. Don't look at the will of another.

C. You can bind the evil spirits that affect one's will. They are subject to the Name of Jesus. Use spiritual weapons against a rebellious will, not carnal or psychological weapons.

D. God can change rebels. He is in the heart-changing business. He has many and varied methods. Intercede-- then trust God!

E. Your harvest depends upon your faithfulness to God and His Word, not on another's will. Join the Spirit in saying, "Come." In interceding for another, don't give up. Expect a big harvest; expect many to yield their will to God.

VIII. ASSIGNMENTS

A. Listen to the tape carefully.

B. Complete the Study Guide Questions.

C. Suggested reading: Destined for the Throne, by Paul E. Billheimer.

STUDY GUIDE QUESTIONS

1.   How does God work through the Church?

2.   Why did Jesus have to die for you spiritually? What Scriptures convince you that He did?

3.   From Scripture answer this question: Does God ever say, "That is enough, they have had ample opportunity. You prayed for them long enough. Stop praying. They have rejected Me"?

4.   The power of God to answer prayer is stronger than a person's free will. Give three Scriptures that give God's positive promises to answer your prayer of faith.

5.   Give a definition of "intercede." What are some effective ways to intercede for others?

6.   What do you do if you have prayed in faith, been faithful in intercession, and the result was not what you had asked for?

7.   Describe the two kinds of wisdom and knowledge from which men can receive information (James 3:13-18).

8.   List as many ways as you can of using God's mighty spiritual weapons.

9.   From the Bible, find three examples of God changing the heart of a rebel.

10.   God sometimes lets people see the results of their rebellion. What are some of the results of rebellion listed in Scripture?

11.   Look for three faith confessions to use for any rebels for which you are interceding.

12.   Someday you will reap a harvest. On what does that harvest depend?

13.   Which Scriptures encourage you most <u>not</u> to give up? Give at least three.

Receive Jesus Christ as Lord and Savior of Your Life.

The Bible says, *"That if thou shalt confess with thy mouth the Lord Jesus, and shalt believe in thine heart that God raised him from the dead, thou shalt be saved. For with the heart man believeth unto righteousness; and with the m outh confession is made unto salvation"* (Romans 10:9,10).

To receive Jesus Christ as Lord and Savior of your life, sincerely pray this prayer from your heart:

Dear Jesus,

I believe that You died for me and that You rose again on the third day. I confess to You that I am a sinner and that I need Your love and forgiveness. Come into my life, forgive my sins, and give me eternal life. I confess You now as my Lord. Thank You for my salvation!

Signed _____ Date _____

Please print.

Name   Mr. & Mrs.
      Mr.
      Miss
      Mrs. _____

Address _____

City _____

State _____Zip _____

Phone (H) (   ) _____

Write to us.

We will send you information to help you with your new life in Christ.
Marilyn Hickey Ministries
P.O. Box 17340 • Denver, CO 80217 • 303-770-0400
www.mhmin.org

TOUCHING YOU WITH THE LOVE OF JESUS!

Marilyn Hickey
PRAYER CENTER

When was the last time that you could say, "He touched me, right where I hurt"? No matter how serious the nature of your call, we're here to pray the Word and show you how to touch Jesus for real answers to real problems.

Call us and let's touch Jesus, together!

303-796-1333

Open 4 a.m.—4:30 p.m. Monday—Friday (MT).

WE CARE!

BOOKS BY MARILYN HICKEY

A Cry for Miracles ($7.95)
Acts of the Holy Spirit ($7.95)
Angels All Around ($7.95)
Armageddon ($4.95)
Ask Marilyn ($9.95)
Be Healed ($9.95)
Blessing Journal ($4.95)
Bible Encounter Classic Edition ($24.95)
Book of Revelation Comic Book (The) ($3.00)
Break the Generation Curse ($7.95)
Break the Generation Curse Part 2 ($9.95)
Building Blocks for Better Families ($4.95)
Daily Devotional ($7.95)
Dear Marilyn ($7.95)
Devils, Demons, and Deliverance ($9.95)
Divorce Is Not the Answer ($7.95)
Especially for Today's Woman ($14.95)
Freedom From Bondages ($7.95)
Gift-Wrapped Fruit ($2.95)
God's Covenant for Your Family ($7.95)

God's Rx for a Hurting Heart ($4.95)
Hebrew Honey ($14.95)
How to Be a Mature Christian ($7.95)
Know Your Ministry ($4.95)
Maximize Your Day . . . God's Way ($7.95)
Miracle Signs and Wonders ($24.95)
Names of God (The) ($7.95)
Nehemiah—Rebuilding the Broken
            Places in Your Life ($7.95)
No. 1 Key to Success—Meditation (The) ($4.95)
Proverbs Classic Library Edition ($24.95)
Release the Power of the Blood Covenant ($4.95)
Satan-Proof Your Home ($7.95)
Save the Family Promise Book ($14.95)
Signs in the Heavens ($7.95)
What Every Person Wants to Know About Prayer ($4.95)
When Only a Miracle Will Do ($4.95)
Your Miracle Source ($4.95)
Your Total Health Handbook—Body • Soul • Spirit ($9.95)

MINI-BOOKS: $1⁰⁰ each
by Marilyn Hickey

Beat Tension
Bold Men Win
Bulldog Faith
Change Your Life
Children Who Hit the Mark
Conquering Setbacks
Don't Park Here
Experience Long Life
Fasting and Prayer
God's Benefit: Healing
God's Seven Keys to Make You Rich
Hold On to Your Dream
How to Become More Than a Conqueror
How to Win Friends
I Can Be Born Again and Spirit Filled

I Can Dare to Be an Achiever
Keys to Healing Rejection
Power of Forgiveness (The)
Power of the Blood (The)
Receiving Resurrection Power
Renew Your Mind
Solving Life's Problems
Speak the Word
Standing in the Gap
Story of Esther (The)
Tithes • Offerings • Alms •
            God's Plan for Blessing You
Turning Point
Winning Over Weight
Women of the Word

Prices are in U.S. dollars. If ordering in foreign currency, please calculate the current exchange rate.

For Your Information
Free Monthly Magazine

☐ Please send me your free monthly magazine, OUTPOURING (including daily devotionals, timely articles, and ministry updates)!

Tapes and Books

☐ Please send me Marilyn's latest product catalog.

Please print.

Name Mr. & Mrs. / Mr. / Miss / Mrs. _____

Address _____

City _____

State _____ Zip _____

Phone (H) ( ) _____

(W) ( ) _____

Mail to:
Marilyn Hickey Ministries
P.O. Box 17340 • Denver, CO 80217 • 303-770-0400

Marilyn Hickey Ministries

Marilyn was a public school teacher when she met Wallace Hickey. After their marriage, Wally was called to the ministry and Marilyn taught Bible studies.

"Today With Marilyn" TV program is broadcast weekdays on TBN, BET, and several independent stations. It is also seen overseas by millions through Christian Channel Europe in the UK, Christian Network TV in South Africa, in Australia on Network 10, and in more than 80 other countries worldwide.

The vision of Marilyn Hickey Ministries is to "cover the earth with the Word" (Isaiah 11:9).

For more than 30 years Marilyn Hickey has dedicated herself to an anointed, unique, and distinguished ministry of reaching out to people—from all walks of life—who are hungry for God's Word and all that He has for them. Millions have witnessed and acclaimed the positive, personal impact she brings through fresh revelation knowledge that God has given her through His Word.

Marilyn has been the invited guest of government leaders and heads of state from many nations of the world. She is considered by many to be one of today's greatest ambassadors of God's Good News to this dark and hurting generation.

The more Marilyn follows God's will for her life, the more God uses her to bring refreshing, renewal, and revival to the Body of Christ throughout the world. As His obedient servant, Marilyn desires to follow Him all the days of her life.

Marilyn and Wally adopted their son Michael; through a fulfilled prophecy they had their daughter Sarah, who with her husband Reece, is now part of the ministry.

Marilyn taught at Denver's "Happy Church" and hosted ministry conferences with husband Wally.

The ministry has expanded to its present headquarters located in Greenwood Village, Colorado.

Marilyn has been the invited guest of government leaders and heads of state from many nations of the world.

In Egypt with Mrs. Anwar Sadat

Marilyn Hickey's Prayer Center handles calls from all over the U.S.—ministering to those who need agreement in prayer.

In Venezuela with former first lady Mrs. Perez

The outreaches of "Outpouring" magazine, Word to the World Bible College and available ministry resources reach people around the world.

Marilyn speaks at Dr. Cho's church in Korea. She is the only woman on his board of directors.

God has opened doors for the supplying of Bibles to many foreign lands—China, Israel, Poland, Ethiopia, Russia, Romania, and Ukraine, just to name a few.

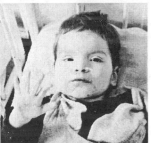

Marilyn and Sarah have a heart for ministering in foreign lands..

Food, Bibles, and water wells have been supplied to many countries, such as Haiti, the Philippines, Ethiopia, Honduras, India, and El Salvador.

Ministry trips and cruises to places such as Indonesia, Russia, Greece, Ukraine, Turkey, and Israel offer short-term missions' opportunities to travel with Marilyn.

Overseas offices in the United Kingdom, Australia, and South Africa provide a base of operations for ministry and partnership throughout these continents.

Marilyn and Sarah have ministered and toured Malaysia, Singapore, Russia, Ukraine, Hong Kong, China, and South Africa. Thousands have attended Encounters and Crusades abroad and in the U.S.

International crusades and Ministry Training Schools in India, Pakistan, Eritrea, and Sudan reach tens of thousands with the good news of Jesus Christ.